Edith Almeda Haigh
1021 Goodrich Ave.
Macalester College
St. Paul
Minn

THE AMERICAN NATION
A HISTORY

FROM ORIGINAL SOURCES BY ASSOCIATED SCHOLARS

EDITED BY

ALBERT BUSHNELL HART, LL.D.
PROFESSOR OF HISTORY IN HARVARD UNIVERSITY

ADVISED BY
VARIOUS HISTORICAL SOCIETIES

IN 27 VOLUMES
VOL. 10

THE AMERICAN NATION
A HISTORY

LIST OF AUTHORS AND TITLES
GROUP I.
FOUNDATIONS OF THE NATION

GROUP II.
TRANSFORMATION INTO A NATION

COMMITTEES APPOINTED TO ADVISE AND CONSULT WITH THE EDITOR

THE AMERICAN NATION: A HISTORY

VOLUME 10

THE CONFEDERATION
AND THE CONSTITUTION

1783–1789

BY

ANDREW CUNNINGHAM McLAUGHLIN, LL.B.

PROFESSOR OF AMERICAN HISTORY IN UNIVERSITY MICHIGAN

WITH MAPS

NEW YORK AND LONDON
HARPER & BROTHERS PUBLISHERS

TO

THE MEMORY OF

MY FATHER AND MOTHER

CONTENTS

xiii

CONTENTS

MAPS

EDITOR'S INTRODUCTION

TO the years from 1783 to 1789, Fiske has given the name of "The Critical Period of American History"; yet it seems doubtful whether it was really a time of such danger of national dissolution as people then and since have supposed. Certainly the trend of this volume is to show a more orderly, logical, and inevitable march of events than has commonly been described. The volume articulates very closely with Van Tyne's *American Revolution* (vol. IX.), taking as a starting-point the defeat of the king's friends in Parliament in the spring of 1782; at the other end the volume leaves for Bassett's *Federalist System* (vol. XI.), the statutes and precedents by which the Constitution was set in motion.

The volume naturally falls into four parts: organization; the government of the Confederation; the constitutional convention; and ratification. In chapters i. and ii., the peace negotiations are described in some detail. Chapter iii., on Imperial Organization, is a luminous discussion of the possibilities of national government in view of the character and political aptitude of the people; it is logically the culmination of the discussions of the

two previous volumes, and the starting-point for
the author's later deductions.

In chapter iv. begins the second part of the
volume, the governmental experience of the Confederation, financial, commercial, diplomatic, paper
money, culminating (chap. x.), in Shays's rebellion
of 1786–1787. Chapters vii. and viii. are given to
an account of the West, continuing the subject
treated by Howard's *Preliminaries of the Revolution*
(chap. xiii.), and Van Tyne's *American Revolution*
(chap. xv.), and emphasizing it as a part of the
new national organization.

Chapters xi. to xvi. describe the movement for
a convention, its culmination, and the work of preparing the Constitution and fitting its parts together. The process of ratification is described in
chapters xvii. and xviii. The Critical Essay deals in
great measure with sources and monographic material.

The special service of this volume is to bring
out the relation of earlier experiences and forms
of government to the final work of the convention.
The Confederation is a preparatory stage, which, in
the author's judgment, was more creditable to the
men of that time than posterity has been willing
to allow. It had viability in itself, and from its
mistakes the framers of the Constitution learned
wisdom. Throughout the book attention is paid
to the capacity and accomplishment of the American
people, and to their working out of tried and familiar
principles into a new and more effective combination.

AUTHOR'S PREFACE

IN the following pages I have sought to bring out clearly the main course of events from the final defeat of Cornwallis to the establishment of the Federal Constitution. In the space allotted me there was no room for the discussion of the episodical or the picturesque, or for the treatment in detail of many topics that might deserve consideration. Everything, or nearly everything, had to be subordinated to the main theme, in order that the story of political achievement might stand out with distinctness; for no history of the American nation would be satisfactory which left in dim obscurity the tale of how the people in the years after the war—when beset with difficulties and troubled by a political order which was unsuited to their needs—proceeded "deliberately and peaceably, without fraud or surprise," to establish a national union and to adjust political powers in a complicated and elaborate system of government. The years under consideration in this volume allowed, if they did not demand, this method of treatment; and I have felt fully justified, therefore, in considering even such themes as the diplomatic relations, or the western movement of population, in connection with the constitutional history of the United States.

I cannot refrain from saying that the centre of my treatment is marked out in the third chapter, which I have called "The Problem of Imperial Organization"; surely the period is seen in its ampler aspects, if the task of forming a substantial union and of solving an intricate political problem is not treated in isolation, but discussed as part of the great question that confronted the English statesmen in 1765 and largely occupied the attention of a generation. The third chapter, therefore, with the chapter on "Proposals to Alter the Articles of Confederation," and the one entitled "The Law of the Land," are, as I have conceived the book, the most important. Though necessarily separated, they should logically supplement one another.

Perhaps I should say, also, that I have taken seriously the wish of the editor that the volumes should be based on original materials. Though I have been helped by many secondary writers, almost nothing is taken from them without verification in the sources; and in many cases the secondary writers are referred to because they contain the original material desired.

I wish to express my appreciation of the scholarly care with which the editor has examined my manuscript and proof. Professor O. G. Libby kindly granted permission to reproduce two maps, first appearing in connection with his valuable monograph on the *Geographical Distribution of the Vote of the Thirteen States on the Federal Constitution, 1787–8.* Mr. James Herbert Russell has been of great service in reading the proofs of these pages, and that fact has given me the comfortable assurance that, whatever other errors I may have inadvertently made, the quotations and references approach absolute exactness.

ANDREW C. MCLAUGHLIN.

THE CONFEDERATION
AND THE CONSTITUTION

THE CONFEDERATION
AND THE CONSTITUTION

CHAPTER I

THE END OF THE REVOLUTION
(1781–1782)

THE defeat of Cornwallis at Yorktown demonstrated the inability of England to conquer America. Throughout the war George III., with characteristic perseverance, had clung resolutely to the purpose of overcoming the rebellious colonists, and when this last disaster came he still spoke of continuing the contest. But the opposition in Parliament gained force daily, and it soon became evident, even to the obdurate monarch, that he must give way.

At the end of 1781 England saw herself surrounded and beset by enemies; Spain, France, and Holland were arrayed in arms against her; no ally on the Continent gave her encouragement or assistance; her colonies were gone; disasters in various parts of the world seemed to bring both ignominy and defeat.

3

The assaults on the ministry were repeated at intervals throughout the winter, and on March 20, 1782, Lord North announced his resignation. He had many times before asked the king to relieve him from office, but he had retained his position because of the solicitation of his sovereign. With him disappeared all purpose of conquering America and all hope of maintaining in its impurity the personal and arbitrary government of George III.[1]

The king was so overcome with chagrin that he actually threatened to flee to Hanover. The royal yacht was said to be in readiness to carry the royal suite across the channel. He assured North that his sentiments of honor would not permit him to send for any of the party of the opposition and personally treat with them; but he soon took heart, and, though he insultingly refused to negotiate with Rockingham except through a mediator, he was ultimately compelled to accept that minister as the head of a new cabinet.[2] Rockingham had been persistently the friend of the Americans. The Whigs whom he represented are said even to have called the American army "our army" and to have rejoiced at American successes.[3] George III. hated

[1] Donne, *Correspondence of George III. with Lord North*, II., 393, 398. See also Van Tyne, *American Revolution* (*American Nation*, IX.), chap. xvii.

[2] May, *Const. Hist. of England* (Am. ed. of 1863), I., 59; *Letters of Horace Walpole* (Cunningham's ed.), VIII., 187; Donne, *Correspondence of George III. with Lord North*, II., 415; Albemarle, *Memoirs of Rockingham*, II., 451–464.

[3] Lecky, *England in the Eighteenth Century*, IV., 76.

them with a virile hatred. Lord North is said to have jokingly remarked that the Whigs had accused him in the past of issuing false bulletins, but that he never issued one so false as that in which his successors announced their accession to office, each paragraph of which began with the words, "His majesty has been pleased to appoint."

Besides Rockingham, who was prime-minister and without whose influence a ministry could not have been formed, Lord Shelburne and Charles James Fox entered the cabinet; the former took the home and colonial departments; Fox, the brilliant debater, the ardent friend of America, was made secretary of state for foreign affairs. It was plain that peace must soon come on the basis of independence for the rebellious colonies; in fact, Rockingham had refused to take office on any other basis.[1] The cabinet, however, was made up of diverse elements, was confronted with intricate problems, and was soon distracted by internal dissension. Fox and Shelburne were incompatible in temperament. Fox was frank, outspoken, and headstrong. Shelburne had the reputation of being insincere and fond of following devious paths to a goal that lay straight before him. False or not, he was a man of ideas and of broad statesmanship, and it is a matter of no small importance for America that there now came into commanding

[1] Fitzmaurice, *Shelburne*, III., 133; Albemarle, *Memoirs of Rockingham*, II., 452.

position a man who could look a big question in the face.

There were various grounds of dissension between the two secretaries, each of whom was suspicious of the other. Among other difficulties arose the question as to the method of treating with America. If the commissioners from the United States were to be considered representatives of a free country, negotiations would naturally be conducted by Fox. If, on the other hand, the states were to be granted their independence only as a result of the treaty, the business naturally fell in Shelburne's department. Fox contended that by a minute adopted on May 23 the cabinet had practically recognized American independence; but to this construction Shelburne could not agree. Fox also felt that the colonial secretary was not acting frankly in the conduct of certain negotiations which Mr. Oswald was carrying on quite informally with Dr. Franklin at Paris. The end came soon. Rockingham, who for some time past had been in ill health, died July 1, 1782; Fox immediately resigned and Shelburne was made prime-minister.

The American Congress had long since made preparations for peace. At first John Adams received appointment as sole commissioner.[1] But Adams was intractable and blunt, and succeeded in getting into difficulties with Vergennes in Paris. The French minister to America, whose business it was to

[1] *Secret Journals of Congress*, October 4, 1779.

look out for his master's interests, secured the appointment of four additional commissioners—Benjamin Franklin, John Jay, Henry Laurens, and Thomas Jefferson.[1] Jefferson at first declined to serve, and, though he accepted a second appointment, he did not, in fact, leave America. Laurens, having been captured by the British in crossing the ocean, was, at the time of his appointment, a prisoner in London, and after his release was unable to take a prominent part in the negotiations for peace. Adams, in the summer of 1782, was busy at The Hague, where he at last succeeded in making a treaty with the Netherlands, winning for himself, to his infinite delight, the title of the "Washington of Negotiations." He, too, was not ready in the spring to take part in the discussions that were beginning at Paris between Franklin and the English representative, Oswald.

Jay had for some time been in Spain, following the Spanish court about and seeking with such humility as he possessed to secure for his country an acknowledgment of independence and the grant of a few much-needed piasters.[2] His experiences had been irritating in the extreme, and when Franklin summoned him to Paris in the spring of 1782 he shook the Spanish dust from willing feet and passed over the Pyrenees to the pleasanter task of negotiating for peace with men that were willing to treat

---

[1] Secret Journals of Congress, June 13, 14, 1781.
[2] Wharton, Dip. Corresp. of Am. Rev., IV., 65, 102, V., 68.

him with respect and consideration.   A good deal of
American history is contained in Franklin's message
asking Jay to come to his aid in France.   "Spain has
taken four years to consider whether she should treat
with us or not," said he.   "Give her forty, and let
us in the meantime mind our own business." [1]

The burden of the early negotiations fell, therefore, on the shoulders of Franklin and of his young
colleague.   Franklin was then one of the most
famous men in Europe.   He was versed in the
methods of diplomacy, for his earlier experiences in
England as colonial agent may well be called
diplomatic, and during his stay in Paris, which was
the centre of continental interest, he had taken
many a lesson.   He was naturally shrewd, discern-
ing, and sagacious.   He had become wonted to
French society, which he doubtless found agreeable.
He was a firm believer in Vergennes's fairness of
purpose, and he was not ready or not willing to
suspect foul play or insidious intrigue.   Jay was
then thirty-six years of age, but he had already
played a conspicuous rôle in politics.   He was
proud-spirited, sensitive, and bold.   His life in
Spain had not been conducive to peace of mind,
and even before he left that country he had gathered
some serious doubts as to the good faith and friendly
purpose of the French ministry.[2]   He did not fit
easily into the life of Paris, but retained an en-

[1] Jay, *Corresp. and Public Papers*, II., 193.
[2] *Ibid.*, 62, 71, 72, 75, 96, 292.

thusiastic patriotism and loyalty to America and American ways. "They" (the French), he said at one time, "are not a moral people; they know not what it is."[1] His firmness, energy, and sagacity admirably supplemented the calm, complacent temper of the more experienced diplomat.

The situation in the spring of 1782 was complicated. The revolt of the American colonies had brought in its train a great European war. France, seeking revenge for the disasters of twenty years before, had made war on England, and had finally succeeded in bringing the elusive court of Spain to take a like step (1779). Holland also had joined the allies. The countries of the north and east were joined in the so-called "Armed Neutrality," which was unfriendly in spirit to Great Britain.[2] For some time France had been bearing the burden of the American war, if, in fact, one could longer call it American; she was at the head of a great alliance against which England with accustomed bravery was fighting sturdily and well. Vergennes, looking out upon the field, had more than one fear that the combination he had arranged with infinite patience and cunning would go to pieces before his eyes, and that France would have little for her pains except ruined finances and the qualified

---

[1] Wharton, *Dip. Corresp. of Am. Rev.*, V., 849; John Adams, *Works*, III., 303.

[2] See Van Tyne, *American Revolution* (*American Nation*, IX.), chap. xvii.

friendship of independent America. The United States was weak, and congressional councils were distracted by rival factions. Spain was eager only for her own gain, and could not be relied on to be either steadfast or considerate. She had entered the war, not for any abstract policy of state, but to win substantial accessions of territory. "The Spanish," said the French minister Montmorin, "like little children, are to be attracted only by shining objects."[1]

Anxious that America should not leave France in the lurch by making an independent treaty with England, the French representative in America induced Congress to instruct the commissioners for peace "to make the most candid and confidential communications upon all subjects to the ministers of our generous ally, the king of France; to undertake nothing in the negotiations for peace or truce without their knowledge and concurrence; and ultimately to govern yourselves by their advice and opinion."[2] These were somewhat humiliating directions; but of course America was bound in honor not to make a separate treaty or to leave France to fight her way to peace as best she might. When Spain entered the war, by the secret treaty with France of April, 1779, it was agreed that one purpose of the war should be certain additions to Spanish territory, and notably the conquest of Gibraltar. Inasmuch

[1] Doniol, *Histoire de la Participation*, II., 798.
[2] *Secret Journals of Congress*, June 15, 1781.

as the purpose of the alliance between America and France had been declared to be the independence of the United States, it is plain that France and Spain, without the knowledge of America, had entered into an agreement which might prolong the war for purely European purposes entirely foreign to American interests or desires. We may doubt, therefore, the wisdom and policy of these instructions from Congress, although the United States was bound by every dictate of honor and good conscience not to abandon France on trivial grounds or for selfish ends.

In the spring of 1782, before Jay came to Paris, and while Fox was still in the cabinet, informal negotiations began between Franklin and Oswald, and by this means certain communications were submitted to Shelburne.[1] Franklin dwelt on the desirability of reconciliation, "a sweet word," and suggested that "reparation" might be voluntarily made by England to those who had suffered peculiarly in the war by the burning of homes and villages. "Nothing would have a greater tendency to conciliate. And much of the future commerce and returning intercourse between the two countries may depend on the reconciliation." With refreshing courage, as if representing a conquering nation, he mildly suggested that England should of her own accord give up Canada. Oswald was in turn told by Shelburne that reparation would not

[1] Fitzmaurice, *Shelburne*, III., 180.

be heard of, and that he was to "make early and strict conditions, not only to secure all debts whatever due to British subjects, but likewise to restore the Loyalists to a full enjoyment of their rights and privileges." "No independence," he was informed, was "to be acknowledged without their being taken care of." He was also told that England must hold as far as the Penobscot River.[1] These instructions formed the core of the British demands, and we thus see at the beginning the subjects that were to be discussed at greatest length and that constituted the most serious obstacles to final agreement: the debts of British merchants; compensation to the loyalists; the northern and eastern boundary. Later there was added to these subjects of controversy the right of the Americans to make use of the Newfoundland fisheries.

Oswald was at last fully commissioned to treat for peace. He was a Scotch merchant, not a trained diplomatist. Owing to his possession of estates in America and his connections with that country, he had been at times consulted by the government during the war.[2] Like Shelburne he was a disciple of Adam Smith, and a man of liberal principles. He was of a mild, temperate, and friendly disposition, but scarcely a match in wits for the talented American commissioners with whom he came into competition.

The first difficulty arose concerning the suffi-

---

[1] Fitzmaurice, *Shelburne*, III., 188, 189.   [2] *Ibid.*, 176.

ciency of Oswald's commission.   He was authorized
to treat with the commissioners of "Colonies or
plantations," and to conclude with "any person or
persons whatsoever, a peace or truce with the said
Colonies or plantations."[1]   To Jay, whom sombre
experiences in Spain had perhaps made unusually
sensitive, such a commission seemed entirely un-
suitable, and he flatly refused to treat seriously with
Oswald on any such basis.   The states had long
since ceased to be colonies or plantations, he asserted, and until England was ready to negotiate
with the United States he would go no further.
Franklin, on the other hand, thought that the
commission was satisfactory enough.

Vergennes agreed with Franklin, and by advising
the Americans to proceed with the negotiations, to
content themselves with the substance and not
make too much ado about the shadow, he aroused
Jay's suspicions.   Jay believed that Vergennes did
not desire the independence of America until all
possible use had been made of her, and that in the
end American interests would be sacrificed to Spain.
In this mood he went so far as to explain to Oswald
that it was good policy for England to render
America independent of France, and that a new
commission recognizing the states as independent
would have the desired effect.[2]   Franklin finally
consented to accept Jay's theory and demand a new

[1] Fitzmaurice, *Shelburne*, III., 249.
[2] Jay, *Corresp. and Public Papers*, II., 372, 373, 381.

commission before beginning formal negotiations for peace.

At this juncture there fell into Jay's hands a copy of a letter written by M. Marbois, a secretary of the French legation in America, to Vergennes. The writer commented on the work of Samuel Adams in raising a strong opposition to any treaty which did not assure to the states the right to the Newfoundland fisheries, and the letter disclosed a very critical, not to say unfriendly, tone toward the United States.[1] Thus for various reasons Jay became convinced that France was willing, if not anxious, not only to keep America from obtaining a share of the fisheries, but to limit the extension of the territory in the west, and that Vergennes was desirous of propitiating the Spaniards at American expense. The dearest object of Spain, as Jay well knew,[2] was to shut off the Americans from the Gulf of Mexico, and to make it almost a closed sea washing the shores of her colonies, which she kept in commercial as well as political subjection to herself. To this end the states must be kept back from the Mississippi and, if possible, confined to the region east of the summits of the Appalachian Mountains.

M. Rayneval, one of Vergennes's secretaries, approached Jay on the subject of the boundaries, saying that as the Americans had no inherent right to the western country they were overbold in

[1] Wharton, *Dip. Corresp. of Am. Rev.*, V., 238–241.
[2] *Ibid.*, IV., 146.

claiming it all. A few days after this conference he sent to the American commissioner a memoir urging a compromise of the conflicting claims of Spain and the United States, and marking off a proposed limit which would deprive the Americans of nearly the whole of the Mississippi Valley.[1] The land south of the Ohio was to be divided into two parts, over the eastern portion of which the United States was to have some sort of control, inasmuch as the Indians inhabiting it were to be under the protection of the United States. Even this portion, however, did not reach to the Mississippi, and the navigation of at least the lower part of the river was evidently to be denied to the American settlers in the west. As to the fate of land north of the Ohio, Spain, the memoir conceded, could have nothing to say. From Rayneval's communication Jay concluded that the French court "would, at a peace, oppose our extension to the Mississippi" and our claim to a free navigation of the river; that she would probably support the British claim to all the country above the thirty-first degree of latitude, and certainly to all the country north of the Ohio; and that in case we should not agree to divide with Spain in the manner proposed, France would aid Spain in obtaining the territory she desired and would agree that the residue should be left to England.[2]

[1] Jay, *Corresp. and Public Papers*, II., 394–398. See map.
[2] *Ibid.*, 398.

Concerning the right to navigate the Mississippi and the title to the western country there had been much discussion in Congress; but in the final instructions the commissioners were not ordered to insist on title to the west or a right to use the river.[1] The American negotiators knew well, however, that Congress desired the land beyond the mountains, and Jay may have had some suspicion that Congress had retreated from its earlier position because of the efforts of the French representatives in America. He was determined, at any rate, that France should not sacrifice the interests of the states to satisfy the hungry maw of Spain.

While matters were in this condition Jay learned that Rayneval, while pretending to go to the country, had secretly departed for London, and he made up his mind that the object of the expedition was to influence Lord Shelburne against America, to discover whether the English would agree to divide the fisheries with France to the exclusion of all others, and to impress upon the English minister Spain's determination "to possess the exclusive navigation of the Gulf of Mexico," and to keep the states from the Mississippi.[2] Promptly and with admirable daring, Jay cast aside all scruples concerning his instructions. Without consulting Franklin,[3] not to say the ministers "of our generous ally, the king

---

[1] Wharton, *Dip. Corresp. of Am. Rev.*, IV., 476, 477.
[2] Jay, *Corresp. and Public Papers*, II., 402.
[3] *Ibid.*, 408.

of France," he prevailed on Benjamin Vaughan, an Englishman and a friend of Franklin, to go to England and show the ministry that it was "the obvious interest of Britain immediately to cut the cords" which tied America to France. The commissioners, Jay said, were determined faithfully to fulfil all engagements of the treaty with the French court, but to be bound by the French construction of their engagements was quite another thing.[1] Vaughan was also urged to make further representations for counteracting the machinations of Rayneval, and to impress on Shelburne the policy of "taking a decided and manly part respecting America."

Without needing to use much persuasion, Vaughan secured the issue of a new commission, authorizing Oswald to treat with representatives of the United States of America. Before the end of September it was brought to Oswald,[2] and negotiations could now commence in earnest. Jay was unwilling to acquaint Vergennes with the course of their proceedings, and Franklin finally, with some reluctance, agreed to break his instructions and to go on without reference to the wishes of France. There is an old story, which may not be true, but which is as good as if it were, because it discloses a real situation, that one day when Franklin and Jay were sitting together Franklin asked, "Would you break your instructions?" "As I break this pipe," said Jay, and he threw the fragments into the fire.

[1] Jay, *Corresp. and Public Papers*, II., 405, 407.   [2] *Ibid.*, 447.

CHAPTER II

THE TREATY OF PARIS

(1782–1784)

WE may now stop to consider whether Jay was justified in the stand he took, and particularly whether his suspicions of French faith were well founded. His refusal to accept Oswald's original commission and to treat for an acknowledgment of independence was probably wise. It amounted to a declaration that America should be treated with as an independent power, and that independence need not be considered in the negotiations as the price of peace. Too much can be made of this episode, for that America really secured better terms simply because her independence was acknowledged before treating may well be doubted. On the other hand, Jay was right, because he was technically so, but chiefly because an evidence of weakness would have damaged his cause. A dignified objection to being considered a delegate from rebellious colonies rather than a plenipotentiary from sovereign states was natural, legitimate, and useful.

The propriety and wisdom of Jay's conduct

toward France constitute a difficult and perplexing problem, which can be understood only after a careful study of many details. One needs to examine all the intricacies of the tangled skein of Revolutionary diplomacy before reaching a conclusion, and then he may find his opinion differing from the judgment of other investigators, for the decision rests on circumstantial evidence and depends on interpretation of personal conduct. First, it may be said that the episode of the Marbois letter, of which much has been said by historical writers, is of little importance. Suspicions have been thrown on its authenticity, but it was probably entirely genuine. Though written in a tone decidedly captious and unfriendly to America, and in that respect not altogether in harmony with other correspondence between Vergennes and his representatives, it was in general accord with French policy; and it is difficult to explain why Jay should have been surprised by it, for before he left America he knew very well that France did not think that the United States should make the possession of the fisheries the absolute condition of a satisfactory treaty.[1]

Concerning the purpose of Rayneval's mission, Jay was in a measure mistaken. Rayneval was sent to interview Shelburne with intent to discover whether certain communications made by Shelburne

[1] Wharton, *Dip. Corresp. of Am. Rev.*, V., 241; Doniol, *Histoire de la Participation*, IV., 177–182.

to De Grasse concerning the basis of peace were to be taken seriously and at full value. He was not formally instructed to discuss American affairs; but the fact of the matter is, he did discuss them and did not hesitate to speak disparagingly of the American claims.[1] No harm was done the American cause, however, for the result of his work was probably to convince Shelburne that, as he had already suspected, the French and Americans were in disagreement. Thus Rayneval encouraged a natural desire on the part of the English to win the United States from attachment to France, and also inspired them to offer favorable terms to the persistent commissioners at Paris. It is not to be wondered at, nevertheless, that Jay believed that Rayneval's purpose was to injure the American cause and assist that of Spain and France. He showed considerable sagacity as well as independence of judgment; in light of the evidence before him he was, perhaps, justified in acting as he did.

And yet in his suspicions of France Jay was only partly right. If we free our minds from the old-fashioned notion that France entered the war and poured out her blood and treasure for the gratification of America and from an amiable zeal for American principles, and if we see that her chief object was to weaken England and to restore in

[1] Wharton, *Dip. Corresp. of Am. Rev.*, V., 821; Doniol, *Histoire de la Participation*, V., 132; Fitzmaurice, *Shelburne*, III., 263–268.

some measure her own prestige, then the action
of France takes on a different aspect, and we do
not so lightly charge her ministers with cunning,
duplicity, and falsehood. Of course, she was not
wasting her substance to please America, and nothing but simple self-complacency would have imag-
ined that such was her object.   For some years
before the summer of 1782 the French had been
bearing the burden of the war.   To accuse France
of treachery under such circumstances, because she
was insistent that the United States must not make
a separate peace, or because she did not wish Congress or the commissioners to set terms and conditions that would prolong the war, is to misunder-
stand the difficulty of her position and to judge of
her conduct solely from the viewpoint of American
desire.   It is necessary to remember that France
was the leader in a great European war for which
she was responsible; and she had good reason for
contending that America should not be regardless
of the interests of the other combatants.

As we have already seen, however, the problem
had been much complicated by the fact that France
had finally induced timorous, selfish Spain to join
in fighting England, and, believing in the need of
Spanish aid, had entered into an arrangement,
which was not, to be sure, in direct variance with
her pledges to America, but which rendered the
consummation of peace more difficult.   Indeed, in
some slight measure this arrangement made the in-

terests of the United States subordinate to those of Spain, all of whose feelings and instincts were hostile to the purposes of the revolting colonies.[1] The terms of the treaty between France and Spain were not known in detail to our commissioners in 1782, but we can now see that France was embarrassed by the pressing demands of her European neighbor, who had entered the war with hesitation, had not contributed much to its success, and wished to come out of it with glory and the lion's share of the booty.

Under the circumstances it was impossible for Vergennes to act as if only American interests were to be considered. He seems to have been sincerely anxious for peace,[2] for France was feeling sorely the burden of the war. He was, moreover, desirous of keeping the friendship of Spain, and, to satisfy her, was quite willing that the Americans should be hemmed in between the mountains and the sea. We must remember that the American claims were, to say the least, exceedingly bold, while Spain's demands for western land were not devoid of reason. There is no evidence that Vergennes had much at heart the narrowing of American territory; he wished, in order to bring peace and to appease Spain, that the claims of our commissioners should be kept just as low as possible. He was not at all anxious to see America playing a conspicuous rôle

[1] Doniol, *Histoire de la Participation*, III., 574–576.
[2] *Ibid.*, IV., 544.

among the nations, and had little dread of her
capacity, but he was also honestly set upon securing
the independence of the states. The lowest limit
that would stand any chance of being acceptable to
the negotiators at Paris or to Congress was the one
he favored.[1] There may be some reason for thinking that he wished to hem in the Americans by the
Appalachians, because he hoped that ultimately
French, rather than Spanish, power would be established in the west.[2] But there seems at present
to be little substantial evidence that any such hope
or purpose really determined his conduct.

As to what course the American commissioners
should have taken, men still differ in opinion. The
instructions, obtained as they were, need not be
taken too seriously, and the commissioners did not
in any way desert France or disregard her peculiar
interests in their negotiations. Jay suspected more
than the truth, and it may possibly be true that he
gained nothing by his breach of instructions and
by conducting the negotiations without the knowledge of France. But if all of the negotiations had
been carried on with the full knowledge of Vergennes, and hence with the full knowledge of Spain,
there is little reason to think that so good a treaty
could have been secured. France certainly would
not have given frank advice in favor of American
demands, and probably in the end the commissioners

---

[1] Doniol, *Histoire de la Participation*, IV., 617–621.
[2] F. J. Turner, in *Amer. Hist. Review*, X., 249 et seq.

would have been obliged to disregard the counsel of the ministers of the king. We may conclude then by saying that Jay was partly right and partly wrong in his suspicions; that France was in a position in which she could not possibly consider only the interests of the United States and give advice for the benefit of America alone; that because of the breach between the commissioners and the French minister the English were induced to treat more freely, more rapidly, and more generously than would otherwise have been the case; that while Vergennes was not altogether frank, and was considering the interests of Spain and France, he was not deliberately, treacherously, and maliciously plotting, as is sometimes charged, to cramp and belittle the United States.

When Oswald's new commission came, late in September, 1782, negotiations began in earnest. Vergennes was not informed as to the details of what was under discussion, and the business in hand moved forward rapidly. Early in October Jay submitted to Oswald a scheme of a treaty,[1] to which the British commissioner gave his consent, and it was sent to England in hopes that it would be acceptable to the ministry. The boundaries were practically the same as those called for by the early instructions of Congress:[2] the northern line, running from the intersection of the forty-fifth

---

[1] Wharton, *Dip. Corresp. of Am. Rev.*, V., 811.
[2] *Secret Journals of Congress*, August 14, 1779.

degree of north latitude with the St. Lawrence to
the south end of Lake Nipissing and thence straight
to the sources of the Mississippi, included a good
deal of what is now Canada; the western line was
the Mississippi. The Americans were assured the
right to enjoy the fisheries, but, on the other hand,
there was no promise on the part of the United
States that the refugees would be compensated or
that the laws regarding confiscations would be repealed, the commissioners declaring that the laws
for confiscation had been made by the individual
states and that Congress had no authority to
stipulate for their repeal.[1]

The draught of the proposed treaty was not acceptable to the ministry. They knew it would be
bitterly attacked in Parliament, if for no other
reason because it contained no promise of aid to
the loyalists, who by adhering to the king's cause had
risked their all, and in many cases had lost their
all, and thousands of whom had been treated with
harshness or driven from the country. The English merchants also to whom debts were owing in
America would expect assurance that they could
make collections; and the boundaries as outlined in
this preliminary sketch were, Shelburne thought, far
too generous to America.[2]

Shelburne, therefore, decided to try again, and
sent Henry Strachey to aid Oswald, and perhaps to

[1] Franklin, *Works* (Sparks's ed.), IX., 426.
[2] Fitzmaurice, *Shelburne*, III., 281, 282.

strengthen the resisting power of this friendly and gracious commissioner. John Adams about the same time came to Paris from The Hague and entered vigorously into the work. The English representatives now insisted upon restoration of property to the loyalists, or their indemnification, and a stipulation for general amnesty. Strachey was not so pliant as Oswald seems to have been. He is "artful and insinuating," wrote Adams. "He pushes and presses every point as far as it can possibly go; he is the most eager, earnest, pointed spirit." [1]

In spite of strong objections and many difficulties another preliminary sketch was agreed upon and taken to England early in November,[2] by which it was agreed that British creditors should meet with no lawful impediments to recovering the sums owing them on debts contracted before 1775. As for the loyalists, the American commissioners would go no further than a stipulation that Congress should recommend to the states so to correct any laws they might have passed regarding the con- fiscation of lands belonging to British subjects as to render the acts consistent with justice and equity. Only the tenacity of Adams retained the guaranty of the right of citizens of the United States to enjoy the fisheries in common with British subjects as "heretofore." The northern and eastern

---

[1] John Adams, *Works*, III., 303.
[2] Wharton, *Dip. Corresp. of Am. Rev.*, V., 851.

boundaries were not far different from those appearing in the earlier draught; the southern boundary
was, as before, the thirty-first parallel from the
Mississippi to the Appalachicola, but a separate
secret article was agreed upon, wherein it was
stipulated that if at the conclusion of the war Great
Britain should retain West Florida, the northern
boundary of this province should be a line through
the mouth of the Yazoo ("Yassous") River, which
is about 32° 25', not far from the present site of
Vicksburg.[1]

The commissioners waited with interest in Paris
for some announcement as to the reception accorded
the new articles in London. There was reason
enough to fear that the refusal to give compensation
to the Tories might destroy all prospects for immediate peace. Jay said that England would be
content with a "tract of land, with a pompous pre-
amble."[2] But the Americans were determined that
nothing favoring the loyalists should be inserted.
And yet something must be done. "We live in
critical moments," wrote Adams. "Parliament is
to meet, and the King's speech will be delivered on
the 26th."[3] Shelburne, indeed, needed to act quickly;
he had to choose between an unsatisfactory treaty
and none at all, and either alternative would be
troublesome. But as the king could not meet

---

[1] Wharton, *Dip. Corresp. of Am. Rev.*, V., 851–853.
[2] John Adams, *Works*, III., 325.
[3] Wharton, *Dip. Corresp. of Am. Rev.*, VI., 65.

Parliament with good face unless able to announce either peace or the continuance of the war, the houses were prorogued for a few days, and Shelburne determined to make another effort for the loyalists and possibly for the fisheries.

When this determination was announced at Paris, wearily over the subject the commissioners went again. The Americans absolutely refused to yield compensation for the Tories and insisted on the right to a share in the fisheries. It was finally brought home to the attention of the Englishmen that they could get no better terms, and a preliminary treaty was agreed to on November 30, 1782,[1] not substantially different from the draught which Strachey had taken to London the early part of the month.

In the treaty as finally agreed upon the boundary was not the same as in the earlier draughts, and, though considered accurate at the time, it in reality left much to be determined by later negotiation. The northeastern boundary was described as "a line drawn due north from the source of Saint Croix River to the Highlands; along the said Highlands which divide those rivers that empty themselves into the river St. Lawrence, from those which fall into the Atlantic Ocean, to the northwesternmost head of Connecticut River." This seemed clear enough, but, in fact, before the lines could be drawn it was necessary to determine which was the St.

[1] Wharton, *Dip. Corresp. of Am. Rev.*, VI., 96–99.

Croix River, which highlands were referred to,
what were the rivers falling into the ocean, and
to which branch of the Connecticut belonged the
northwestern head of the river. From the Connecticut the line ran along the forty-fifth parallel to
the St. Lawrence, thence through the Great Lakes
and connecting waters to the Lake of the Woods.
From the most northwestern point of the Lake of
the Woods the line ran due west to the Mississippi—
an impossible boundary—down the river to latitude
thirty-one degrees, and thence east, by that parallel
and by the line which is now the northern boundary
of Florida, to the ocean. The secret article mentioned before was retained, whereby the United
States agreed, in case Great Britain at the conclusion of the war should "recover or be put in
possession of West Florida," to accept as its southern
boundary from the Mississippi to the Appalachicola
a line running through the mouth of the Yazoo.
Heedless of the fact that the mouth of the Mississippi was in the hands of unhappy Spain, the eighth
article of the treaty declared that the navigation
of the river from its source to its mouth should be
free to Americans and British alike. The grant of
this privilege of navigation England based on her
treaty with France of 1763.

The success of the American negotiators was
phenomenal; they won practically every contested
point. "You will notice," wrote Vergennes to
Rayneval, "that the English buy peace rather than

make it. Their concessions, in fact, as well in the matter of the boundaries as in that of the fisheries and the loyalists, exceed all that I could have thought possible." [1] The peace was received with enthusiasm in America, as well it might have been; for how the country that had in many ways wearied of the war and of strenuous well-doing could have had the hardihood to expect so much is difficult to see. [2]

Some members of Congress, it is true, were disposed to criticise the conduct of the commissioners. [3] But such complaints were of little moment, for in reality the course followed by the negotiators worked France no injury. The articles of agreement of 1782 were preliminary only, and it was distinctly understood that the final treaty should not be signed until France was ready to close the war.

Vergennes wrote in a tone of injured magnanimity to Luzerne, who repeated to Congress his master's sentiments. But Vergennes could complain of naught save the exhibition of discourtesy and lack of confidence. His letter to Franklin was a dignified rebuke: "You are wise and discreet, sir; you perfectly understand what is due to propriety; you have all your life performed your duties. I pray

[1] Circourt, *Histoire de l'Action Commune*, III., 50.
[2] Jay, *Corresp. and Public Papers*, III., 40.
[3] Madison, *Papers* (Gilpin's ed.), I., 407; Wharton, *Dip. Corresp. of Am. Rev.*, VI., 333, 334.

you to consider how you propose to fulfill those which are due to the King." An adroit letter, at once frank and insinuating, in the best form of experienced diplomacy, was sent by Franklin, acknowledging that the Americans had been guilty of neglecting a point of *bienséance*, and intimating that he hoped the notion of the Englishmen that they had divided the allies would prove unfounded.[1] So little did the French minister feel aggrieved that he consented almost immediately after this interchange of letters to afford the United States a new proof of the friendship of the king by granting a loan of six million livres for the year 1783, and this although France was much oppressed with the expenses of the war, and although the financial burdens that were rolling up were beginning to foretell the great revolution that awaited her.

To discuss the question as to which one of the commissioners is deserving of chiefest credit would be useless; we all must recognize the fact that Jay, with admirable boldness, took the weightiest responsibility and bore the heaviest burden in the anxious days before Adams came from The Hague. Adams, whose rare words of praise are like apples of gold in pictures of silver, was warm in his enthusiasm for Jay's valor: "Nothing that has happened since the beginning of the controversy in 1761 has ever struck me more forcibly, or affected me more intimately, than that entire coincidence of principles

[1] Wharton, *Dip. Corresp. of Am. Rev.*, VI., 140, 143, 144.

and opinions between him [Jay] and me." [1] But
until further evidence is produced we are also
bound to believe that Jay was somewhat too suspicious of France, for if in the end American independence had not been secured Vergennes would
have been discredited in Europe, and there is as
yet no evidence that he had much at heart the
limitation of America's territory, even if on the
whole he was inclined to sympathize with Spain in
her contention for the west. Franklin, it should be
noticed, had laid the plans for the negotiation, and
there is no good reason for thinking that he would
have easily surrendered any of the American claims.
Easy-going he was, and possibly too much inclined
to trust the Frenchmen, who of course had their own
interests to look after, but he was shrewdness itself,
and had spent a long life in studying human nature
and learning its lessons.

In January, 1783, England concluded preliminary
articles of peace with France and Spain. Gibraltar,
the chief object of Spanish desire, was not surrendered to Spain, but Minorca and the Floridas were.
France, for all her sacrifices, obtained but little.
She had entered the war hoping to crush forever the
power of her rival across the channel; she had acted
with energy and spent money with profusion. Con-
firmation of a few petty fishing privileges, the establishment of "full right" to two dreary islands off
the coast of Newfoundland, abrogation of an article

[1] Adams, *Works*, III., 336.

in the treaty of Utrecht stipulating that Dunkirk should not be fortified, certain territories in India which she was destined soon to lose, and a few other concessions from Great Britain, seem slight recompense for the strenuous efforts of France to regain her old prestige by helping the American colonies to independence, and by humbling the nation that had stripped her of her possessions twenty years before.[1]

Though it is difficult to see how America could have won independence without France, though Spanish aid was won only by dangling "shining objects" like Gibraltar temptingly before the eyes of the court at Madrid, and though France planned the campaigns, furnished troops, and paid money, the French king received little for his pains, and within ten years after this treaty England was ready to fight again, seemingly as vigorous and as self-reliant as of yore. If the American Revolution was a popular uprising on this side of the water, in Europe it was pre-eminently a war conceived in the cabinets of kings, and fought out for policies of state that in the end proved illusory.

The definitive treaty of peace,[2] concluded on September 3, 1783, and ratified by the Congress of the Confederation in January, 1784, was simply a repetition of the preliminary articles of November, 1782. America was now possessed of a wide territory and

---

[1] *Annual Register*, 1783, pp. 322–338.
[2] *Treaties and Conventions of U. S.* (ed. of 1889), **375–379.**

every apparent opportunity for peace and progress.
Could England have rested content with her loss and
treated her former colonies with nobleness and justice, could America have forgotten her animosity
and believed that not all Englishmen were bullies,
could the spirit which actuated Oswald, Jay, and
Franklin at Paris have been perpetuated, many of
the trials of the future might have been avoided.

CHAPTER III

THE PROBLEM OF IMPERIAL ORGANIZATION
(1775–1787)

THE end of the war did not end America's trials.
The next few years were crowded with perplexities; men that could think were anxious and
troubled. Before the people who had broken away
from Britain and had announced their own political
beliefs could take full advantage of the opportunities lying at their door, the wreckage left by the
war had to be cleared away; they had to find suitable political organization, overcome the disastrous
influence of civil commotion, look the toil of the
future fairly in the face, and begin seriously to prac-
tise the principles of self-government, which many
were apt to forget were not far different from the
principles of self-control.

The Revolution, if correctly understood, was
much more than a separation from Great Britain; it
was more even than the establishment of so-called
free institutions as over against monarchical institutions. To understand the task of political and social
organization, we must remember that the Revolution had been a civil war. No notion could be

35

more erroneous or lead us into greater difficulties in our endeavor to appreciate the trials that ensued after the war was over than the notion that the Revolution had been merely a contest between America and Great Britain, that it was a great popular uprising of a united people indignant and righteously angered at the prospect of tyranny. As a matter of fact, while a majority of the Americans sympathized with the so-called patriot cause, only a small minority were actively interested and ready really to sacrifice their material comfort for an ideal. A large number, almost equal to the enthusiastic patriots, were stanch loyalists, willing to do service for George III., to fight, if need be, in his armies, to give up their property and go into exile rather than surrender the name of Englishmen or prove traitors to their king. A third large group, fond of the good things of this world and not anxious about the success of either side, had shown a readiness to drink British Madeira at Philadelphia or New York, or to sell their produce for bright British guineas, while the American army, hungry and cold, ill-clad — if clad at all — were starving and shivering at Valley Forge or dying of small-pox at Morristown.

An interesting glimpse of this Revolutionary struggle is obtained from Washington's letter to Congress,[1] in which he speaks of Howe's success in Pennsylvania (1777). Washington had been moving

---

[1] Washington, *Writings* (Ford's ed.), VI., 80.

through a country in which it was difficult for the
Americans to gain intelligence because the people
were "to a man disaffected," while forced marches
and rapid movements of the troops were impossible
because a great number of the soldiers were without
shoes. Washington, not Howe, was in the enemy's
country. It was, therefore, from the distressing influences of civil strife that America had to free herself in the days of readjustment after the peace,
when the troops were withdrawn, the Continental
army was disbanded, and the people were left to look
in upon themselves and wonder what manner of folk
they were.

The loyalists were many—perhaps nearly, if not
quite, a third of the population.[1] Many of them
were, moreover, or had been when the war began,
men of substance and of position. On the whole,
they came from the conservative classes, who disliked rebellion for itself and because they had something to lose. Men that were looking for a chance
to wipe out their old debts and had hopes of getting
something ahead in the general overturning were
not apt to be Tories. The people that were banished
from Boston were members of the old families of the
commonwealth.[2] Greene reported to Washington
that two-thirds of the property in New York City

[1] Van Tyne, *Loyalists*, 94–105; Tyler, "The Party of the
Loyalists in the American Revolution," in *Amer. Hist. Review*,
I., 27–29; Flick, *Loyalism in New York*, 182; Van Tyne, *Ameri-
can Revolution*, chap. xiv.

[2] Tyler, in *Amer. Hist. Review*, I., 31.

and its suburbs belonged to Tories,[1] and one is constrained to feel that in the confiscation by which loyalists' property was taken during the war there was a tinge of more than patriotic enthusiasm or even of partisan hostility; there was greed for the spoils of the enemy.

We must not understand from this that the Tories were all educated gentlemen and the Whigs miscreants and ruffians; but if we see aright the difficulty of the situation after the peace, we must at least appreciate the fact that in the war there had been a great social upheaval, that many of the wisest, ablest, and most substantial citizens had been driven into exile, and that no country could afford to lose the services of such men as moved away to England or passed over into Nova Scotia or settled in Canada to be the Pilgrim Fathers of the Dominion—no country, above all, that was forced to establish lasting political institutions and to undertake a great constructive task that might well have proved too heavy for the most efficient and the most creative nation in the world. This expulsion of tens of thousands of loyalists was well likened by a contemporary to the expatriation of the Huguenots on the revocation of the Edict of Nantes.[2] From that expatriation France has not yet recovered. Could America easily get on without the one hundred thousand men, women, and

---

[1] Washington, *Writings* (Sparks's ed.), IV., 86, *n.*
[2] Grant, *Memoirs of an American Lady* (ed. of 1846), 283.

children who were killed in the wars, died in prison, or suffered banishment because they had been faithful to the cause of King George? Could she prosper politically without the help of those disfranchised Tories that survived the trials of the war and remained to face the ill-will of their neighbors? To a country, then, which had known the agony of civil strife, which had been confiscating the property of its own citizens, which had seen thousands of its prosperous people impoverished or driven across the seas, came the duty of finding stable, trustworthy, and free institutions for a vast territory.

The political task that confronted the people when independence from Great Britain was declared was in its essence the same that had confronted the British ministry ten years before—the task of imperial organization. Britain had been able to find no principles that suited the colonists or that in the long run suited herself. The learned Mansfield or the faithful Grenville could do no more than assert the sovereignty of Parliament and declare that all power rested at Westminster. The Americans were not content with this simple declaration of law; they insisted on other rights, on an imperial order in which not all legislative power was gathered at the centre. When at length independence came, when the colonies were states, and especially when the war was over, what was America to do? Could the Americans, who had scolded England so roundly and broken away from her control, find imperial organization themselves without giving up all they had contended for? Could they reconcile local liberty with central authority and real unity? The work was a momentous one, of great significance to mankind, and it must be done, if at all, by a distracted country emerging from civil war.

Though the Americans had been contending, as they claimed, for established English principles, the war had in part rested on theories of government and of society which, if carried to their logical conclusion, meant primeval confusion. The ultimate position of the Americans in their argument with England in the years preceding the war had been based on "natural rights," on the assertion that there are certain inalienable rights which no government could take away, rights which had been reserved as untransferable when the individual entered society and when the social compact was formed. The notion that liberty and right existed before government was easily changed into the notion that government, and indeed all the conventionalities of society, had grown at the expense of liberty and the right of the individual. In Tom Paine's *Common Sense*, the most popular book of that generation, this Revolutionary philosophy was admirably set forth. In its pages one could read that government is a necessary evil, and that palaces of kings are built on the ruins of the bowers of paradise. If men believed this, they naturally be-

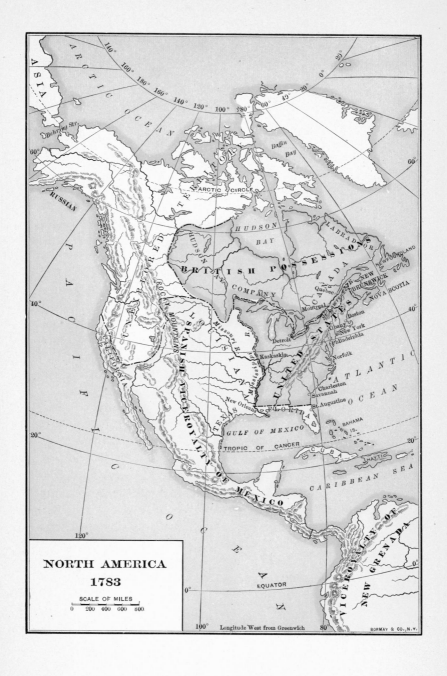

NORTH AMERICA
1783

SCALE OF MILES

0   200 400 600 800

BORMAY & CO., N.Y.

Longitude West from Greenwich

lieved that a return to nature would be a return to happiness; and if, because of sinful man, government, an evil in itself, was necessary, it should be looked on with suspicion and guarded with jealous care. Such philosophy was of wide influence in that generation and the next. Even a man like Jefferson was ready to talk nonsense about fertilizing the tree of liberty with the blood of tyrants, and about the advisability of occasional rebellions, which ought not to be too much discouraged.[1] In the days when such thoughts were current, it was difficult to argue for efficient government and to point to the necessity of punishment and restraint.

The men of those days could not quite see that if the Revolutionary principles were made complete, if the popular institutions were established, if the people were to be the real rulers, there could be no antithesis between government and people, inasmuch as the people were the government, the possessors of the final political authority; what was called government was merely the servant of a power superior to itself. To limit this servant and to make it weak and ineffective was to limit the people. This fact was not comprehended; it took time for the full significance of the democratic idea to come home to men. And this was natural in the light of the long struggle for liberty; it was natural, if it is true that the Revolution was but one of the great movements in English history for a freer life and

[1] Jefferson, *Writings* (Ford's ed.), IV., 362.

for a freer expression of the individual. How could men at once realize that, if the circle was now complete, if they were now the government, there was no need to struggle against government? "It takes time," said Jay, "to make sovereigns of subjects." [1] But many there were besides who believed in individualism pure and simple, the right of the individual to do as he chooses. They did not care where government rested; they wished themselves and their neighbors let alone. All these influences were making, not for imperial organization, not for law and system, but for personal assertion, for confusion that might threaten the foundation of all reasonable order. If these influences were overcome, it must be because the wise and the strong succeeded in winning control.

During the war, it is true, the states had formed new state constitutions,[2] and it will not do to underestimate the importance of the fact that these fundamental laws were made, and that the people discovered and began to make use of the constituent convention—this, after all, is the most significant fact of the American Revolution. But in a measure the theories of the day were a real source of danger even to the states themselves, and the time might come when the men in the individual states would anxiously turn to national authority for relief. It was, moreover, much easier for the people to allow the

---

[1] Jay, *Corresp. and Public Papers*, III., 211.
[2] Van Tyne, *American Revolution*, chap. ix.

state governments to wield power than to grant any to the nation. The local authority was near at hand, and in its new dignity was not very different from the old colonial administration. The war had been begun against a general government; why should implicit obedience be paid to the Congress of the United States, clamoring for power and for taxes as George III. and Lord North had never dared to do?

So far we have seen several different circumstances that must be taken into consideration in interpreting the task of the American people in the years of national readjustment: the harassing and demoralizing experiences of a war which was at once a civil war and a revolution; the banishment and voluntary emigration of thousands of its most intelligent and substantial citizens; the political thinking of the time, which the course of the war had intensified—thinking that, if allowed to ferment in shallow-pated citizens, might endanger the stability of society itself; and, lastly, the fact that the war had been waged to support local governments against a general government. Amid all of these difficulties America was imperatively called upon to organize its empire, if we may use the word to convey the meaning of the vast territory stretching from the St. Croix to the St. Mary's and westward to the Mississippi—an empire inhabited by thirteen distinct groups of people in large measure ignorant of the lives and thoughts of one another.

In solving this problem the United States was at once aided and hindered by its geographical make-up and its history. Geographically separated from Europe by thousands of miles of space and many weeks of time, the Americans felt isolated from the rest of the world, and must perforce have been impressed with the thought of a common destiny; but separated as the states were from one another, when the people were thinking of themselves and not of Europe, they must have felt their differences more keenly than their similarities. South Carolina was so remote from Virginia that we might almost think of her as belonging to the West-Indian group of colonies rather than to the continental. The Declaration of Independence was known in Paris almost as soon as in Charleston. The hardy Yankee seamen who buffeted the winds off stormy Hatteras must have felt far from home when they sailed into the harbor of Wilmington or Savannah. A Georgian knew little of New York or Massachusetts. Life on the plantations of Virginia was far different from life in the little settlements of New England. When John Adams, leaving his fireside in Braintree, went to Philadelphia as a delegate in Congress, the letters which he sent home were welcomed as tidings from a " far country." "Of affairs of Georg[i]a," wrote Madison to Jefferson in 1786, "I know as little as of those of Kamskatska." [1] When we add to all this the

[1] Madison, *Writings* (Hunt's ed.), II., 261.

fact that the colonies were established at different
times and from different motives, and that climate,
soil, and industrial life varied greatly from Maine to
Georgia, we are so impressed by the diversity that
union seems almost beyond the verge of possibility.
And yet political unity was a necessity; any form of
political order not expressing the fact of real inter-
dependence and essential oneness of purpose was
insufficient if America was to organize her empire.

Without modern means of communication, without railroads or telegraphs, the states were also
without good highways of any kind. The road
between Boston and New York was not very bad,
but in the most favorable weather the traveller
making the trip must spend four days in a clumsy,
uncomfortable coach, giving up more time and
much more comfort than he would now expend
in passing across the continent.[1] The highways of
Pennsylvania were often almost impassable, and
travel on them was little less than misery.[2] South
of the Potomac the roads were still worse; there
even bridges were a luxury. Even on the much-
travelled route between the north and the south
the mails were infrequent. Three times a week
throughout the summer they passed between Portland, Maine, and Suffolk, Virginia, but from Suf-

[1] Brissot de Warville, *Travels in America*, I., 97; Quincy, *Life
of Josiah Quincy*, 37.

[2] "Letters of Phineas Bond," in Am. Hist. Assoc., *Report*,
1896, p. 522; *Pa. Archives*, 1st series, X., 129.

folk southward only twice a week in the summer and once a week in winter. Inhabitants of towns out of the main course of travel were more isolated than are now secluded hamlets in the heart of the Rockies. Into the great west beyond the Appalachian range a few courageous men had gone and established their homes; but this vast region was a wild and almost trackless forest. A man in the little village of Louisville was often ignorant for months at a time of what was going on at New York or Boston, knowing no more of the internal affairs of the sea-coast towns than "what our friends are about in the other world."[1]

To such a people, then, thus distracted and thus divided, came the problem of imperial organization. One fact aided them materially: the states were alike in structure; they had the same political inheritance; the fundamental ideas of English liberty and law, taking root in congenial soil, had grown strong in every section; men in all the states thought in the same terms and used the same phrases. Even their Revolutionary philosophy with its notion of absolute rights was a product of English history. Moreover, events, relentless facts, were showing the way to sound union; there could be no real peace and prosperity till political organization was in harmony with industrial and social needs. If the people were reluctant, union on a proper basis was to be established by "grinding necessity."

[1] N. Y. Hist. Soc., *Collections*, 1878, p. 233.

The important process of making state constitutions was pretty well completed four years after the Declaration of Independence, but the formation of a national system was not so simple. For some years after the Declaration the affairs of the Union were conducted by a Congress of delegates on whose discretion or authority there were no constitutional restraints; hence Congress did, not what was needed to be done, but what it was able to do or thought it wise to attempt, at times showing energy and intelligence, again sinking into sloth and incompetence. During these years America was acting under an unwritten constitution, and, in spite of the inability of Congress, establishing precedents of some weight and importance.

On March 1, 1781, Maryland, the last of the thirteen states, signed by its delegates the Articles of Confederation, and henceforward the powers of Congress were clearly outlined.[1] The first form of imperial organization was that of a "perpetual Union," a "league of friendship" between states. To care for the interests of the Confederation, a Congress was provided, to be made up of delegates annually chosen in the states. Each delegation was entitled to one vote; Rhode Island had as much influence in the affairs of America as Massachusetts or Virginia. Congress had authority to decide on peace and war, to carry on hostilities, to manage

[1] For the process of forming the Articles of Confederation, see Van Tyne, *American Revolution*, chap. xi.

all diplomatic matters, to build and equip a navy, to borrow money and emit bills of credit, to make requisitions on the states for men and money, to appoint naval officers and superior military officers, to establish and regulate post-offices, to determine the alloy and value of coin, and to perform some other duties supposed to be of general interest. This was a generous allotment of authority, but its exercise was carefully guarded, since no vote, except to adjourn from day to day, could be carried except by a majority of all the states, while the consent of nine states was required to carry any measure of special importance. Unless nine states agreed, Congress could not engage in war or enter into treaties or alliances, or coin money or borrow money, or make appropriations, or appoint a commander-in-chief, or, indeed, even determine on the sums of money for which it would ask the states.

The better to secure mutual friendship and intercourse, it was especially provided that the free inhabitants of each state should be entitled to all the privileges and immunities of citizens in the several states. Sundry restraints were placed upon the states; they were not to enter into treaties, confederations or alliances, interfere in foreign affairs, or engage in war without the consent of Congress, unless actually invaded. These and similar prohibitions marked with some clearness the line of demarcation between the reserved power of the states and the authority granted to Congress. Congress was the

final resort on appeal in all disputes between the
states, its authority to be exercised by the establishment of a special court or board of arbitration whose
decision was decisive of the question at issue.   The
Articles were in many ways dissimilar to the state
constitutions; in fact, there is no evidence that
their framers intended to follow the examples of
the states.   There was no effort to establish a government with distinct branches; all the authority
granted was in the hands of Congress, which was,
however, authorized to appoint an executive committee to sit when Congress itself was not in session.

This simple arrangement, a confederation of sovereign states, performing certain functions through
a body of delegates, proved in the course of a short
time so inadequate that it is easy to pass these
Articles by with an amused smile at their utter un-
fitness for the work at hand.   As a matter of fact,
they were in many respects models of what articles
of confederation ought to be, an advance on previous
instruments of like kind in the world's history.
Their inadequacy arose from the fact that a mere
confederacy of sovereign states was not adapted to
the social, political, and industrial needs of the time.

In one important particular the Articles were of
profound significance: with remarkable care they
separated the particular or local powers from those of
general character; and let us notice that on the wisdom and the accuracy with which this division is
made must depend the permanence of any plan of

imperial organization. Under no conditions, of course, would the states surrender all political authority to any central government; but by the Articles of Confederation they granted nearly every power that was really of a general or national character. Two powers that the central authority much needed were withheld: the power to raise money and the power to regulate commerce—the very ones about which there had been so much discussion before the war. "Let the king ask for money," the colonists had said to Parliament, "and we will pay it." This plan of imperial organization was to prove a very lame one when applied on this side of the Atlantic; Congress was to try this plan, to call for money, plead for it, implore attention, and remain penniless. But few years were needed to show the necessity for general control of commerce if the Confederation were to be more than a name, or if the states were not to change from rivals into open enemies. In spite of all this, as far as the mere division of powers was concerned, the Articles were not far from perfection, and in any plan for a broader and better system this allotment of authority would be of the utmost service.

Of course the Congress of the Confederation, made up of delegates from states, could not pass effective laws or enforce its orders. It could ask for money but not compel payment; it could enter into treaties but not enforce their stipulations; it could provide for raising of armies but not fill the ranks; it could borrow money but take no proper measures for repayment; it could advise and recommend but not command. In other words, with some of the outward seemings of a government, and with many of its responsibilities, it was not a government.

The Articles, as we have seen, provided for no executive department. They did provide for the appointment of a member of Congress to preside over its sessions; but in fear of kingly authority, it was stipulated that no one person should serve as president more than one year in any term of three years. They also provided for the appointment of civil officers for managing the general affairs of the United States under the direction of Congress. And yet the course of the war had already proved how unfit for general administrative duties were the whole body of delegates or committees of members,[1] and as a result a movement for the establishment of executive departments began even before the Articles went into effect.

The office of postmaster-general, an inheritance from the colonial days, existed from the beginning of the war. In the early part of 1781 the offices of secretary for foreign affairs, superintendent of finance, secretary at war, and secretary of marine were created.[2] To the second position Robert Morris,

---

[1] Guggenheimer, " The Development of the Executive Departments, 1775–1789," in Jameson, *Essays in the Const. Hist. of the U. S.*

[2] *Journals of Congress*, January 10 and February 7, 1781.

of Pennsylvania, whose knowledge of business and finance had already been of great service to the country, was appointed. After considerable delay, caused by the customary factional controversies between the cliques of Congress, General Benjamin Lincoln was made secretary at war. He did not take the office until January, 1782. Nothing of consequence was done with the department of marine, probably because of the old difficulty of selecting anybody that would suit the wrangling factions, and the whole department was turned over to the superintendent of finance, who already had more than any one could do in managing the distracted finances of the Confederation. Robert R. Livingston, of New York, was made foreign secretary, but retained his position only till June, 1783. He was succeeded the next year by John Jay, who showed skill in handling the intricate diplomatic questions of the time, and perhaps even more wisdom in impressing on Congress the importance of his position. By insisting on the dignity of his office and by making use of its privileges, he brought it into prominence and helped to give it a real value and significance.[1] Inadequate as the Articles were, constitutional organs were gradually growing. Administrative failures and experiments were showing the way to a more effective and satisfactory system.

[1] Jameson, *Essays in the Const. Hist. of the U. S.*, 161–165.

CHAPTER IV

POVERTY AND PERIL

(1781–1783)

THE adoption of the Articles gave no assistance to Congress in securing money. It had managed to hobble along in the past, now begging alms of France, now ordering the printer to issue more paper, again obtaining some assistance by requisitions from the states. But if the Confederation was to maintain even the semblance of credit abroad or of dignity at home, it must have money. In February, 1781, even before the Articles had been adopted by Maryland, the states were asked to vest in Congress the power to levy a five-per-cent. import duty; the income thus arising was to be used for paying the debts and interest on the debts contracted or that might be contracted on the faith of the United States for supporting the war.[1] To this request most of the states gave their consent promptly, but Rhode Island, on whose acquiescence much depended, after some hesitation refused to allow such an encroachment on her cherished liberties. The impost, she declared, would bear

---

[1] *Journals of Congress*, February 3, 1781.

hardest on the commercial states; officers unknown
to the free law of the state would be entitled to come
within her limits; and, lastly, to grant to the Congress a power to collect money, for the expenditure
of which it need render no account to the states,
would render that body independent and endanger
the liberties of the United States.[1]   Such reasoning
as this manifested the virile feeling of local liberty
which underlay the Revolution, and was a good
example of how well the states had learned the
lesson of opposition to taxation.   Though the war
was not yet over, Rhode Island feared that Congress
might attack her liberties!   Within a short time
Virginia, which had at first granted Congress the
desired authority, repealed her act, for fear that the
sovereignty of the state would be injured and the
liberties of the state put in jeopardy.[2]

Men like Richard Henry Lee, of Virginia, were
now strongly opposing the growth of Congressional
power.   To inspire jealousy in the states was a
simple and safe route to popularity; an orator or
politician could so easily enlarge upon the dearest
liberties of the people, speak of the bloodshed and
ideals of the war, and pose as the defender of freedom against the machinations of government.
There was already a real controversy between local
and continental politics,[3] which was to last long

---

[1] Staples, *R. I. in the Cont. Cong.*, 400.
[2] Hening, *Statutes*, X., 409, 451.
[3] Hamilton, *Works* (Hamilton's ed.), I., 356.

after Lee and the fearsome Rhode-Islanders were buried. The failure to get the states to agree to give Congress the power to raise money was discouraging in the extreme; but there was a body of intelligent, large-minded men in the country who would not be beaten, and they determined to persist rather than give their country over to ignominy.[1]

To overestimate the need of money would be difficult; money was needed for everything: to pay the troops, to pay the civil servants, to pay the interest on the public debt, to pay the anxious and needy creditors. "Imagine," wrote Morris, "the situation of a man who is to direct the finances of a country almost without revenue (for such you will perceive this to be) surrounded by creditors whose distresses, while they increase their clamors, render it more difficult to appease them; an army ready to disband or mutiny; a government whose sole authority consists in the power of framing recommendations."[2]

To float more paper money was no longer feasible, for the past issues had depreciated so rapidly that even to keep track of their vanishing value was a difficult intellectual task. It is not easy to say when this money had ceased to circulate commonly or how much it was worth at a given time. Jefferson says that by the end of 1781 $1000 of Continental scrip was worth about one dollar in

[1] Madison, *Papers* (Gilpin's ed.), I., 239.
[2] Wharton, *Dip. Corresp. of Am. Rev.*, VI., 203.

specie.[1] Certainly when the Congress of the Confederation was asking for funds the old paper was valueless; an enterprising barber used some of it to paper his shop;[2] a crowd of men and boys, parading the streets of Philadelphia one day, used Continental bills for cockades in their hats and were accompanied by an unhappy dog which had been covered with tar and decorated from head to tail with "Congress" paper dollars.[3] Evidently to turn out more money of this kind might add to the amusement of the populace, but would little avail the superintendent of finance.

To borrow money had never been easy, and it was now a matter of difficulty. France had been generous in her loans and gifts, but the war bore heavily on her income and her patience. Even after the signing of the preliminary articles of peace Vergennes had consented to grant aid, but he could not help remarking that when his majesty had done so much to help America in her time of "moral infancy," she ought now in her maturity to support herself.[4] France could not go on lending money forever; but what hope was there that the Americans would realize that fact, stop their recrimination, and pay their debts? Men that ought to have known better spent their time, not in talking for honesty,

---

[1] Jefferson, *Writings* (Ford's ed.), IV., 154.
[2] Breck, *Historical Sketch of Continental Paper Money*, **15**.
[3] Moore, *Diary of Am. Rev.*, May 7, 1781.
[4] Sparks, *Dip. Corresp. of Rev.*, XI., 172.

but in maligning Morris, charging the troubles
upon him, as if he could make money or ruin
American credit.[1]   To rely on France and Holland
ought to have been humiliating; but there were many
Americans who were quite willing that France
should bear the burden, though it was by no means
a light one.   Taxation in America had become irksome in the extreme.   Morris pleaded and planned
and labored with the states to little purpose; to
talk to them, he said, was like preaching to the dead.

By January, 1783, the finances of the country
were in a deplorable condition.   Morris informed a
committee of Congress, appointed to confer with
him in secret, that his foreign account was already
overdrawn three and a half million livres, and that
further draughts were indispensable "to prevent
a stop to the public service."   In desperation he
proposed to draw again, relying on the friendship of
France and the hope of proceeds from a loan in
Holland.[2]   This was a bold game—to draw on funds
that did not exist, to rely on the friendship of a
nation already overloaded with its own burdens.
But, bold as it was, there was nothing else to be
done, and Congress decided to try it.   This resolution, marking as it does the depth of want and
the height of financial audacity, deserves to be
quoted in full: "Resolved unanimously, That the
superintendent of finance be and he is hereby au-

---

[1] Sumner, *Financier and Finances of Am. Rev.*, II., 97.
[2] Madison, *Papers* (Gilpin's ed.), I., 251.

thorized, to draw bills of exchange, from time to time, according to his discretion upon the credit of the loans which the ministers of the United States have been instructed to procure in Europe, for such sums, not exceeding the amount of the money directed to be borrowed, as the publick service may require." [1]

Soon after this Morris determined to resign, and sent to Congress a strong letter: "To increase our debts while the prospect of paying them diminishes, does not consist with my ideas of integrity. I must, therefore, quit a situation which becomes utterly insupportable. . . . I should be unworthy of the confidence reposed in me by my fellow citizens if I did not explicitly declare that I will never be the minister of injustice." [2] He offered to remain, however, a short time, in hopes of improvement, and, indeed, he was prevailed on to retain the position till November of the next year.[3] In a letter to Washington, written February 27, 1783, he said that Congress wished to do justice, but the members were "afraid of offending their States." [4] That was the root of the difficulty, and conditions were not likely to improve. Morris tried to impress on Congress the wholesome conviction that there was no more hope of European aid. "Whatever may be the ability

---

[1] *Secret Journals of Congress*, I., 253, January 10, 1783.

[2] Wharton, *Dip. Corresp. of Am. Rev.*, VI., 229.

[3] Sumner, *Financier and Finances of Am. Rev.*, II., 95 et seq.; Oberholtzer, *Robert Morris*, 200, 209.

[4] Wharton, *Dip. Corresp. of Am. Rev.*, VI., 266, 267.

of nations or individuals," he said, "we can have no right to hope, much less to expect the aid of others, while we show so much unwillingness to help ourselves. It can no longer be a doubt to Congress, *that our public credit is gone.*" [1] He estimated the public debt, not including the cartloads of Continental paper or the "arrearages of half pay" due the army officers, or various other debts classed as "unliquidated," "being the moneys due to the several States and to individuals in the several States," at over $35,327,000.[2]

Throughout the winter of 1782–1783 the conditions in the country were full of danger. It will be remembered that there was no assurance that the war would not be renewed, and it was necessary still to maintain the army. The main body of the troops was gathered at Newburg on the Hudson. The soldiers were better fed and clothed than they had been in the past,[3] but spending the winter in dreary and rugged hills in idleness, wearily watching the British in New York, was not a pleasing occupation. The patience of the soldiers had been indeed marvellous; but now that peace was at hand they were growing weary of want and penury. The officers had been promised half-pay for life,[4] but nothing had been done to carry out the pledge, and

---

[1] Sparks, *Dip. Corresp. of Rev.*, XII., 342.
[2] Wharton, *Dip. Corresp. of Am. Rev.*, VI., 282.
[3] Washington, *Writings* (Ford's ed.), X. 153.
[4] *Journals of Congress*, October 21, 1780.

the common soldiers lacked even the support of generous but unfulfilled promises. In behalf of themselves and of the soldiers of the army, the officers at Newburg drew up an address (December, 1782) and sent it by delegates to Congress. "We have borne," they said, "all that men can bear—our property is expended—our private resources are at an end, and our friends are wearied out and disgusted with our incessant applications." The tone was menacing because it declared a real and imminent danger, but it was respectful and noble. Congress was told plainly that further experiment on the patience of the soldiers would be perilous.[1]

Strong and incisive as were the letters of Morris and the other officials, they give little notion of how trying and menacing those days were. It is plain that thoughtful men were weighed down with forebodings. Some that knew the situation thought that the army had already secretly determined not to lay down its arms until its reasonable demands were satisfied.[2] Hamilton believed that Washington was daily growing unpopular from his known dislike to unlawful measures, and that leading characters were doing what they could to undermine him. The truth seems to be that Hamilton[3] himself, and others generally patriotic, were not altogether sorry to see the army restless. Perhaps, they

[1] *Journals of Congress*, VIII., 225–228, April 29, 1783.
[2] Madison, *Papers* (Gilpin's ed.), I., 350.
[3] Hamilton, *Works* (Hamilton's ed.), I., 346–348.

thought, this might bring Congress to energetic action and the states to their senses if nothing else
would. Hamilton wrote a patronizing letter to
Washington, telling him that the "claims of the
army, urged with moderation, but with firmness,
may operate on those weak minds which are influenced by their apprehensions more than by their
judgments, so as to produce a concurrence in the
measures which the exigencies of affairs demand."
He hoped that Washington's influence would keep
"a *complaining* and *suffering army* within the
bounds of moderation." [1]

A bolder and more dangerous tone was taken by
Gouverneur Morris, a young man of immense energy, enthusiasm, and self-confidence, then acting
as assistant to Robert Morris; he looked at the
danger of an army uprising almost with hope.
"The army," he wrote to Jay, "have swords in
their hands. You know enough of the history of
mankind to know much more than I have said, and
possibly much more than they themselves yet think
of. I will add, however, that I am glad to see things
in their present train. Depend on it, good will arise
from the situation to which we are hastening . . .
although I think it probable, that much of convulsion will ensue, yet it must terminate in giving to
government that power, without which government
is but a name." [2]

[1] Hamilton, *Works* (Hamilton's ed.), I., 328.
[2] Sparks, *Gouverneur Morris*, I., 249.

If the army were disbanded without steps being taken to pay them, and if the soldiers were sent home to demand pay of the individual states, they would not be likely to retain any particular affection for Congress, under whose direction they had fought and from whom they vainly sought for well-earned wages. The dispersion of the army would mean the dissolution of a natural centre of general patriotism and affection. Morris, and probably Hamilton also, was anxious, therefore, that the army should not become thirteen armies. Morris had the temerity to write to Greene, who was then in the south, and also to Knox,[1] at Newburg, intimating that the army must stand together and not be divided. "If the army," he said to Greene, "in common with all other public creditors, insist on the grant of general permanent funds for liquidating all the public debts, there can be little doubt that such revenues will be obtained." Greene was as patriotic as anybody, but he saw the peril clearly. "When soldiers advance without authority, who can halt them? We have many Clodiuses and Catilines in America, who may give a different direction to this business, than either you or I expect."[2]

This correspondence does not mean that Hamilton and Morris were bent on raising an insurrection; they wished to consolidate the public debts and to

[1] Hatch, *Administration of Am. Rev. Army*, 163, 164.
[2] Sparks, *Gouverneur Morris*, I., 250–252.

have it clearly understood that the Union, not the states, was responsible for payment, If this were accomplished, a firm and durable bond of union would be created. Probably Morris wished the army to present requests for pay in such form that they would have the effect of threats; it may be that he was willing to see even more dangerous steps taken.[1] Whatever the decided intention of Morris and those that thought with him, in discussing the intervention of the soldiers they were playing with fire. And yet the army, although full of combustible material, was patriotic and right-minded. "The army generally have always reprobated being thirteen armies," wrote Knox. "Their ardent desires have been, to be one continental body, looking up to one sovereign." "It is a favorite toast in the army, 'a hoop to the barrel,' or, 'cement to the union.' . . . As the present constitution is so defective, why do not you great men call the people together, and tell them so. That is, to have a convention of the States to form a better constitution?"[2]

While Congress was lamenting and discussing, the situation at Newburg was growing more serious. At no time during the Revolution was the American cause in a more desperate situation than in the early part of 1783. On March 10, 1783, an anonymous paper was circulated suggesting a meeting of the officers of the army for the following day, to

[1] Sparks, *Gouverneur Morris*, I., 250–252.
[2] *Ibid.*, 256; Brooks, *Henry Knox*, 169, 170.

consider their grievances and to take steps to bring an end to their sufferings. It was written with very unusual skill and in language calculated to excite the anger and awaken still further the resentment of the soldiers, who with much justice felt that they had sacrificed their comfort and were now treated with scorn and contumely. "Can you then consent to be the only sufferers by this revolution, and retiring from the field, grow old in poverty, wretchedness, and contempt? Can you consent to wade through the vile mire of dependency, and owe the miserable remnant of that life to charity, which has hitherto been spent in honour!—If you can—GO —and carry with you, the jest of tories and the scorn of whigs—the ridicule, and what is worse, the pity of the world. Go, starve, and be forgotten! But if your spirit should revolt at this; if you have sense enough to discover, and spirit enough to oppose tyranny under whatever garb it may assume; whether it be the plain coat of republicanism, or the splendid robe of royalty, if you have yet learned to discriminate between a people and a cause, between men and principles—awake; attend you to your situation and redress yourselves. If the present moment be lost, every future effort is in vain; and your threats then, will be as empty as your intreaties now."[1]

[1] *Journals of Congress*, April 29, 1783; Washington, *Writings* (Sparks's ed.), VIII., 555 – 558; Hatch, *Administration of Am. Rev. Army*, 197–199.

No better, no more vehement and virile English was written by the generation that produced Burke and Junius, and one is tempted to forget the offence in admiring the capacity of the offender.   The paper seems to have been written by John Armstrong,[1] aide-de-camp to General Gates; but though the hands were the hands of Esau, the cunning and the force were probably supplied by more conspicuous men.   If the pompous Gates was not the chief conspirator, he was at least the figurehead.

Washington discovered that the address had been circulated and at once appreciated the danger. General orders were issued calling for a meeting at a later day, in hopes that in the mean time the passion excited by the inflammatory address might have somewhat subsided.   The senior officer in rank, who could, of course, be none other than the re-doubtable Gates himself, was called on to preside at the meeting.   At the appointed hour Washington appeared.   The scene is one of the most dramatic in our history.   The commander was in fear lest the passions of the army, inflamed by insidious suggestions and stimulated by real injustice, should lead them to turn upon the government or seek to compel the states to pay them their dues; civil war of the most odious and distressful kind might well ensue.   As he took his place at the desk he drew " his written address from his coat pocket, and

---

[1] Hatch, *Administration of Am. Rev. Army*, 161; *U. S. Magazine and Lit. and Polit. Repository*, January, 1823, 37–41.

his spectacles, with his other hand, from his waist-coat pocket, and then addressed the officers in the following manner: 'Gentlemen, you will permit me to put on my spectacles, for I have not only grown gray, but almost blind, in the service of my country.' This little address, with the mode and manner of delivering it, drew tears from [many] of the officers."[1]

The paper was a manly, eloquent, telling appeal to the patriotism, judgment, and patient generosity of the officers; it was a stinging rebuke for the cowardly conspirators who were plotting to disgrace the army and ruin the country. "And let me conjure you," he said at length, "in the name of our common country, as you value your own sacred honor, as you respect the rights of humanity, and as you regard the military and national character of America, to express your utmost horror and detestation of the man, who wishes, under any specious pretences, to overturn the liberties of our country, and who wickedly attempts to open the flood gates of civil discord, and deluge our rising empire in blood."[2] Upon the conclusion of the address the whole assembly was in tears.[3] Washington withdrew and resolutions were then adopted expressing unshaken confidence in the justice of Congress and the country, declaring that the officers of the American army

---

[1] Cobb, in Washington, *Writings* (Ford's ed.), X., 170; see also Pickering, *Pickering*, I., 431.
[2] Washington, *Writings* (Ford's ed.), X., 173, 174.
[3] Lossing, *Schuyler*, II., 427, *n.*

received with abhorrence and rejected with disdain the infamous proposals of the anonymous circular, and respectfully requesting Washington to urge upon Congress the prompt attention to their claims. And thus, " that body of officers, in a moment, damned with infamy two publications, which, during the four preceding days, most of them had read with admiration, and talked of with rapture." [1]

Without more substantial assets than good intentions Congress found itself in an embarrassing situation. While the army was clamoring for wages, the opposition to giving the officers half-pay for life reached in some portions of the land incredible height, causing in New England, Madison said, " almost a general anarchy." In lieu of this method of payment, therefore, Congress determined to offer full pay for five years,[2] and ere long the soldiers were given new promises and steps were taken to disband the army. But the fear of the soldiery, which aroused the sturdy patriots who had bided safe at home during the war, did not die out with the disappearance of the army; the Society of the Cincinnati, an order formed to perpetuate the memories of the Revolution and to preserve the friendships " formed under the pressure of common danger, and in numerous instances cemented by the blood of the parties," [3] awakened the dread of many gloomy-

[1] Letter of March 16, 1783, in Pickering, *Pickering*, I., 440.
[2] *Journals of Congress*, March 22, 1783.
[3] Brooks, *Henry Knox*, 175.

minded citizens, who shuddered at the spectre of an hereditary order.

The veterans who had "borne the heat and burden of the war" went home in good order, "without a settlement of their accounts, or a farthing of money in their pockets." But there was mutiny among the Pennsylvania troops who were stationed at Lancaster. Some eighty of these "soldiers of a day"[1] marched upon Philadelphia, and, though not directly threatening Congress, placed that body in a humiliating position. Just how perilous the situation was it is now difficult to say, but certainly while the authorities in the city were timidly negotiating for days with the band of mutineers, who had found their unerring way to the wine-bottles and the ale-casks of hospitable Philadelphia, the plight of Congress was unenviable and disagreeable. Feeling that its dignity was injured, and not unwilling to rebuke the Pennsylvania authorities, it passed over the river to Princeton,[2] and there for a time continued its helpless process of recommendation and appeal. The event, though not particularly serious in its consequences, was a dramatic representation of the helplessness of the Congress, whose representatives abroad were asking for favors and expecting to be treated as the representatives of a great sovereign nation.

Though the war was over, the year 1783 was full

[1] Washington, *Writings* (Ford's ed.), X., 272.
[2] *Journals of Congress*, June 21 and 30, 1783.

of discouragement; notwithstanding the urgent calls for money, the states did not respond. Morris sent out to the governors a letter of appeal; up to June 13 his payments had exceeded his receipts by more than $1,000,000. "How, indeed, could it be otherwise," he asked, "when all the taxes brought into the treasury since 1781 did not amount to seven hundred and fifty thousand dollars?"[1] For the year 1782 Congress asked for $8,000,000, and for the year 1783 it asked for $2,000,000; but by the end of the latter year less than $1,500,000 had been paid in. A committee which was appointed to consider the matter spoke of the distress and poverty of the people "just relieved from the ravages of predatory armies, returning from an attendance on camps, to the culture of their fields—beginning to sow, but not yet having reaped."[2]

The fact is, however, that the people were not in destitution. There is abundance of contemporary evidence to show that at the end of the Revolution the people were living with more ease and circumstance than before the war. "The people," wrote Morris to Franklin, "are undoubtedly able to pay, but they have easily persuaded themselves into a conviction of their own inability, and in a Government like ours the belief creates the thing."[3] The trouble was not poverty, but commercial confusion,

[1] Wharton, *Dip. Corresp. of Am. Rev.*, VI., 611.
[2] *Journals of Congress*, report of April 5, 1784.
[3] Wharton, *Dip. Corresp. of Am. Rev.*, V., 774.

vicious politics, and a native disinclination to pay taxes. "The necessity of the present application for money," Morris said in 1782, and his remark held true for the next five years, "arises from the necessity of drawing by degrees the bands of authority together, establishing the power of Government over a people impatient of control, and confirming the Federal Union of the several States by correcting defects in the general Constitution." [1]

On the disbanding of the army Washington addressed a long letter to the states, in which he frankly spoke of the condition of the country and the need of respectable government. "This is the favorable moment to give such a tone to our federal government, as will enable it to answer the ends of its institution, or this may be the ill-fated moment for relaxing the powers of the Union, annihilating the cement of the confederation, and exposing us to become the sport of European politics, which may play one State against another, to prevent their growing importance, and to serve their own interested purposes." [2] The letter was courteously received by the states, and it may have had some influence for a time. Things were to grow worse, however, before they grew better. It was already evident that the Confederation was a failure, though efforts to amend the Articles gave no prospect of success; and Congress grew steadily more helpless as the months went by.

[1] Wharton, *Dip. Corresp. of Am. Rev.*, V., 774.
[2] Washington, *Writings* (Ford's ed.), X., 254–265.

CHAPTER V

COMMERCIAL AND FINANCIAL CONDITIONS
(1783–1786)

MORRIS, as we have seen, declared in 1782 that the people were quite able to pay taxes, but had persuaded themselves of their poverty. All through the critical years after the peace this outcry against taxes and this lament over poverty continued, and yet there seems to have been little excuse for it. Some tribulation there was, but that the country was forlorn, destitute, and poverty-stricken is far from the truth.[1]

When the Revolution began it brought at the outset a necessity for industrial and chiefly for commercial readjustment. The trade of New England was, of course, badly deranged. Men were thrown out of employment and property was destroyed. The New England merchants and sailors, however, did not stand about in idleness waiting for the skies to clear. Some of those whose living had been made from the sea moved off into the forest to begin life anew on the frontier; the capital

[1] Chastellux, *Travels in No. Am.*, I., 47, II., 255; Jay, *Corresp. and Public Papers*, III., 223.

and labor of the people "flowed back from the coasts towards the interior of the country, which has profited rapidly by the reflux."[1]   But the fishermen and sailors were not altogether driven from the sea, for hostilities had scarcely commenced when it was seen that war had its chances for gain no less than peace. Privateering was an exciting and lucrative calling, full of interest for the seaman and of fascination for the vessel-owner.   Fast-sailing ships were fitted out in the New England ports, and the Yankee skippers soon showed aptitude for the new trade.   In the year 1776, it is said, three hundred and forty-two English merchantmen were captured by American privateers; in the course of the war Boston alone commissioned three hundred and sixty-five vessels,[2] and to Salem came as many as four hundred and forty-five prizes.   Thus many of the New England seamen and vessel-owners found new, interesting, and lucrative employment which brought money and supplies into the country.   An illustrative experience is that of Elias Hasket Derby, who at the outbreak of hostilities owned a small fleet with which he had been carrying on a profitable trade.   Seeing his business broken up and ruin staring him in the face, he did not spend much time in repining, but fitted out his ships as privateers. The end of the war found him rich and prosperous.[3]

[1] Chastellux, *Travels in No. Am.*, II., 237, 250.
[2] Winsor, *Memorial Hist. of Boston*, III., 118.
[3] Weeden, *Econ. and Soc. Hist. of New Eng.*, II., 776–778.

But after the war was over what were the privateersmen to do? How were the owners to use their ships or employ their capital? Evidently it was necessary to pause and take breath, and there was doubtless a short time when the trade of New England was dull if not stagnant. The whale-fisheries were ruined by the war, and it would take years to build them up to their old place; the cod-fisheries, too, were in bad condition.[1] The whole situation was now altered, for the tradesmen could not at once fall back into the normal methods of peace, and, moreover, the conditions prevailing before the war no longer existed. England was no longer the guardian of American commerce; her old acts of navigation and her old commercial policy, under which, however loud the complaint, American trade had in one manner or another grown tremendously, were now the acts and the policy of a rival nation.

In former years the New-Englanders had carried rum and some other commodities to the British possessions at the north, but by an act passed in 1784 the commerce with Newfoundland was almost entirely prohibited.[2] They had also sent large quantities of oil to London, had sold their ships, built of New England lumber, to pay the debts of their merchants, and had carried on a trade with the West Indies. Soon after the war the king

---

[1] Letters of Higginson, in Am. Hist. Assoc., *Report*, 1896, I., 723, 729.   [2] 25 George III., chap. i.

was authorized by Parliament to issue orders for the regulation of the American trade; and at different times orders in council were issued, which were on the whole fairly liberal and did not by any means apply the old navigation laws in their full vigor. The trade in American ships with the British West Indies was, however, practically prohibited, and England, desirous of encouraging her own whale-fishery, did not permit the importation of American oil.[1] As a result of these regulations the American shipping interests suffered much.

The Americans, with all their adaptability, insisted on following, when possible, the old lines of trade, and especially the old direct trade with England,[2] just as they had done before the war in accordance with the navigation laws about which there had been so much complaint. They insisted on buying in British markets, and they did not properly develop their trade with the other countries of Europe. But even the direct trade with England was naturally less than before the war, and the balance was of course much in England's favor.[3] Because of the retention of the frontier posts in British hands—for these were not given up at the close of the war—a large portion of the fur-trade, which had brought in considerable profit, was confined to the British companies and merchants.

---

[1] Sheffield, *Observations* (ed. of 1784), App., 340–345.
[2] Adams, *Works*, VIII., 323.
[3] Pitkin, *Statistical View of the Commerce of the U. S.*, 17, 30.

All this affected chiefly the New England carrying-trade, and points to a derangement of the old conditions and a need of adjustment. But the south, too, was suffering in a measure; it had recently been in the hands of the enemy and was much torn by civil strife; many thousands of slaves had been carried away by the British. The life of the plantation was therefore considerably disturbed, and the conditions necessitated or seemed to necessitate the introduction of more slaves; time was needed to get new supplies, "to rebuild their houses, fences, barns, etc., . . . and to repair the other ravages of the war." [1] The exportation, therefore, of southern products diminished in amount and value in the first few years after the war.[2] The decrease in ship-building was a discouraging sign of the general situation throughout the country.[3]

Of course it took time for commerce to find new outlets and for business to adapt itself to the close competition and careful bargaining of ordinary times after the excitement and risk of war. Some things the merchants of the north soon proceeded to do; they once again adjusted themselves to facts, not without loud outcries and not without ultimate profit. Ere long the hardy privateersman entered lustily into foreign trade; for the privateering, after

---

[1] Jefferson, *Writings* (Ford's ed.), IV., 204.
[2] Drayton, *View of South Carolina*, 167; *Am. State Papers, Com. and Nav.*, I., 32, 33.
[3] "Letters of Phineas Bond," in Am. Hist. Assoc., *Report*, 1896, I., 638.

all, was but an interlude, a passing stage, between the great negro and rum trade of the earlier days and the European and Oriental traffic that rapidly grew in importance in the first decade after the war. In February, 1784, the *Empress of China* sailed from New York for the Far East, and the next year the enterprising Derby sent out *The Grand Turk* for the Isle of France and Canton. With continental Europe a profitable trade was springing up. Sixty American vessels entered the port of Lisbon in 1785 from American and foreign ports and only seventy-seven European vessels from the same ports;[1] and with France and some of the other continental countries the traffic was considerable. In this way and in others the people were finding new industrial organization, making good such losses as they had suffered in the war, and reaching out for a new prosperity, which could only come in its fulness, however, when the political system gave assurance of protection and opportunity.

At the end of the war, in some portions of the country, if not in all, there was no dearth of money. Probably never throughout the course of colonial history had there been so much specie as circulated in the country immediately after the withdrawal of the English troops. For it must be remembered that during eight years and more the English exchequer had been sending its sovereigns to America,

---

[1] *Dip. Corresp.*, *1783–1789* (3-vol. ed.), II., 577.

that France had freely lent her gold,[1] that the American farmer and merchant had received the bright guineas and *louis d'or* of the foreign armies without even the appearance of hesitation. When we remember the merry winter that Howe spent at British expense in the "rebel capital," we know how some specie got into circulation in the states. Some of this money left the country soon after the peace, for there was an enormous influx of European goods; markets were glutted and merchants cried aloud for buyers.[2]   It has been estimated that in the three years succeeding the war at least £1,260,000 in coin went to England.[3]   But in spite of the rising fear of paper money, which of course tied knots in the purse-strings of those who had good money, and notwithstanding all sorts of obnoxious laws that threatened the creditor with loss, commerce and industry were by no means lifeless.

To know, therefore, just what the situation was in 1785 or 1786 is difficult; but probably we are justified in saying that commerce had grown in vigor and was ready to enter upon a course of great activity, if it could be reasonably safe from the harassing perils of paper money and the annoyance of tender-laws, and could rely on the protection of a good government that could pass proper regulations for trade and form respectable treaties with

---

[1] Wharton, *Dip. Corresp. of Am. Rev.*, VI., 341.
[2] Tench Coxe, *View* (Philadelphia, 1794), 49; Sheffield, *Observations* (ed. of 1784), 248.   [3] *Pa. Gazette*, July 19, 1786.

foreign governments. Though the trade, especially of New England, was badly deranged, the commerce and industry of the country were by no means in a hopeless condition. Everywhere were indications of improvement, even if in some places the ravages of war had not been overcome. The main danger to commerce, and the cause of possible disaster, was the paper-money craze, of which we shall speak in another chapter. Trouble, confusion, and lament there were, and for complaint there was some reason; but, if we believe the testimony of many persons of insight, there was not poverty or destitution.

"Population is encreasing," Charles Thompson reported to Jefferson, "new houses building, new lands clearing, new settlements forming, and new manufactures establishing with a rapidity beyond conception, and what is more, the people are well clad, well fed, and well housed. Yet I will not say that all are contented. The merchants are complaining that trade is dull, the farmers that wheat and other produce are falling, the landlords that rent is lowering, the speculists and extravagant that they are compelled to pay their debts, and the idle and the vain that they cannot live at others cost and gratify their pride with articles of luxury." [1]

To expect to borrow money abroad without making any effort even to provide means of paying interest was absurd, and the failure of the five-percent. impost scheme of course made the prospect of

---

[1] N. Y. Hist. Soc., *Collections*, 1878, p. 206.

relief darker.[1] In April, 1783, soon after Morris declared that American credit was hopelessly at an end, Congress made another effort to procure a steady means of income "as indispensibly necessary to the restoration of public credit." The states were requested to alter the Articles of Confederation so as to invest Congress for twenty-five years with the power to levy for federal purposes a small duty on imported goods, with the express understanding that the income should be used only for the discharge of the principal and interest of the debt;[2] they were also requested to establish for a term of twenty-five years and to appropriate to the discharge of the public debt some substantial and effectual revenue, according to such plans as they might deem convenient. Each was asked to pay in this manner its proper proportion of $1,500,000 annually. With these requests was a recommendation that the section of the Articles of Confederation providing that quotas of taxes for federal purposes be in proportion to the value of lands within their respective limits should be altered, so that in the future the taxes should be applied by the states in proportion to the whole number of free inhabitants and three-fifths of all other persons, except Indians not taxed.

In spite of all efforts and though the need was sore, the recommendations were not followed by

[1] Franklin, *Works* (Sparks's ed.), IX., 459.
[2] *Journals of Congress*, April 18, 1783.

the states. Each watched the other warily, fearing that its neighbor might win some commercial advantage. Three years after the measure was laid before the states for adoption, seven states—New Hampshire, Massachusetts, Connecticut, New Jersey, Virginia, North Carolina, and South Carolina—had granted the impost in such a manner and under such restrictions that if the other states had made similar grants the plan of the impost might immediately have gone into operation. But Pennsylvania and Delaware had consented to the measure with the proviso that it should not go into effect until all of the states passed laws in conformity with the whole revenue system proposed. Only two of the states—Delaware and North Carolina—acceded to the system in all its parts; and four—Rhode Island, New York, Maryland, and Georgia—did not decide in favor of any part of the system. Assured that no money could otherwise be secured, Congress appealed again to the states as late as 1786, urging them to pass laws for the carrying out of the plan and pleading with them for authority to collect the impost.[1]

The financial condition of the Confederation was by this time deplorable. From requisitions $2,457,-987.25 were received by Congress from November 1, 1781, to January 1, 1786; for the last fourteen months of this period the income was but $432,897.81, which was at the rate of $371,052 per year, a sum short of

[1] *Journals of Congress*, February 15, 1786.

what was necessary "for the bare maintenance of the
federal government on the most economical establishment, and in time of profound peace." [1]
Unless the country was to be rated as hopelessly
bankrupt from sheer unwillingness to pay taxes,
something had to be done, inasmuch as $577,000
was due for interest on foreign loans before June
1, 1787; from that time forward, for some years,
interest and capital due on the foreign debt alone
amounted to over $1,000,000 annually. The total
debt, foreign and domestic, which amounted in 1784
to over $35,000,000, was growing by the addition
of unpaid interest, which of course rolled up rapidly; the arrears of interest on the domestic debt
increased from $3,109,000 in 1784 to $11,493,858
before the end of 1789, while the principal alone
of the foreign debt increased from $7,830,517 to
$10,098,707 in the same time. [2] Conditions would
have been even worse without the aid of the Dutch,
who were of constant assistance, lending the strug-
gling Congress in these five years $2,296,000, and
thus in a measure supporting the public credit of
America in Europe.

Meanwhile the income from taxation was scarcely
sufficient to pay the running expenses of the government, while Congress was doing little more than
performing the functions of a stately debating

[1] Report of committee, *Journals of Congress*, February 15, 1786.
[2] Bullock, *The Finances of the U. S., 1775–1789*, in University of Wisconsin, *Bulletin*, Hist. Series., I., 145, *n*, 181, 187.

society.   Money was needed for everything—to pay
the servants of the government at home and its
representatives abroad, to secure immunity from
attack from the Barbary pirates on the ocean and
from the Indians on the frontier, to save the country
from the shame of defaulting in interest.   "The
crisis has arrived," said a committee of Congress, in
February, 1786, "when the people of these United
States, by whose will, and for whose benefit the
federal government was instituted, must decide
whether they will support their rank as a nation, by
maintaining the public faith at home and abroad;
or whether, for want of a timely exertion in establishing a general revenue, and thereby giving
strength to the confederacy, they will hazard not
only the existence of the union, but of those great
and invaluable privileges for which they have so
arduously and so honorably contended." [1]

The penury of the government was so patent that
men listened to this eloquent appeal.   "Oh! my country!" exclaimed Jeremiah Belknap, of New Hampshire.   "To what an alarming situation are we reduced, that Congress must say to us, as Joshua did
to Israel, 'Behold, I set before you life and death.'
. . . We must be drove to our duty, and be taught
by briars and thorns, as Gideon taught the men of
Succoth." [2]   The states were at last moved by

[1] *Journals of Congress*, February 15, 1786.
[2] *Belknap Papers*, I. (Mass. Hist. Soc., *Collections*, 5th series,
II.), 431, 432.

the appeal of Congress, and all but one of those that had not acted granted the impost before the end of 1786. Governor Clinton, of New York, however, politely refused to do anything, declaring that he did not have the power to summon the legislature except on extraordinary occasions.[1]

In New York, as in Virginia, there was a strong party opposed to growth of the national authority and exceedingly jealous for the power of the state. Clinton was the leader of this party, and opposed to him was Hamilton, who worked unceasingly for a broader appreciation of the duties and responsibilities of Congress. Hamilton prepared a petition, which was widely circulated, asking the adoption of the revenue scheme, and declaring that all the motives of public honor and reputation demanded that New York yield.[2] The petition had no effect, and when the next year he took his place in the legislature of the state his eloquent speeches won him laurels but not converts; the opposition in the legislature, without replying to Hamilton's argument, simply voted against him, which led to the remark that the "impost was strangled by a *band of mutes.*"[3] Much labor must yet be done by Hamilton, Schuyler, and Jay before New York could be brought to take a liberal view of continental politics, or indeed to do her plain duty.

[1] *Journals of Congress*, August 23, 1786.
[2] Hamilton, *Works* (Hamilton's ed.), II., 333, 334.
[3] Hamilton, *Hist. of the Rep.*, III., 228.

The commerce of the country, though by no means insignificant,[1] was in the mean time, as we have already seen, in considerable confusion because of the heavy importations of foreign goods. Men were now feeling the pressure of debt, and the restraints put on American trade by the British orders in council were irksome in the extreme. The merchants and vessel - owners of the north chafed at England's restrictions, which limited the market for American oils and cut off our communication with the West Indies. As early as April 30, 1784, Congress passed resolutions declaring it advisable to meet the restrictions of England with similar restrictions, and requesting the right for fifteen years to pass a navigation act, and thus prohibit the importation or exportation of any goods in ships belonging to or navigated by subjects of any power with whom the United States should not have a treaty of commerce. Authority was also asked to prohibit during the same time the subjects of any foreign state, unless authorized by treaty, from bringing into the United States merchandise which was not the produce or manufacture of the dominions of their sovereign.[2]

There was considerable excitement and interest on this matter, especially in the north. The mer-

---

[1] Jay, *Corresp. and Public Papers*, III., 153, 154; Am. Hist. Assoc., *Report*, 1896, I., 726–729; *Senate Ex. Doc.*, 34 Cong., 1 Sess. (1856), No. 107, p. 41.

[2] *Journals of Congress*, April 30, 1784.

chants of Boston, much wrought up over the subject, and naturally resorting to pre-Revolutionary methods, entered into agreement not to import English goods.[1] The Boston men felt strongly that something must be done to invest Congress with powers of retaliation, for it was plain enough that a navigation law passed by Massachusetts alone would simply drive commerce to other ports. So strongly did Massachusetts feel the need of some general regulation that the general court in July, 1785, passed resolutions favoring a convention to revise the Articles of Confederation.

But, on the whole, the request of Congress for power to pass a navigation act met with a cold reception in the states. They acted with great deliberation, as if some foreign power rather than their own representatives were asking for authority. Two years and a half after Congress had asked for the power, all of the states had in one form or another acted in the matter, but some of them had burdened their grants with so many qualifications and conditions that Congress was compelled once again to issue an appeal (October 26, 1786). On the whole, the middle states favored the measure, the eastern states were anxious to have it adopted, while in the southern states there was much difference of opinion.[2] The planters feared that the authority would be used by Congress for the benefit of

[1] Bancroft, *Hist. of the Const*, I., 188.
[2] Madison, *Writings* (Hunt's ed.), II., 180.

northern commerce and to the injury of southern interests.

Refusing to grant power to Congress, the states could not themselves act in unison. Some of them had passed their own acts in regulation of commerce,[1] but such independent measures were ineffectual. "The States are every day giving proofs," said Madison, "that separate regulations are more likely to set them by the ears, than to attain the common object.[2] In fact, their laws were confusing and conflicting. There seemed at times to be little desire to reach a common basis for the regulation of commerce or the levying of imposts. Too often legislation was shaped rather by jealousy and the hope to win trade away from a neighboring state than by principles of wise policy or foresight.[3]

In the mean time Congress could do little or nothing. A good part of the time not enough states were represented to allow action of any kind. On only three days between October, 1785, and the following April were there nine states on the floor.[4] Resolutions and letters sent to the state governments were quite without effect. The next year (1786–1787) there was not a quorum for months. "The

---

[1] Bancroft, *Hist. of the Const.*, I., 191.

[2] Madison, *Writings* (Hunt's ed.), II., 227.

[3] Cf. *Laws of New Jersey* (1800), 54; *Laws of New York* (1886), II., 65; *Pennsylvania Acts* (1785–1786), 85; *Laws of Delaware*, II., 831–837.

[4] King, *Life and Corresp. of King*, I., 133.

civil list begin to clamour," said King, in April, 1786, " — there is not money to pay them. . . . The handful of troops over the Ohio are mutinous and desert because they are unpaid. The money borrowed in Europe is exhausted and this very day our Foreign Ministers have it not in their power to receive their salaries for their support." [1]

Evidently not much longer could the futile Confederation hang together. The ablest men, looking about them and seeing the danger, realized that the crisis was near. "Even respectable characters" were talking "without horror" [2] of monarchy. Jay, much disturbed by the spirit of faction, the greed for money, the disregard of public duty, was uneasy and apprehensive, more so than during the war. Even those who complained of industrial derangement were willing to say that the trouble was largely with the people, whose habits of thrift and economy had been disturbed by the war, and with the incompetent Congress which had "scarcely the . . . appearance of a Government." [3] But the times were teaching their lessons. "Experience has taught us," said Washington, "that men will not adopt and carry into execution measures the best calculated for their own good, without the intervention of a coercive power. I do not conceive we can exist long

[1] King, *Life and Corresp. of King*, I., 134.
[2] Washington, *Writings* (Ford's ed.), XI., 55.
[3] Am. Hist. Assoc., *Report*, 1896, I., 740.

as a nation without having lodged some where a power, which will pervade the whole Union in as energetic a manner as the authority of the State governments extends over the several States." [1]

[1] Washington, *Writings* (Ford's ed.), XI., 53, 54.

CHAPTER VI

DIPLOMATIC RELATIONS

(1783–1788)

WHILE the Confederation was troubled with
poverty and discontent at home, its foreign
relations were far from satisfactory; for here again
the incompetence of Congress was shown, making
it difficult to reach satisfactory conclusions with
other powers. The nations of Europe were in no
mood to take the trouble of pleasing the United
States. France felt little or no interest in the
political career of the country for whose cause she
had been ostensibly fighting; she had little ex-
pectation that America would soon play a prominent
rôle among the nations, and she had no desire to see
the young republic push forward to prosperity and
influence. The French statesmen were not unwilling to offer opportunities for trade, but were disappointed at the tendency of American merchants
to carry on their commerce with England. English
statesmen were cold and critical or absolutely unfriendly. They could see little to be gained by a
consideration for the upstart republic which had
been so anxious to cast aside the guiding hand of

the mother-country. Spain respected America, perhaps, somewhat more than before the war; and her ministers may have wondered whether they had shown superior intelligence in treating the American representatives abroad with such masterly hauteur; but with this new respect, if such there was, came no addition of friendliness nor any purpose to surrender a portion of her policy. If she disliked and distrusted the states when they were fighting her detested enemy, England, she liked them no more when they had won their independence and were setting up titles to lands skirting her precious colonies on the Gulf of Mexico.

Some of the other European states showed an occasional gleam of interest in the possibility of securing some hold on the western trade. With Portugal especially there grew up an important commerce; Adams had succeeded in getting a treaty with Holland, even before the peace; in 1783 one was made with Sweden; and in 1785 a treaty of commerce was made with Prussia. But perhaps the Barbary pirates really had the most intelligent appreciation of the fact that the United States were no longer British colonies, and they naturally confined their attention to the seizure of American ships and seamen, an occupation in which they indulged with their customary success.

The most serious diplomatic questions that arose were, in their essentials, those which had proved most perplexing and troublesome during the Rev-

olution. Throughout the war Spain had haughtily
refused to recognize the independence of the states
or to enter into a treaty of alliance. Wishing to
retain a monopoly of their colonial commerce, and
fearing that the aggressive Americans would encroach upon their colonies, the anxious Spaniards
had watched the course of the Revolution, vexed by
irreconcilable fears and incompatible hopes, longing
to see England humiliated and destroyed and dread-
ing to see the impertinent rebels succeed.

When the treaty between England and the United
States was published, Spain saw much cause for
fault-finding. Her claims in the southwest, which
she had for some years been steadily asserting and
gradually extending, were by the treaty quietly
ignored, for the line agreed on in the treaty ran
down the Mississippi to the thirty-first parallel and
thence by this parallel to the Appalachicola. England asserted at the same time the right of both
England and America to navigate the Mississippi
from its source to the gulf. In these cessions Spain
had no intention of acquiescing. For some years
she had been making much ado about the western
country and the Mississippi, and even if the French
ministers, with a half-amused shrug of the shoulders,
were willing to recognize the results of the astute
diplomacy of Jay and the other audacious Americans, Spain certainly would not yield up her claims.
Less superciliously, but not less obstinately than
before, she adhered to the purpose by cunning and

by force to keep the western Americans away from
her possessions; for the cardinal principle of the
Spanish colonial policy was monopoly and seclusion.
The idea of allowing the Americans to traffic with
her subjects or to introduce into her colonies the
dreadful notions of freedom was intolerable.

The secret clause of the treaty of 1783 could not
long be kept from the knowledge of Spain. It was
soon known at Madrid that America had promised,
in case England in her negotiations with the other
combatants succeeded in holding West Florida, to
accept as her southern boundary between the
Appalachicola and the Mississippi a line running
through the mouth of the Yazoo.[1] The knowledge
that such an arrangement had been made may
have added to the ill-humor of Spain; but her
wrath needed no stimulus; her course of opposition
to the United States had been for years consistent
and unflagging. She did not long delay in letting
Congress know that she had no intention of abiding
by the boundaries that England had set or of admitting the right of the Americans freely to navigate
the Mississippi to its mouth. In the summer of
1784 Congress was formally warned that England
had no right to make such generous cessions at a
time when the two borders of the river were held
by the arms of Spain;[2] and that, until the limits of
Louisiana and the two Floridas should be settled

[1] See above, chap. ii.
[2] *Secret Journals of Congress*, December 15, 1784.

and determined, American citizens, by seeking to
navigate the Mississippi, would only expose their
vessels to confiscation. Naturally this news was
not relished by Congress. Its members had been
debating the western land question for years, and
when England surrendered practically all that
was asked from her they were not pleased to find
Spain standing in the way as unreasonably as
ever.

Spain did not content herself with formal warn-
ings. On this subject she was in earnest; on this
one matter her ministers had convictions. She was
determined to hold fast to her colonies, even though
they were strangled in her grasp. There were various methods open to her, and she was under strong
temptation to use all of them: first, to carry on
frank and fair diplomatic negotiations, backed by a
maintenance of her authority on the river and in the
disputed territory; second, to intrigue with the
Indians, who by sundry well-known methods could
be induced to make the life of the western pioneer
unpleasant and his residence in the Mississippi
Valley unattractive;[1] third, to stir up dissatisfaction
among the American settlers, and by bribes and
threats help to bring about the separation of the
western territory from the eastern states. Spanish
gold looked good and fair to the average westerner,
whose currency was often nothing better than
otter skins or whiskey, and it was not hard to find

[1] Gayarré, *History of Louisiana*, **III.**, 185–192.

those whose consciences did not revolt at the sight of a reasonable bribe.

In the early summer of 1785 Don Diego de Gardoqui came to Philadelphia as the first Spanish minister, presenting a commission authorizing him to treat with the United States concerning boundaries and to settle all differences on that subject.[1] To John Jay, the secretary for foreign affairs, Congress intrusted the duty of carrying on the negotiations. Inasmuch as Jay had in the past taken such an independent stand against Spanish presumption, he might well have been expected to be especially opposed to the Spanish claims in the Mississippi Valley. But in Gardoqui Jay found a foeman worthy of his steel. The wily Spaniard, knowing the feebleness of Congress, probably aware of the intrigues on the frontier, and conscious that no harm could come to the Spanish cause by delay, so long as Spain actually held the country in dispute, was unyielding to the last degree.

Before the negotiations were begun Jay had written Lafayette that the Kentucky settlements were increasing "with a degree of rapidity heretofore unknown in this country,"[2] and that they would continue to increase notwithstanding the attempt of anybody to prevent it. And yet, perhaps, in spite of all he had done before, Jay did not quite appreciate the fact that the right to navigate the

---

[1] *Secret Journals of Congress*, July 20, 1785.
[2] Jay, *Corresp. and Public Papers*, III., 138.

Mississippi must be speedily secured. It was no longer a theoretical right affecting American pride and ambition and only vaguely touching American life, for now the great western wilderness, to which, when the Revolution began, only a few hardy hunters and adventurers had found their way, was being rapidly peopled. With that patient endurance, that marvellous disregard of danger, which have characterized the frontiersman in our history, men were moving into the new country, following Boone's old wilderness road through eastern Tennessee, or floating down the Ohio to found settlements in the attractive land of Kentucky. In 1785 the inhabitants of the latter region were estimated to be more than twenty thousand persons,[1] and the population was increasing with a remarkable rapidity that surprised even those who were used to the ease of American movement. "Do you think to prevent the emigration from a barren country loaded with taxes and impoverished with debts, to the most luxurious and fertile soil in the world?" wrote an exuberant pioneer at the Falls of the Ohio to a friend in New England. "You may as well endeavour to prevent the fishes from gathering on a bank in the sea which affords them plenty of nourishment."[2] Of course these self-reliant and eager frontiersmen

[1] Lewis Brantz, "Memoranda of a Journey in the Western Parts of the United States in 1785," in Schoolcraft, *Indian Tribes*, III., 342; see Roosevelt, *Winning of the West* (1st ed.), III., 16.

[2] *Secret Journals of Congress*, April 13, 1787 (paper viii.).

could not long be kept from using the Mississippi and following its current to the gulf.

Jay was instructed to insist on the recognition of the thirty-first parallel and the free navigation of the Mississippi to its mouth, rights guaranteed by the treaty with England.[1] Over this question he and Gardoqui debated and haggled until Jay was weary. In February of 1786 he reported that the discussions were still in progress and that American rights on the Mississippi could be secured only "by *arms*, or by *treaty*."[2] Doubtful of the success of the negotiations, he was, nevertheless, anxious that the matter should not be precipitated by rash demands or by inconsiderate action in the west, for the time was not come for war, and the building up of the western country and the gradual regulation of the affairs of the nation would enable America to attain its ends. The fact is, the negotiations were becoming more and more disagreeable. Gardoqui flatly informed Jay that the king refused to recognize the treaty of 1783 as binding him. Then from polite circumlocutions he resorted to unambiguous threats, reminding Jay that the friendship of the king could win in considerable measure the friendship of Morocco and Algiers, and calling to mind the fact that America was in debt to Spain.[3]

Jay in desperation asked for a special committee of Congress to advise and instruct him. In August

[1] *Secret Journals of Congress*, August 25, 1785.
[2] *Ibid.*, February 28, 1786.   [3] *Ibid.*, August 3, 1786.

he made a long report. Spain, he said, was ready
to make a favorable commercial treaty, but would
not yield an inch on the western question. What,
then, was to be done? America was in no condition
to fight and could not disgracefully surrender her
claims. But one thing was left, Jay thought, and
that was to enter into a treaty limited to a duration
of twenty-five or thirty years, securing commercial
advantages, and stipulating that the United States
would forbear the use of the Mississippi below its
boundaries. Unless some such step were taken, the
secretary declared, he could see no hope, at least
not until the American nation should "become more
really and truly a nation" than it was in those disconsolate months of 1786. "For, unblessed with an
efficient government, destitute of funds, and without publick credit, either at home or abroad, we
should be obliged to wait in patience for better days,
or plunge into an unpopular and dangerous war
with very little prospect of terminating it by a
peace, either advantageous or glorious."

One of the stipulations of this proposed commercial treaty was to the effect that, inasmuch as
America was often in need of gold and silver as a
circulating medium, his Catholic majesty would
agree to order in this country the masts and timber
for his royal navy and pay for them in specie.
Nothing could more lucidly show the apparent
magnificence of decrepit old Spain, whose whole
colonial empire, built on a principle of seclusion and

selfishness, was on the very brink of ruin, and, on
the other hand, the humiliating poverty of young
America, whose feet were already set on the highway
to wealth and imperial grandeur.

Heated debates ensued in Congress. The southern states voted solidly against Jay's proposition,
for they still claimed land beyond the Alleghenies,
and their citizens were passing over into the great
valley. The northern states just as unanimously
voted to relieve the secretary from his former instructions, which directed him to insist on the
boundaries of the treaty with England and on the
navigation of the Mississippi; for the New-Englanders were naturally anxious for a commercial
treaty and were not solicitous about the southwest.
Twelve states were in attendance, and Jay was openly supported by a vote of seven; but it was a question as to whether less than nine states could give
him authority to make a treaty. Certainly nine
states would be needed to ratify any agreement he
should reach. A candid examination of Jay's em-
barrassment will convince the reader that he was
not weak. His difficulties were stupendous; a
large portion of the burden of the government was
thrown on his uncomplaining shoulders, and he
toiled honestly and ably. Congress was fit for
little, and the country was woful and distracted.
And yet men on the frontier and the self-complacent
men in the east spoke of resisting Spain's demands
and defending American rights.

Some wise men even in the south admitted that there was no haste, and the wisest of them all said frankly, more than once, that until there was time to open and make easy the ways between the Atlantic states and the western country the obstruction of the Mississippi would not be harmful. "There is nothing," wrote Washington to Lee, "which binds one county or one State to another, but interest. Without this cement the western inhabitants, who more than probably will be composed in a great degree of foreigners, can have no predilection for us, and a commercial connexion is the only tie we can have upon them."[1] But the Virginians, as a rule, were indignant that the north should seize the advantage of a commercial treaty and barter away the rights of the south. Even the mild-mannered Madison was near to anger,[2] and Patrick Henry was reported to have remarked "that he would rather part with the confederation than relinquish the navigation of the Mississippi."[3] Coming at a time when efforts were being made to solidify the Union and to increase the power of the national government, the Mississippi question, which could indeed be solved only by national growth and national authority, increased for a period the particularistic spirit and put obstacles in the way of those who were working for union and government.

---

[1] Washington, *Writings* (Ford's ed.), X., 488.
[2] Madison, *Writings* (Hunt's ed.), II., 262 et seq.
[3] Lee, *Arthur Lee*, II., 321.

The people of the west were out of patience with the delay and annoyed at the notion of surrendering the navigation of the Mississippi. "To sell us, and make us vassals to the merciless Spaniards, is a grievance not to be borne,"[1] said one. There was danger of war, brought on by the impatient frontiersmen, who fretted at being hemmed in by the mandate of Spain. Moreover, ambitious conspirators were beginning to contemplate alliance or political connection with Spain,[2] or at least the separation of the Kentucky country from the Union. The most adroit of the plotters was James Wilkinson. He had been an officer in the Revolution, and with other traders and sharpers had recently moved to Kentucky to make his fortune, and no methods were too dishonorable to suit his purpose. Scarcely thirty years of age, he was already well entered on the career of corruption which won him the well-deserved reputation of being the most finished rascal in American annals. A copy of a paper by Wilkinson announcing his allegiance to the king of Spain has been found in the Spanish archives. In the end he did not accomplish much, though doubtless he was satisfied so long as he lined his pockets with Spanish gold. It is hard to-day to take the plots of the conspirators very seriously, for, out of patience as they were, the people of Kentucky were too loyal to break away from the Union. But they

[1] *Secret Journals of Congress*, April 13, 1787 (paper viii.).
[2] *Amer. Hist. Review*, IX., 490 et seq.

had no sympathy with schemes for giving more power to the central authority when they heard that Congress was actually considering the possibility of surrendering the use of the great river that formed their outlet to the sea.

During the winter of 1786–1787 negotiations between Jay and Gardoqui dragged wearily on. The Spaniard would not yield on the main points at issue, and the following spring Jay still believed that the only way out of the difficulty was to promise not to navigate for a time the lower course of the river. But he reported that the negotiations were "dilatory, unpleasant and unpromising." [1] Nothing was done until, under better conditions, the Americans with a new government were able to speak with more assurance. In the meantime population continued to pour into the valley, and the day could not be far distant when the demand of the west for the free use of the Mississippi must be obeyed.

While Spain was occupying the southwest and denying that America had any title to territory as far south as the thirty-first parallel, England, in her turn, was quietly holding the frontier forts on the northern boundary within the limits marked out by the treaty of peace. By the retention of these strategic positions from Lake Champlain to Michilimackinac English influence over the Indians was made secure and English traders were enabled to

[1] *Secret Journals of Congress*, April 13, 1787, September 16, 1788.

retain their hold on the fur-trade in a rich and extensive region. For some years after the peace, therefore, and indeed through the whole of the period covered by this volume, a large portion of American territory was held by England and Spain in simple disregard of the treaty. The settlers in the region south of the Ohio plotted with Spain or threatened to fight her, and meanwhile grew in numbers and strength; into the north for seven years after the peace there was almost no immigration, and for some years after that the presence of the English within the limits marked off by the treaty was a constant cause for irritation.

In 1785 John Adams, who was then in Paris, was appointed minister to England. He went to London in hopes that he could enter into some commercial agreement satisfactory and helpful to the United States, persuade England to withdraw her troops from our territory, and secure indemnity for the exportation of the negroes from America after the peace in plain violation of the treaty.[1] He had a hard task before him. If at the close of the war there had seemed some chance that the English, hating the Spaniards and the French with a manly hatred, would be especially considerate of the welfare of their kinsmen across the sea, hope of any such good temper soon disappeared. Adams was probably as

---

[1] For this whole subject, see McLaughlin, " Western Posts and British Debts," in Am. Hist. Assoc., *Report*, 1894, 413–444; *Dip. Corresp., 1783–1789* (3-vol. ed.), II., 340.

well fitted as any one could be to undertake the task assigned him. If English ministers were blunt and self-satisfied, no less was Adams. It never occurred to him to fawn and flatter or to be ashamed of the young, distracted country he represented; and in power of lucid, forceful expression or in knowledge of public law he had few, if any, superiors among the English statesmen of the time.

The residence in England began auspiciously. In June[1] Adams was presented to the king and was courteously received. His words were well chosen, and seem to have deeply affected the monarch, who had not ceased to mourn the loss of his colonies. Adams expressed the hope that he could be instrumental in "restoring an entire esteem, confidence, and affection; or, in better words, the old good nature and the old good humor between people who, though separated by an ocean, and under different Governments, have the same language, a similar religion, and kindred blood." The king, after polite words of commendation and a declaration that he had done in the past only what he felt it his duty to do, assured Adams that he would be the first to meet the friendship of the United States. "The moment I see such sentiments and language as yours prevail, and a disposition to give this country the preference, that moment I shall say, let the circumstances of language, religion, and blood have their natural and full effect."

[1] *Dip. Corresp.*, *1783–1789* (3-vol. ed.), II., 368–371.

The mission thus pleasantly begun was, however, destined to prove almost fruitless. The English ministers were leisurely and deliberate, while Adams with remarkable humility and praiseworthy persistence sought to discover why England did not give up our territory. In October he wrote to Jay: "I have the honor to agree fully with you in your opinion, that 'it is manifestly as much the interest of this country to be well with us as for us to be well with them'; but this is not the judgment of the English nation, it is not the judgment of Lord North and his party, it is not the judgment of the Duke of Portland and his friends, and it does not appear to be the judgment of Mr. Pitt and the present set."[1] He found the Englishmen confident that America could do nothing, neither raise a revenue, nor exclude shipping of foreign nations, nor build a fleet, and in truth they were not far from right.

Finally, nearly five months after his dramatic interview with the king, Adams succeeded in getting from the retentive ministers some notion as to their intentions. Lord Carmarthen told him that the frontier posts would not be delivered till "the debts were paid." "Paid! my Lord!" ejaculated Adams; "that is more than ever was stipulated."[2] It was February,[3] however, before the ministry gave an explicit answer to the American demands. The

[1] *Dip. Corresp.*, *1783–1789* (3-vol. ed.), II., 478-482.
[2] *Ibid.*, 484.   [3] *Ibid.*, 581.

fourth article of the treaty stipulated that creditors of either country should find no lawful impediment to the recovery of their debts. To this article Carmarthen said America had paid little attention, and it would be foolish to suppose that England was obliged to carry out her promises if the United States was not under a similar obligation. Further satisfaction than this Adams could not get. He returned home in 1788 without a treaty and without much hope that England would deviate by a hair from the path which seemed to her the best-suited to her own gain.

Doubtless England refrained from entering into a commercial treaty because she believed the enforcement of navigation laws would put money in her merchants' pockets, and because she believed that, notwithstanding restrictions on West-Indian trade, she could secure and hold her commerce with the United States. She was, moreover, in no haste to deliver the western posts so long as their retention gave her traders opportunity to control the fur-trade. But withal it must be remembered that the states had done little to promote good feeling. Their treatment of the loyalists after the peace was outrageous, while, in utter disregard of the treaty, they placed in one form or another impediments in the way of the collection of British debts. Jay declared that there had not been a single day since the ratification of the treaty on which it had "not been violated . . . by one or other of the

States."[1] "I suspect," he said to Adams, in speaking of the disorder and lawlessness in America, "that our posterity will read the history of our last four years with much regret."

Before the Revolution a large portion of the flour and fish exported from the United States found its best markets in the Mediterranean ports.[2] But now the Barbary powers felt at liberty to seize American vessels and imprison the seamen. A number of men were held for ransom and handsome prices demanded for their liberty. Agents were sent to make peace and to see about the succor of the prisoners, but accomplished nothing. Algiers had twenty-one captives, for whose release was demanded the sum of $59,496.[3] America had no funds to spend in redeeming its citizens from slavery, and its statesmen could do no more than ponder on the possible effect of war. A Tripolitan ambassador appeared in London, and with him Adams had a series of remarkable interviews, the humor of which appealed even to the serious mind of the American minister. "His Excellency made many inquiries concerning America, the climate, soil, heat, and cold, etc., and observed, 'it is a very great country, but *Tripoli is at war with it.*'" He said "that Turkey, Tripoli, Tunis, Algiers, and Morocco were the sovereigns

[1] Jay's report, *Secret Journals of Congress*, October 13, 1786; Jay, *Corresp. and Public Papers*, III., 214.
[2] *Am. State Papers, For. Rel.*, I., 104.
[3] *Am. State Papers* (Wait's ed., 1817), X., 43.

of the Mediterranean, and that no nation could
navigate that sea without a treaty of peace with
them."[1] The sum of 30,000 guineas was mentioned as the price of a treaty, making for the four
Barbary powers, if all accepted the terms, 120,000
guineas. Jefferson went over from Paris to London,
and in company with Adams had conferences with
the stately Abdrahaman, who repeated his demand
for 30,000 guineas, plus a little *douceur* of £3,000 for
himself.[2] A treaty was made with Morocco at the
beginning of 1787; but the relations with the other
Barbary states could not be arranged. America was
too poor to pay and could not make up her mind
to fight, and so this question, like others, awaited
the establishment of a national government.

All this, like everything else one touches during
the dismal period, discloses the helplessness of the
confederacy. The English at first were actually
curious to know whether Congress or the states individually had the right to negotiate,[3] and until
1791, eight years after the peace, sent no minister to
America; Spain felt no fear save from the aggressive,
ambitious spirit of the western settlers; the Barbary
powers found the taking of American seamen an
easy but not a lucrative employment.

---

[1] *Dip. Corresp.*, *1783–1789*, II., 567; Adams, *Works*, VIII., 374.
[2] Jay, *Corresp. and Public Papers*, III., 197.
[3] *Dip. Corresp.*, *1783–1789*, I., 574.

CHAPTER VII

FOUNDING A COLONIAL SYSTEM
(1783–1787)

DURING the dreariest days of the Revolution, when it was often uncertain whether independence could be maintained, when British armies were occupying much of American territory, when Washington had not the troops or the equipment to beat the enemy back, there was much discussion concerning the ownership of the land beyond the mountains. For the ownership of the west was not only the source of diplomatic controversy and perplexity; it was also between the states themselves a topic for prolonged dispute. There would seem to have been little haste about determining the ownership of the almost uninhabited wilderness; but it is not strange that a nation which in less than a century was to reach out and occupy a continent and push its settlements three thousand miles beyond the Appalachians should, at the beginning of its existence, be confronted with a land problem and find its earlier political organization complicated with disputes about territorial titles.

The parties to this internal controversy were on

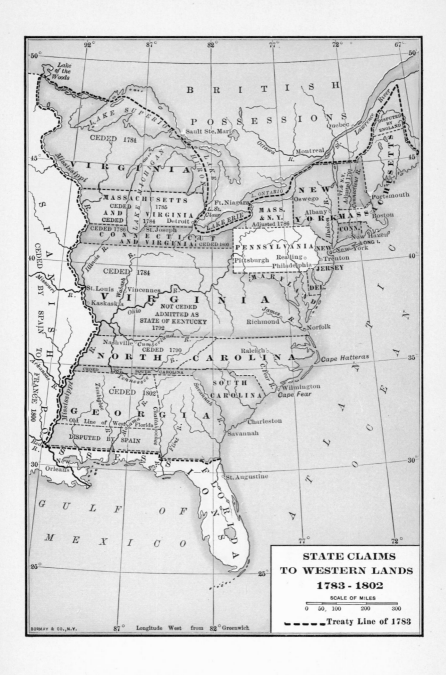

STATE CLAIMS
TO WESTERN LANDS
1783 - 1802

SCALE OF MILES

0   50   100   200   300

▄ ▄ ▄ ▄ ▄Treaty Line of 1783

one hand Congress, on the other hand the seven states — New York, Massachusetts, Connecticut, Virginia, North Carolina, South Carolina, and Georgia—which laid claim to this western country. The other six states asserted either that Congress already had rightful authority or that Congress should be given it for the public good. The long debates over this subject in Congress and the state legislatures were important, because much more was involved than the mere question of ownership; the whole great problem of territorial expansion, of the management and organization of new communities beyond the limits of the old commonwealths, was finding solution.

Fearing the strength and influence of the states which claimed the vast territory beyond the mountains, Maryland at an early day proposed that Congress should have the right to "fix the western boundary of such states as claim to the Missisippi or south sea; and lay out the land beyond the boundary so ascertained into separate and independent states from time to time as the numbers and circumstances of the people thereof may require." [1] This was a proposition of immense importance, for Maryland refused to agree to the Articles of Confederation so long as other states asserted their claims to the wide region beyond the

[1] *Journals of Congress*, October 15, 1777; Adams, *Maryland's Influence upon Land Cessions* (*Johns Hopkins University Studies*, III., No. I.), 22.

mountains. Early in 1780 New York[1] expressed a readiness to give up her claims, which at the best were vague; and Congress the next September[2] urged all the states to take like action. The next month Congress passed a momentous resolution declaring that the lands ceded or relinquished to the United States by any state should be disposed of for the common benefit of the United States and be settled and formed into distinct republican states which should become "members of the federal union, and have the same rights of sovereignty, freedom and independence, as the other states."[3]

Connecticut, desiring to promote the liberty and independence of the "rising Empire," next promised a cession.[4] Then Virginia, whose claim was based not only on her old charter but on the military achievements of George Rogers Clark, expressed a willingness to yield title[5] to all the territory north of the Ohio. Although Virginia's cession was coupled with conditions that were not acceptable to Congress, Maryland, expressing her confidence in the justice of her sister states, finally entered into the Confederation. Her delegates in Congress signed the Articles March 1, 1781.[6] Though not all the

---

[1] *Journals of Congress*, March 1, 1781.
[2] *Ibid.*, September 6, 1780.
[3] *Ibid.*, October 10, 1780.
[4] *Ibid.*, October 12, 1780. See Regents of University of N. Y., *Report on Boundaries of N. Y.* (1874), I., 157.
[5] *Journals of Congress*, September 13, 1783.
[6] *Ibid.*, February 12, 1781.

states had as yet declared their readiness to give up their claims in full, such a surrender was sure to come, and the Confederation was to have title to an imperial domain beyond the mountains. Moreover, the principle had won acceptance that the settlers in the west should not be held permanently in colonial subjection to the mother-states of the seaboard, but should from time to time be formed into self-governing commonwealths.

We need not trace in detail the history of the cessions that were formally made after the Articles were signed. Acrimonious discussion did not end with the signing of the Articles, but step by step the difficulties were cleared away. In 1782[1] Congress accepted the New York cession of all territory west of a meridian running through the most western bend or inclination of Lake Ontario. Virginia ceded freely all claim to the territory north and west of the Ohio, stipulating substantially in the language of Congress that the territory so ceded should be laid out and formed into "distinct republican states, and admitted members of the fœderal union, having the same rights of sovereignty, freedom, and independence, as the other states."[2] April, 1785, the delegates in Congress from Massachusetts executed a deed of cession[3] of all claims west of New York; and in 1786 Massachusetts came

[1] *Journals of Congress*, October 29, 1782.
[2] Hening, *Statutes*, XI., 326–328.
[3] *Journals of Congress*, April 18, 1785.

to an agreement with New York ceding jurisdiction but retaining ownership in western New York. Connecticut, sore and wrathful over a decision of a court of arbitration in 1782 denying her claim to northern Pennsylvania, adhered to her western claims till 1786, and then gave up all save a strip known as the Western Reserve,[1] running from the western boundary of Pennsylvania westward one hundred and twenty miles along the south shore of Lake Erie, a valuable piece of fertile land containing three million two hundred and fifty thousand acres. In 1800 the jurisdiction over the Western Reserve was surrendered to the United States.[2]

With the exception of the Western Reserve, Congress had, therefore, by 1786, full title to all the land north of the Ohio. South of the Ohio the seaboard states, basing their claims on their old charters, still asserted ownership westward as far as the Mississippi. But Congress now owned many millions of acres, and this ownership constituted a common interest and a tangible indication of the unity of the nation. It remained for Congress to work out a plan of settlement and to carry out the principles which it had already announced.

Even before the Revolution there was much interest in the settlement of the west; there was a

[1] *Journals of Congress*, September 14, 1786.
[2] Report at length by John Marshall, for a committee of Congress, in *Am. State Papers, Public Lands*, I., 94–98.

belief that the country would be rapidly peopled
and that much revenue could be derived from the
sale of lands. Impressed with the value of the
western country, Congress offered bounties in land
to those who would enlist [1] in the war, and this, too,
before the states consented to give up their claims
to the territory beyond the mountains. When the
Confederation was completed and the states began
to make their deeds of cession, the country north
of the Ohio was practically unoccupied by settlers
from the older states; but as the war neared its end
there was renewed interest in plans for colonization
and renewed hope that by one mode or another the
western lands could be disposed of for paying the
debts of the Confederation and replenishing its
empty coffers.[2]

The first plan of any importance for the organization and settlement of the northwest was drawn
up by Timothy Pickering and other army officers
at Newburg as early as April, 1783. The idea was
to form a community on the frontier capable of
defending itself against the Indians, and to give
Congress the opportunity of fulfilling its promises
of bounties to the officers and soldiers of the army.
The plan seems to have contemplated nothing less
than the formation of a state beyond the Ohio, the
adoption of a constitution before settlement, the
total exclusion of slavery from the limits of the

[1] Cutler, *Cutler*, I., 122.
[2] Barrett, *Evol. of Ord. of 1787*, 4, 5, with references.

commonwealth, and its immediate admission into the Union;[1] but the petition sent to Congress, judging by Rufus Putnam's draught, spoke of marking out a "tract or teritory sutable to form a distinct goverment (or Colloney of the United States)—in time to be admited, *one* of the *Confedirated States of America.*"[2] Little is known of the project beyond the general purposes of its framers, who, for some reason, apparently made no great effort to carry out their plans. Soon afterward (June, 1783) an ordinance for the organization of the west was introduced into Congress, but nothing was done with it, and though it contained some significant provisions it is now of interest chiefly because it was the first scheme for western colonization introduced into Congress and because it shows that ideas of importance were taking shape.

More definite action was taken in March, 1784,[3] when by Virginia's cession Congress held unquestioned title to at least a large portion of the lands north of the Ohio. An ordinance draughted by Jefferson was brought before Congress: the western lands "ceded or to be ceded" were by this plan to be divided into states; besides a strip just west of Pennsylvania, the territory covered was all the land between the meridian running through the western cape of the mouth of the Great Kanawha on the east

[1] Pickering, *Pickering,* I., 457, 546–549; Cutler, *Cutler,* I., 159–174; Buell, *Memoirs of Putnam,* 215.   [2] *Ibid.*
[3] Cutler, *Cutler,* II., 407 et seq.; *St. Clair Papers,* II., 603 et seq.

and the Mississippi on the west, and extending from the thirty-first parallel to the international boundary at the north. A second meridian running through the lowest point of the Falls of the Ohio and several east and west lines were to divide the whole area into sixteen different states; or if the framers intended, as there is some reason for believing, that South Carolina and Georgia should extend westward to the second meridian, into fourteen states.[1]

By this plan the settlers were not immediately to form a state and enter the Union, as the proposers of the earlier plan may have desired; they were, "either on their own petition, or on the order of Congress," to meet together for the purpose of establishing "a temporary government," and when any state had twenty thousand free inhabitants it was to receive from Congress authority to establish a permanent constitution and government. Not until a state should have as many free inhabitants as should be at the time contained in "the least numerous of the thirteen original States" was it to have the right to be admitted into the Union. Thus we see that by the spring of 1784 there had been brought forward the two essential ideas of the American colonial system: temporary government with a large measure of self-government for the colony; and the ultimate admission of the colony into the Union on terms of equality with the older members.

[1] Cutler, *Cutler*, II., 407 et seq; Staples, *R. I. in the Cont. Cong.*, 479.

In Jefferson's plan, as first introduced, it was declared that in all this western country "after the year 1800 of the Christian æra there shall be neither slavery nor involuntary servitude . . . otherwise than in punishment of crimes, whereof the party shall have been duly convicted to have been personally guilty." The restriction, it should be noticed, was evidently intended to cover not alone the territory north of the Ohio but the territory south as well.[1]

The southern states, however, from whose older portions people were already moving into the interior beyond the mountains, were not ready to dedicate the west to freedom. When the Ordinance was under discussion a delegate from North Carolina moved to strike out the antislavery clause. Jefferson in his own delegation voted for the retention of the provision, but he was overruled by his colleagues. The vote of North Carolina was divided. Virginia, South Carolina, and Maryland voted to strike out the clause, and though six northern states voted for its retention, they were defeated, inasmuch as seven states were needed to establish the law.[2]

Without this important provision, therefore, and also without a list of high - flown names for the states which Jefferson had suggested — Metropotamia, Assenisipia, Polypotamia, Pelisipia, etc.— and with slight changes in the boundaries of the

---

[1] For first draught of the report, see Randall, *Jefferson*, I., 397–399.   [2] *Journals of Congress*, April 19, 1784.

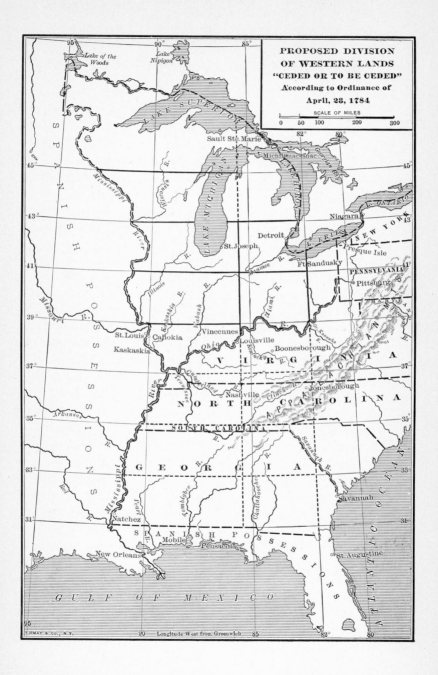

PROPOSED DIVISION
OF WESTERN LANDS
"CEDED OR TO BE CEDED"
According to Ordinance of
April, 23, 1784

SCALE OF MILES

0   50   100   200   300

proposed states which apparently reduced their number, the Ordinance was passed[1] April 23, 1784. It never went into effect; but it has its significance as one of the early attempts to organize the west, and perhaps still more because of the effort to exclude slavery.

Some of the northern men were not willing to rest content with the decision of Congress. Pickering called the attention of Rufus King, of Massachusetts, to the omission of the antislavery clause from the Ordinance of 1784. "To suffer," he said, "the continuance of slaves till they can gradually be emancipated, in States already overrun with them, may be pardonable, because unavoidable without hazarding greater evils; but to introduce them into countries where none now exist—countries which have been talked of, which we have boasted of, as asylums to the oppressed of the earth—can never be forgiven." [2]

Prompted by Pickering's letter, King introduced an antislavery resolution in Congress. The resolution was referred to a committee of which King was chairman, which on April 26 reported a resolution declaring that after the year 1800 there should be no slavery in the territory covered by the Ordinance of 1784, but that fugitives from service should not, by escaping into the new states, obtain their freedom. These propositions were not

---

[1] *Journal of Congress*, April 23, 1784.
[2] Pickering, *Pickering*, I., 510.

made into law; they peacefully slept on the secretary's docket, like so many hundreds of other resolutions, but they deserve attention because there seems to be immediate connection between them and the final regulations governing the northwest.[1]

A dread of western influence, a fear that the new states of the interior would imperil the interests of the old states on the coast, now arose to complicate the situation and make the task of organization more difficult. Monroe, then serving as a member in Congress, took a trip into the west, and became convinced, after a rapid and superficial examination, that large portions of the country were so unattractive and valueless that they would not for ages contain a sufficient number of inhabitants to entitle them to membership in the Confederation. "A great part of the territory," he declared, "is miserably poor, especially that near lakes Michigan and Erie and that upon the Mississippi and the Illinois consists of extensive plains which have not had from appearances and will not have a single bush on them, for ages."[2] In light of these supposed facts he advocated reducing the number of new states. And this proposition, or at least the sentiment it represented, had influence in determining the number of commonwealths ultimately formed north of the Ohio.

---

[1] Pickering, *Pickering*, I., 510; *Journals of Congress*, March 16, 1785; Barrett, *Evol. of Ord. of 1787*, 28.

[2] Monroe, *Writings* (Hamilton's ed.), I., 117.

The subject of the organization of the west came up time and again for consideration in Congress in the two years that followed the adoption of the Ordinance of 1784; but decision was delayed, though it is apparent that the final ideas were forming. The ultimate step was hastened and the complete plan of organization was determined on, not because Congress was ready to act on general principles, but because there was need of satisfying the demands of men who were intent on a scheme for western settlement, and wished their status determined before embarking on a financial enterprise.

The Ohio Company, made up of New England men, was formed in Boston, March 3, 1786. Its directors were General Rufus Putnam, who had served creditably in the Revolution, General Samuel H. Parsons, also a Revolutionary officer, and lastly Manasseh Cutler, a doctor of divinity, who, with a penchant for botany and a love for natural philosophy, had also an aptitude for business and was not above turning an honest penny in a land-speculation which bade fair to be remunerative and interesting. This company was organized for purchasing land in the west and promoting settlement.[1] The New-Englanders were already moving into the "northern frozen deserts," Cutler said, and to turn their faces to the new west it was necessary only to tell them of the temperate climate and fertile land of the Ohio country.

[1] Articles of agreement, in Cutler, *Cutler*, I., 181–184.

In the spring and early summer of 1787 Congress at various times discussed a draught of a new ordinance for the western territory, but, moving with its customary circumspection, it had reached no results, when Dr. Manasseh Cutler appeared in New York, where Congress was sitting, and put up at the hostelry of the "Plow and Harrow" in the Bowery (July 5).[1] Cutler came commissioned to buy land, and the simple proposition to that effect must have sounded sweet in the ears of Congress, even though the purchase was to be made, not in hard cash, but in certificates of public indebtedness. Probably the attractive prospect of disposing of land hastened the action of Congress, for on July 13 was passed the Ordinance of 1787, which, because of its wise provisions and liberal terms, has justly been considered one of the most important documents in our history. It was the consummation of long discussion and much effort, and laid down a series of fundamental principles of great significance in building up the Union west of the mountains. After providing that for the purpose of temporary government there should be at first but one district northwest of the Ohio, the Ordinance provided for the liberal descent and conveyance of estates. For the temporary government there were to be a governor, a secretary, and three judges appointed by Congress; the governor and judges were to have authority to adopt and publish such laws

[1] Cutler, *Cutler*, I., 228.

of the original states as they thought suited to the needs of the district. As soon as there should be five thousand free male inhabitants of full age, a general assembly might be brought into being, to consist of the governor, a legislative council, and a house of representatives with power to legislate.

Then followed in the Ordinance a series of fundamental declarations similar to the bills of rights that had been framed as part of the constitutions of some of the states, granting freedom of religious worship, assuring the benefits of habeas corpus, trial by jury, proportionate representation, and the conduct of judicial proceedings according to the common law. It declared that no man should be deprived of his liberty or property except by the judgment of his peers or the law of the land; that full compensation should be made for property taken or services demanded by the public; that no law ought ever to be made which would interfere with or affect private contracts that had been previously formed; and, in happily chosen words, that, as religion, morality, and knowledge are necessary to good government and the happiness of mankind, schools and the means of education should forever be encouraged. Not less than three nor more than five states were to be organized within the territory, and when any state had a free population of 60,000 it was to be admitted into the Union on terms of equality with the old states. The most famous, though possibly not the most important clause of the Ordinance, was one excluding slavery: "There shall be neither slavery nor involuntary servitude in the said territory, otherwise than in the punishment of crimes, whereof the party shall have been duly convicted." Provision was made, however, for the reclamation and return of any person escaping into the territory from whom labor or service was "lawfully claimed in any one of the original states."

The Ordinance was a great state paper. It is true that, even had it not been framed, slavery could probably not have gained a permanent footing in the northwest. But it prevented the introduction of slavery in early years when settlers were moving into the region, it assured the development of the northwestern states unembarrassed by the slavery issue, and, not less important than all else, it stated a principle and established a precedent. There was value, too, in proclaiming in simple, straightforward language the fundamental principles of civil liberty and sound maxims concerning education and religion. By the passage of the Ordinance, Congress fulfilled its earlier promise, that, if the western lands were ceded, free republican states would be formed. By providing for temporary government and the ultimate admission of the states it laid the foundations of the American territorial system.

CHAPTER VIII

FOUNDING OF NEW COMMONWEALTHS
(1787–1788)

WHEN the Ordinance was passed, eighteen delegates were in attendance in Congress, representing eight states — New York, Massachusetts, New Jersey, Delaware, Virginia, North Carolina, South Carolina, Georgia—five of them south of Mason and Dixon's line, yet there was but one dissenting vote, and that came from Abraham Yates, of New York. Nathan Dane, of Massachusetts, had expected opposition to the antislavery clause, and he added it almost at the last moment because he found the southern delegates favorably disposed.[1] But this does not mean that the southerners necessarily believed at that time in excluding slaves from all the western land. The Ordinance did not refer to the land south of the Ohio, and in considering the northwest the south was in part influenced by political motives, in part by industrial and commercial considerations. Grayson, of Virginia, who was himself an opponent of slavery extension, wrote to Monroe that "the clause respecting

[1] King, *Life and Corresp. of King*, I., 290.

slavery was agreed to by the southern members for the purpose of preventing tobacco and indigo from being made on the northwest side of the Ohio, as well as for several other political reasons." [1]

Concerning the authorship of this important document there has been much discussion. On this interesting question there seems to have been little comment at the time, for the Ordinance was passed by a moribund Congress, from which most of the talent was already withdrawn. Credit has at times been ascribed to Cutler, and one might expect to find in his detailed journal full information on the whole subject. He took a lively interest in his journey to New York, but he describes in his diary everything but the one thing which we should like to know; he tells of wine dinners, of pleasant companions, of entertaining and well-dressed young women, but of the excellences of this fundamental Ordinance he says nothing at all. He did propose some amendments to the report pending in Congress; [2] he did meet the committee in charge; [3] and he may well have advocated the insertion of the fundamental maxims of liberty, for he well knew the monetary value of having it well understood that certain principles of freedom were to obtain in the western country; but his diary would lead one to think that it was the shrewd bargain for

---

[1] Bancroft, *Hist. of the Const.*, II., 437.
[2] Cutler, *Cutler*, I., 293.
[3] Poole, in *No. Am. Rev.*, CXXII., 254.

the purchase of land that filled his mind and thoughts.

Nathan Dane, a member of Congress and of the committee, claimed in his later years the credit of the authorship, and his case is fairly clear.   He may have been influenced by Cutler; he was surely influenced by other men, for a large part of the Ordinance was a condensation of portions of the Massachusetts constitution of 1780;[1] but he, more than any other man, draughted the Ordinance of 1787,[2] and his name should not be forgotten in the list of makers of the American nation.   Credit should also be given to Rufus King, who, though not in Congress when the Ordinance was passed, was at least responsible in part for the most famous clause in it, the clause prohibiting slavery.[3]   But of course, when all is said, the credit of authorship cannot be given to two or three men; the significance of the Ordinance lies in the fact that it was the result of a long effort to settle the western question.   In many of its essentials it was—like other great historical documents momentous in human annals—the product of years.   It crystallized the principles of colonial organization about which men had been disputing for a generation.   Even the slavery clause had been considered and discussed more than once

---

[1] Barrett, *Evol. of Ord. of 1787*, 55 et seq.
[2] King, *Ohio* (ed. of 1903), 422; Dunn, *Indiana*, 205–210; King, *Life and Corresp. of King*, I., chap. xv.
[3] *Ibid.*, 286 et seq.

before the summer days of 1787 when Dr. Cutler appeared on the scene and spoke of buying millions of acres of wild land on the Ohio.

Dr. Cutler proved a capable and efficient agent. A few days after the passing of the Ordinance,[1] Congress authorized the sale of the western land on terms that were acceptable to the Ohio Company. He was also instrumental in making a purchase for the Scioto Company, a land-grabbing combination which has left a malodorous history behind it. The whole bargain constituted, said Cutler, "the greatest private contract ever made in America."[2]

Preparations were now made on an extensive scale for the settlement of the northwest. Arthur St. Clair was appointed by Congress governor of the new territory, which stretched from the western limits of Pennsylvania to the Mississippi and from the Ohio northward to the international boundary. In the year 1788 a body of New-Englanders made their way over the mountains, and with large flat-boats floated down the Ohio and founded the town of Marietta at the mouth of the Muskingum. "No colony in America," said Washington, "was ever settled under such favorable auspices. . . . Information, property, and strength, will be its characteristics."[3]

In the course of the legislation concerning the western territory, two or three important steps were

[1] *Journals of Congress* (ed. of 1823), IV., App. 17 et seq.
[2] Cutler, *Cutler*, I., 326.
[3] Washington, *Writings* (Ford's ed.), XI., 282.

taken that we have not yet referred to. In 1785
Congress passed an ordinance for ascertaining the
mode of disposing of lands in the western territory.[1]
It contained a number of significant provisions, and
was the beginning of the admirably complete and
simple land system of the United States, providing for the establishment of townships six miles
square, each of which should be divided into thirty-
six sections one mile square. Moreover, the act
provided that the lot number sixteen of every
township should be reserved for the maintenance of
public schools within the township. This provision
was included in the arrangement made with the
Ohio Company, and it was also expressly stipulated
that the company should set aside two townships
for a university and one section in every township
for the support of religion.[2] This was the foundation
for the broad policy of popular education and the
beginning of the free school and university system
of the west. Doubtless we see here the New-Eng-
land idea, and one that appealed to the business
instinct of the men who were forming the new
settlement; the formation of townships and the
grant of land for public purposes would furnish in-
ducements for " neighborhoods of the same religious
sentiments to confederate for the purpose of purchasing and settling together."[3]

[1] *Journals of Congress*, May 20, 1785.
[2] *Ibid*. (ed. of 1823), IV., App.; Cutler, *Cutler*, I., 319.
[3] Bancroft, *Hist. of the Const*., I., App., 425.

We have thus seen what preparations were made for building new commonwealths north of the Ohio: before settlements were made an elaborate plan of colonial organization was devised, providing for temporary government and for ultimate admission into the Union; a definite grant of territory was secured from Congress, and in accordance with well-matured arrangements a body of settlers left their eastern homes and moved over the mountains to form new settlements. The early method of building up the southwest was much different from this: there was no waiting for Congressional authority; the extension of the border depended on independent enterprise. A few bold hunters and restless adventurers pushed on into the wilderness with the instinct of the hopeful, land-loving, adventurous American frontiersman, and built palisades and clustering log-houses in the forests of Tennessee and Kentucky. The movement was spontaneous and natural, and did not rest on prearranged system or harmonize with any logical notion of colonial establishment. The pioneer, relying on his rifle as his title-deed, moved with his companions on into the unoccupied forests, prepared to hew his way to comfort and prosperity, and to build up civil government as the needs disclosed themselves.

The topography of the country influenced in considerable measure the history of state-making south of the Ohio. While the framers of the ordinances in Congress were marking out states by parallels and meridians, the western settler was feeling the inevitable force of geography. There was a movement to form a new state in the western portion of Pennsylvania and Virginia, a movement that was in part made good nearly a century later by the division of the Old Dominion. At an early day the settlers in this region, "separated by a vast, extensive and almost impassible Tract of Mountains, by Nature itself formed and pointed out as a Boundary between this Country and those below it," sought to be established as "a sister colony and fourteenth province of the American Confederacy."[1] There was, as we shall see, a movement to establish an independent state in what is now eastern Tennessee but was then western North Carolina, a section separated from the older state by the Appalachian range and different in its make-up from the lower land of western Tennessee. The frontiersman who turned his face to the great "western world," to use his own phrase, must have felt, even without words, that the west, separated by the mountain-chain from the Atlantic basin, could not long remain subservient to the older commonwealths of the coast. And yet at the same time he felt the unity of the great valley.[2] In the coming years, in spite of strong objection to restraint and in spite of an independent and buoyant spirit, the western man

[1] Document in Crumrine, *Hist. of Washington County, Pa.*, 187; quoted in Turner, "Western State-Making in the Revolutionary Era," in *Am. Hist. Review*, I., 83. [2] *Ibid.*, 75.

was on the whole loyal to the Union and national in his sympathies.

The settlement of the southwest began even before the Revolution. The region was not won simply by the bold diplomacy of our commissioners at Paris. While the war was in progress little bands of settlers, heedless of peril and careless of privation, were step by step moving on into the western wilderness, building homes by the side of the rivers that flowed westward and southward to the gulf. In all the negotiations, bickerings, and conspiracies that occupied the minds of so many men — Spaniards, Frenchmen, and Englishmen alike—for the twenty-five years that ensued between the French treaty of alliance in 1778 and the treaty of 1803, which brought us Louisiana, one fact could not be neglected: the western pioneer with his rifle and his powder-horn had built blockhouses and palisades in the heart of the Mississippi Valley. The perils that were encountered, the sufferings that were borne by these winners of the west, form an essential and vital part of American history.

One is at a loss to understand the restless energy with which these rough woodsmen pushed forward to make new homes in the solitudes of Kentucky and Tennessee. For years together the Indians were hostile; every little settlement had its tale of horror, of men murdered at their work, of children carried into captivity, of the plowman shot in the field or the harvestman as he stored his grain, of

sudden attack and spirited defence, of scalping and
torture, of ceaseless, hourly, unremitting danger.
And yet, in spite of suffering and disaster, men
that had seen their homes burned, their children
murdered before their eyes, went on quietly with
their work.[1] Clearing was added to clearing; houses
were built farther in the wilderness; little communities of self-reliant men and women sprang into
existence in the primeval forests of the great valley.
These woodsmen were the vanguard of English
civilization; these men of the "back country" were
in the forefront of American achievement.

Soon after the treaty of Fort Stanwix (1768), by
which the Iroquois gave up their claim to lands
between the Tennessee and the Ohio, Daniel Boone
was on his way "in quest of the country of Ken-
tucke"; and in 1770 a settlement was made on
the Watauga, a head-water of the Tennessee River,
under the leadership of James Robertson, a man
of rare force of character and boundless energy.
In 1772 he was joined by John Sevier, who was
"well fitted for this wilderness work," strong yet
jovial, at once an Indian fighter, a statesman, and a
gentleman. These two men were the founders of
Tennessee. Their settlement was in the attractive
upland valley bounded on the west by the Cumberland Mountains, on the east by the ridge of the
Alleghenies, which separated them from the parent

[1] See the letter of James Robertson, in *Am. Hist. Mag.* (Nashville, 1896), I., 83.

state. In their isolation the settlers soon needed a government, and they proceeded to form one.[1] One can find no more striking fact in American history, nor one more typical, than the simple ease with which these frontiersmen on the banks of the western waters, on the threshold of the central valley of the continent, finding themselves beyond the reach of eastern law, formed an association and exercised the rights and privileges of self-government. Under their articles of association the settlers seem to have lived until taken under the government of North Carolina soon after the outbreak of the Revolution (1776). The land, however, did not belong naturally to the coast but to the Mississippi region, and in later years became part of Tennessee.

The Watauga settlers, though separated by miles of forest from their neighbors east of the mountains, were not altogether cut off from the older regions, but ere long settlements were made in the heart of the more distant wilderness. Following Boone's trace, the famous Wilderness road over Cumberland Gap and on into the north and west, hardy, courageous woodsmen with their families made their way to found new homes in Kentucky. In 1775 Boonesborough was established, a lonely island in the great forest, two hundred miles from the eastern settlements. Blockhouses were likewise built and land was cleared at Nashborough, now Nashville, on the

[1] Ramsey, *Annals of Tenn.*, chap. ii.; Haywood, *Civil and Pol. Hist. of Tenn.* (ed. of 1823), 41.

broad bend of the Cumberland (1780).　Here again
the foundation of government was not, as at the
north, a document drawn up in the older settlements by legislative authority; the settlers took
nothing with them but their courage and a determination to build houses in the wilderness.
When they needed laws for protection, as a "temporary method of restraining the licentious," they
drew up a compact, not intending to establish an
independent state, but, till recognized and cared
for by Carolina, to supply for themselves "the
blessings flowing from a just and equitable government."[1]

Thus before the end of the Revolution permanent
settlements were established beyond the mountains,
although as yet no separate state was formed, for the
eastern states still claimed dominion; there was everywhere in these western settlements strong self-
reliance and democratic self-government. It could
be only a short time before independent commonwealths would be established.

The most famous movement for the establishment of a separate state was made by the settlers
near the head-waters of the Tennessee shortly after
the Revolution was ended.　Separated from North
Carolina by the mountains, this region, as we have
said, had a geographic individuality of its own.
In 1784 North Carolina ceded her western lands

[1] Ramsey, *Annals of Tenn.*, I., 194.　Cf. the compact in Putnam, *Middle Tenn.*, 94.

to Congress, with a proviso, however, that until Congress accepted the cession the sovereignty should remain in the state, and two years were allowed for the acceptance of the cession. North Carolina had for some time taken no tender interest in the transmontane settlements. With that complaisant superiority which often marks the man who has stayed at home when speaking of those who have had the enterprise to move, some of the men of the old state had declared the pioneers were nothing but the "off-scourings of the earth"[1] and "fugitives from justice."

The westerners felt themselves abandoned, but were not accustomed to shed tears because left to their own devices. They probably supposed that Congress had practically assured them statehood by passing the Ordinance of 1784, and they proceeded themselves to organize a state. "If we should be so happy," they said, "as to have a separate government, vast numbers from different quarters, with a little encouragement from the public, would fill up our frontier, which would strengthen us, improve agriculture, perfect manufactures, encourage literature and every thing truly laudable. The seat of government being among ourselves, would evidently tend, not only to keep a circulating medium in gold and silver among us, but draw it from many in-

[1] Quoted in a statement of their case by the Franklin general assembly, 1785. See Alden, "The State of Franklin," in *Am. Hist. Review*, VIII., 277; *Pennsylvania Packet*, May 21, 1785.

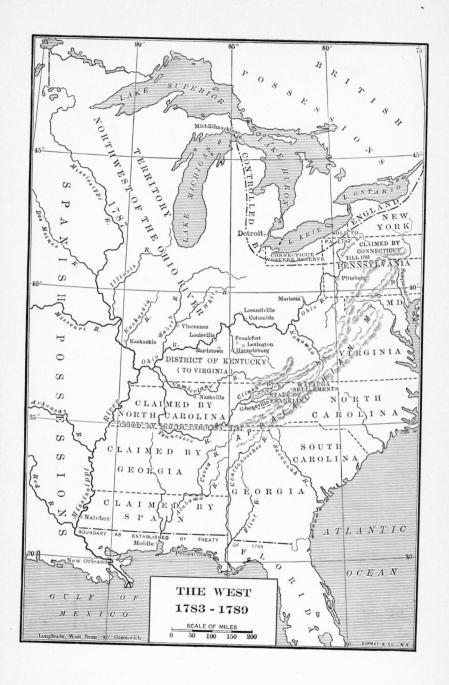

THE WEST
1783 - 1789

SCALE OF MILES

0   50   100   150   200

Longitude West from 90 Greenwich

BORMAY & CO., N.Y.

dividuals living in other states, who claim large
quantities of lands that would lie in the bounds of
the new state."[1] This simple statement, full of
quaint economy and charged with the enthusiasm
and idealism of the frontiersmen, brings before us
much that was characteristic of the hopeful west.
No wonder, with such prospect of monetary and
literary improvement, they did not hesitate to establish an independent commonwealth.

Before final action was taken, North Carolina
withdrew her act of cession. In spite of this, and
though persistence meant rebellion, the western
men drew up a constitution modelled after that of
the parent state (1785), and, adopting the name
of Franklin, sought recognition from the Congress
of the Confederation. One of their first acts was
to provide for taxes and to show, if not the need
of literature and all things laudable, at least the
primitive condition of society and the absence of
gold and silver, whose presence was so much desired. Taxes were made payable in otter, deer, and
beaver skins,[2] in well-cured bacon, in clean tallow,
in distilled rye whiskey, in good peach or apple
brandy, and in like useful and cheering commodities.
North Carolina protested against this separate organization; Congress of course did nothing; and
Franklin led a troubled life for about four years,
giving up its pretence of independence in 1788.

[1] Ramsey, *Annals of Tenn.*, 288, 289.
[2] *Ibid.*, 297.

In Kentucky, then a district of Virginia, there was throughout this time considerable restlessness and discontent. Some of the settlers, with Wilkinson at their head, were engaged in some sort of a mysterious intrigue, disreputable at the best, with the Spanish authorities in New Orleans. Others desired a separation from Virginia and admission into the Union as a state. Nothing definite was accomplished, however, before the end of the period of the Confederation. June 1, 1792, Kentucky entered the Union.

Despite this restlessness of the frontiersmen, and despite the plottings of ambitious schemers like the unspeakable Wilkinson, the story of early western settlements is a story of American achievement. During the Revolutionary era the American people had expanded and laid the foundations for new commonwealths in the valley of the Mississippi, which offered homes for countless thousands; the Congress of the Confederation had at last become possessed of property, and, incorrigibly incompetent in all other directions, succeeded in drawing up a wise and noble plan for colonial expansion. The settlers themselves, who were now pouring over the mountains, were showing remarkable political sagacity. Rough, uncouth, lawless, as many of the adventurers were, the great body of them were home-seekers, bent on improving their fortunes, and they gave evidence withal of a native instinct for government and order. Unlovely as was the

raw frontier in some of its aspects, there was no
danger that these enterprising pioneers would found
hopeless, forlorn settlements in the wilderness; the
history of American achievement in the Mississippi
Valley was to be different from the French or
Spanish.   Only when the importance of this movement is grasped do we see how much the Americans
accomplished in the eventful years from 1774 to 1788:
they won their independence from Britain, began
with astounding courage and zeal the occupation
of the "western world," worked out the principles
of territorial organization, and, almost without
knowing it themselves, prepared the outlines of a
system which assured the facile extension of their
power from the Atlantic coast across the continent.

CHAPTER IX

PAPER MONEY

(1781–1788)

ALL through the period of which we have been speaking, the monetary conditions of the country were in confusion. There were so many different kinds of money in circulation that to calculate the value of any piece was a serious arithmetical problem. There were moidores, doubloons, pistoles, gold johanneses, English and French crowns, English guineas, and Spanish dollars. The standard in transactions with Great Britain was the pound sterling, but the coins most commonly used were the Spanish milled dollars—Captain Flint's "pieces of eight." In such a state of disorder and depreciation was the currency of the times, and so much did terms differ from state to state, that the dollar was worth six shillings in New England and Virginia, eight shillings in New York and North Carolina, seven shillings sixpence in Pennsylvania, five shillings in Georgia, and thirty-two shillings sixpence in South Carolina.[1]

[1] Sparks, *Gouverneur Morris*, I., 274; Sparks, *Dip. Corresp. of Rev.*, XII., 91.

To make matters worse, counterfeiting was much practised, so commonly, in fact, that the wary trader might well have taken almost as much time for testing his money as for selling his goods. "Enclosed are one hundred Dollars of new Emission Money," wrote Gerry to King in 1785, "which Colonel Steward desired me to have exchanged for Specie. Pray inform him they are all counterfeit."[1] Good coin, moreover, was too valuable and rare to be allowed to circulate unmutilated. Clipping and shearing were so commonly practised that, as Washington complained, if an end were not put to the business a *pistareen* would be converted "into *five* quarters" and a man be forced to "travel with a pair of money scales in his pocket, or run the risk of receiving gold at one fourth less by weight than it counts."[2]

Some efforts were made to improve the coinage, but without immediate result. Gouverneur Morris, while acting as assistant to Robert Morris, drew up a scheme for decimal currency,[3] and Jefferson, at the head of a committee of Congress, considered similar plans.[4] In the summer of 1785 Congress announced that the smallest coin should be of copper, of which two hundred should pass for a dollar, and the "several pieces . . . increase in a decimal ratio,"[5] and on August 8, 1786, a full plan

[1] King, *Life and Corresp. of King*, I., 87.
[2] Washington, *Writings* (Ford's ed.), X., 493.
[3] Sparks, *Gouverneur Morris*, I., 273 et seq.
[4] Jefferson, *Writings* (Ford's ed.), III., 446.
[5] *Journals of Congress*, July 6, 1785.

of coinage was adopted. Congress endeavored in some measure to remedy the evil by providing for a mint and by fixing the value of the coin to be struck.[1] But it is needless to say that practically nothing was done.

Amid all the genuine distress caused by the war, by heavy taxes, and by the need of a sound and reliable circulating medium, came still greater trouble caused by the restlessness of the people, by the honest-minded but uneasy poor, and by the debtors who sought an avenue of escape. The times were indeed hard for a man that was once down; imprisonment for debt was common; the jails were dreadful and filthy; the processes of the courts were expensive and summary. Some quick method of paying old debts, some way of getting rid of the truly formidable consequences of either idleness or misfortune, was naturally sought after, and, following the precedents of earlier days, there was a demand for paper money, tender-laws, and other measures of relief. The years 1785 and 1786 are therefore marked by the rise of a paper-money party in the states, intent on remedying the supposed evil of the day, "a scarcity of money." To be sure, a good deal of specie had been drawn from the country by the recent heavy importations of merchandise; but the natural result of strenuous efforts to introduce a cheap currency was to drive specie out of circulation. The greater

[1] *Journals of Congress*, October 16, 1786.

the agitation, therefore, the more serious the difficulty.

The truth is that in this paper-money agitation
we see the most serious danger of those dreary days,
when nearly everybody was grumbling, and when
the wise and prudent feared even for the foundation
of society itself; for with the paper-money faction
everywhere were enrolled, not alone the unhappy
and the deluded, but also all those uneasy elements
that opposed the extension of federal authority and
believed in law only as a means of securing some
selfish and niggardly end. The paper-money agitation had much more than a mere financial or business significance; here were gathered together the
malcontents and the dangerously restless. As conservative men watched the growing discontent they
grew closer together and saw more clearly the need
of a strong hand and a firm government to insure
domestic tranquillity.

While a good many men saw as clearly as the
ablest economists of to-day the impossibility of
making something out of nothing, and while many
able and honest men argued strongly and vehe-
mently against the criminal folly of trying to supply currency or to restore prosperity by a recourse
to the printing-press, thousands of lusty throats
clamored unceasingly for relief. Some miscreants
had doubtless made money with considerable ease
during the war, and there was reason for dissatisfaction with the money-sharps who had taken

advantage of the necessities of their neighbors. But the argument of the needy or shiftless was easy: the property of the United States had been protected from destruction by the joint exertion of all, it ought therefore to be the common property of all. The man that opposed this creed was declared to be "an enemy to equality and justice," who should "be swept from the face of the earth." "They are determined," wrote Knox to Washington, October 23, 1786, "to annihilate all debts public and private, and have agrarian laws, which are easily effected by the means of unfunded paper money, which shall be a tender in all cases whatever."[1]

All this mad reasoning was in some degree the natural product of a war against authority, a war which had brought a social upheaval and was based on ideas of personal right and liberty antagonistic to authority. As soon as those who had profited by the disturbed conditions, or who had fallen into extravagant or negligent habits, saw that conditions were resuming their old form, that the industrious were to reap the fruits of their industry, and that the indolent and improvident were likely to suffer the natural consequences of idleness and sloth, they began to cry out against the existing order. First, the grant of full pay for five years to the Revolutionary officers was the object of attack; then the weight of public taxes, the scarcity of money, and the cruelty

[1] Drake, *Henry Knox*, 91, 92; see also *Mass. Centinel*, December 9, 1786.

of creditors who were calling for their dues.[1] Thus
paper money was the panacea for all their ills.
"Don't be influenced by anybody's talking and
nonsense," said one patriotic debtor, addressing his
fellow-citizens in Connecticut. "Choose for your-
self. Choose then without favor or affection men
of simplicity, not men of shrewdness and learning;
choose men that are somewhat in debt themselves
that they may not be too strenuous in having laws
made or executed for collection of debts, nothing
puts a poor, honest man so much out of ready money
as being sued, and sheriffs after him. Choose such
men as will make a bank of paper money, big enough
to pay all our debts, which will sink itself (that will
be so much clear gain to the state)."[2] When a great
body of men are preaching the righteousness of the
confiscation of property, the stability of society is
threatened, even though the method of confiscation
be simply the depreciation of the currency for the
benefit of the discontented poor.

Some of the states, in spite of the popular excitement over supposed financial ills, refused to go
back to paper. Connecticut had issued paper at
the outbreak of the war, but was now well out of
the trouble and steadfastly refused to burn her
fingers anew. Massachusetts was feeling sorely the
derangement of her trade, and within her borders

[1] Hart, *Contemporaries*, III., 192.
[2] *New Haven Gazette*, March 22, 1787, quoted in Libby,
Geographical Distribution of the Vote on the Federal Const., 58.

were thousands of surly malcontents who grumbled without ceasing and threatened unsparingly; but she, too, was not allured into seeking peace and prosperity by the practical confiscation of credits. New Hampshire, Virginia, Delaware, and Maryland likewise resisted, though in each was a powerful party eagerly working for paper.

The cheap-money faction in Virginia was strong and persistent; but fortunately the state contained a body of capable men who were not afraid to enter the conflict and to call things by their right names. One of the noteworthy points of Virginia politics was the fact that the best men had from the beginning been leaders, had taken part in political controversy, and were not accustomed weakly to yield obedience to the shouts of an uneasy mob. When in 1775 men like Thomas Hutchinson were driven from Massachusetts and the other colonies, the sober men of property in Virginia were the leaders of the populace.

In 1786 the head of the conservatives in the Virginia legislature was Madison. He was at his best in discussing a subject like this, which did not require great knowledge of finance or of practical business, but did need a clear mind, a sound conscience, a patriotic spirit, and an ability to see the relations between legislation and morality. At no time in his career, perhaps, did Madison do more valiant or more valuable service for his country than in these trying days of the Confederation when there were so many social and political perils

on every hand. He was able, industrious, and full
of confidence, one of that company of young men
to whom the upheaval of the Revolution had given
opportunity, and who did so much for establishing the Union and setting her feet on the way to
prosperity. His delicate perceptions, his scholarly
tastes, his historical and legal knowledge, his simple
appreciation of right, his sense of justice, were now
devoted to the interests of his country. He did
not hesitate to declare that the issuing of paper
money was pernicious, that it sowed dissensions
among the states, destroyed confidence between individuals, discouraged commerce, enriched sharpers,
vitiated morals, reversed the end of government,
which is to reward the best and punish the worst,
and that if Virginia followed the example of other
states in adopting paper, she would help to disgrace
republican government in the eyes of mankind.
Virginia, to her honor, announced by her house of
delegates that an emission of paper money would
be "unjust, impolitic, destructive of public and
private confidence, and of that virtue which is the
basis of Republican Government."[1]

In a plan allowing the taxes of the year to be
paid in tobacco, or, more properly in "inspectors
receipts or notes for good merchantable crop tobacco,"[2] Madison reluctantly acquiesced, for fear
that "some greater evil under the name of relief

---

[1] Madison, *Writings* (Hunt's ed.), II., 277, 281.
[2] Hening, *Statutes*, XII., 258.

to the people would be substituted."[1] His yielding was, perhaps, a characteristic piece of weakness,
but it should be noticed that the plan of having
government warehouses was one of long standing,
that tobacco receipts or "promissory notes" had
not uncommonly circulated as money within a
limited area in the colony, and that, in fact, this
great, fragrant crop had in great measure played the
rôle of gold and silver in the financial history of the
colony. The plan of issuing receipts that in fact
constituted money was not so very different from
the system in force in the latter part of the nineteenth century, whereby "silver certificates" were
given out as receipts for a deposit of bullion.[2]

Even in New Hampshire, where the sound-money
party finally won a decisive victory, and where there
was on the whole a peaceful and law-abiding spirit,
there were days of distress and anxiety. The state
was heavily in debt, was almost hopelessly behind
in its payments to the federal treasury, and was not
entirely recovered from the past demoralization of
its currency. The air was filled with complaints
of the discontented, with grumblings over taxes, and
with denunciation of courts and lawyers.[3] "Your
Supplicants have great cause to Mourn," declared
one petitioning town, "when by Reading and Information they are Convinced of the happiness,

[1] Madison, *Writings* (Hunt's ed.), II., 301.
[2] Ripley, *Finan. Hist. of Virginia* (Columbia College *Studies*,
IV.), 150.   [3] Belknap, *Hist. of N. H.*, II., 457 et seq.

those People enjoy . . . Whose Legislative Bodies
have emitted a Paper Currency." But when the
people considered "the immense Treasures" expended in the war, "the hosts of their beloved
fellow Citizens" that had fallen, "the rivers of
human blood with which the earth " was "wantonly
crimsoned," and when they reflected that though
the " din of war " was no more heard, they could not
find the "golden prize—the dear earned promised
happy day," then they were disconsolate indeed.
Instead of the "blessings of peace," though they
sought them "diligently with tears," they found
misery; they were in a "labyrinth of difficulty and
distress, like Issachar of old crouching under the
weight of complicated burdens."[1]

In September of 1786 an armed mob some hundreds strong, demanding paper money, asking for
distribution of property, and clamoring against government, surrounded the meeting-house in Exeter,
where the legislature was in session, and threatened
to hold the lawmakers prisoners till their demands
were complied with. Fortunately the citizens of
Exeter and the neighborhood were not in a mood to
sympathize with rioting. The mob, first frightened
by stratagem into retreat, was the next day dis-
persed by a band of citizens and militia.[2] Thus

[1] *Town Papers of N. H.*, XI., 122, 123, 488.
[2] Bell, *Hist. of Exeter*, 96; *Historical Mag.*, 2d series, V., 37;
"An Account of the Insurrection in the State of New - Hampshire—Written by a Gentleman who happened to be present,"
in *Boston Mag.*, III., 401-404.

the state was saved from disgrace if not from humiliation. Even before the insurrection the legislature had determined to submit a paper-money measure to the towns of the state for their approval. In spite of the clamor of those who pointed to the "Elysian fields" in other states as "contrasted with the bondage" of New Hampshire,[1] good sense prevailed; the measure was emphatically rejected by the people.[2]

The conservative party, therefore, in the end was safely victorious, but the mob that disturbed the peace of placid little Exeter was but illustrative of the dangers of the time. There was inflammable material in every state. The hoarse laments of the unhappy, who wished for the promised days of plenty and complained that gold and silver had "taken wings and flown to the other side of the Atlantic," who demanded that ease and prosperity be brought to each man's door by legislative enactment, were heard not alone in the grumbling town-meetings of New Hampshire.

Under the sway of the paper-money party seven states entered on the difficult task of legislating their people into financial blessedness by the simple means of making money, a task which many seemed to believe was the most useful employment of popular government. Of all the states, Rhode Island, with a talent for the dramatic, adopted the

[1] Belknap, *Hist. of N. H.*, II., 467, quoting *New Hampshire Gazette*, July 20, 1786.   [2] *Early State Papers of N. H.*, XX., 772.

most radical measures. The condition of the
state was doubtless distressing, for nowhere else
had the war wrought such havoc. Newport had
been a flourishing seaport before the Revolution:
hundreds of vessels each year sailed thence to
Europe or to the West Indies, or carried cargoes of
rum to the slave coast, to bring back across the
Atlantic the black ivory of Africa. Many scores
of little trading-ships sailed from Narragansett Bay
to traffic along the coast. There were then in
Newport oil and candle factories, ropewalks, sugar
refineries, and as many as twenty-two distilleries to
produce the New England rum that formed the
great staple of trade.[1] At the close of the war the
town was almost in ruins and its commerce shat-
tered.   Trade was beginning to revive in a measure,
and Providence was gaining something of what
Newport had lost; but the state had great burdens,
much augmented by a spirit of independence, fault-
finding, and absurd self-assurance.

Rhode Island had been founded as a home of the
"otherwise minded," and for some time it had been
playing that rôle with conspicuous success in both
domestic and continental politics. It had already
experimented much with paper money, but there
were many who had not lost faith in what Jay
called "the doctrine of the political transubstantia-
tion of paper into gold and silver."[2] The merchants

[1] Arnold, *Hist. of R. I.*, II., 300.
[2] Jay, *Corresp. and Public Papers*, III., 215.

and tradesmen of the larger towns opposed the issuing of more paper, but the country people as strongly favored it. At the polls the countrymen were successful, and the legislature immediately passed a bill for the emission of bills of credit which were to be issued to the freeholders of the state, on the security of landed property of twice the value of the loan. The scrip was made legal tender in payment of debts. The inevitable difficulties, of course, ensued, for the creditors, reversing the time-worn practice, sought to escape their debtors for fear of being paid in worthless money. To make escape impossible, a law was passed declaring that a debtor might pay into court a sum which he asserted he owed to a creditor, and that after due notice to the creditor the debt should be considered discharged. But this was not enough. The paper depreciated, and the legislature, not to be baffled, passed a bill making it an offence punishable by fine to refuse to take the scrip.[1]

The condition of the state during these days was deplorable indeed. The merchants shut their shops and joined the crowd in the bar-rooms; men lounged in the streets or wandered aimlessly about with no hope of employment. A French traveller who passed through Newport about this time gives a dismal picture of the place: idle men standing with folded arms at the corners of the streets; houses

[1] Bates, *R. I. and the Union*, 125, 126; Arnold, *Hist. of R. I.*, II., 521.

falling to ruins; miserable shops offering for sale nothing but a few coarse stuffs or baskets of gnarly apples; grass growing in the streets; windows stuffed with rags; everything announcing misery, the triumph of paper money, and the influence of bad government.[1] The merchants had closed their stores rather than take payment in paper; farmers from neighboring states did not care to bring their produce and receive nothing but Rhode Island scrip. Some of the countrymen sought to starve the tradesmen into a proper appreciation of the simple laws of finance by refusing to bring their produce to market.

To help enforce the law requiring acceptance of paper in payment, the legislature now went one step further and provided for a summary trial of an offender before a court composed of at least three judges. No jury was to be summoned, but conviction was to be determined by the majority of the judges.[2] There now occurred a very interesting incident. One John Weeden, a butcher of Newport, refused to accept John Trevett's paper money in payment for meat. In any well-regulated community of reasonable sobriety and sense a butcher is not expected to sell his meat unless he wishes to, but in Rhode Island in 1786 such a refusal was a

---

[1] Brissot de Warville, *Travels* (ed. of 1794), I., 118; see also "Diary of John Quincy Adams," in Mass. Hist. Soc., *Proceedings*, 2d series, XVI., 459.

[2] *Records of State of R. I.*, X., 213.

penal offence, and John Weeden, at the instance of Trevett, was haled before the court and charged with breach of the law. He was ably defended by learned counsel, one of whom was James M. Varnum, a lawyer of talent, and for some time a member of Congress.

In a forceful argument to the court, Varnum laid down principles of constitutional law of great significance, which are now recognized as fundamental and all-important in American jurisprudence. "The legislative," he declared, "have the uncontrollable power of making laws not repugnant to the constitution. The judiciary have the sole power of judging those laws, and are bound to execute them; but cannot admit any act of the legislative as law, which is against the constitution." [1] The legislature derives all its authority from the constitution, but must not violate the constitution, as was done by an act depriving citizens of the right to trial by jury. "This court," he said, "is under the solemn obligations to execute the laws of the land, and therefore can not, will not consider this act as a law of the land." [2] Inasmuch as Rhode Island was still working under its old colonial charter, and had not a new constitution plainly established by the will of the people, Varnum's contention was peculiarly bold. But the court sustained the argument, declaring that the "information was

---

[1] Coxe, *Judicial Power and Unconst. Leg.*, 242.
[2] *Ibid.*, 236.

not cognizable before them." The judgment of the court plainly rejected the statute as void because contrary to the constitutional authority of the legislature.

The lawmakers, outraged by the conduct of the court, summoned the judges to appear before them.[1] At the hearing the judges ably defended their position, contended manfully for the independence of the judiciary, and asserted the unconstitutionality of the statute. After hearing the defence, the assembly voted that it was not satisfied with the reasons given by the judges in support of their judgment; but the judges were finally allowed to leave the presence of the assembly without further reproof and without impeachment. The court had given to the public a lesson regarding sense, liberty, and the function of the judiciary in a free commonwealth. Though the decision of the court helped to restore confidence and give hope, Rhode Island for some time after this was the prey of prejudice, jealousy, and ignorance. At the next election only one of the judges of the superior court was re-elected.

[1] Varnum, *Trevett vs. Weeden;* Thayer, *Cases on Constitutional Law,* I., 73.

CHAPTER X

SHAYS'S REBELLION
(1786–1787)

BAD as were the follies of petulant Rhode Island, they seem to have caused little dismay to the conservative men of other states; but events were at the same time taking place in Massachusetts which startled sober - minded and law - abiding citizens everywhere. The air of that state was heavy with the murmurs of the discontented. It is not easy to say in a word what the trouble was; for though the taxes were high and the indebtedness of the state large, Massachusetts doubtless had at that very moment the foundation for reasonable prosperity. Crops were good,[1] commerce, though in some respects disarranged, was reviving, manufactures were growing in number and increasing their product. But the demon of depreciated money had left its curse upon the state, the old continental money was fit only for kindling fires, much of the specie had left the country, and good, hard money was kept in close confinement. There was real need of a circulating medium; at any rate,

[1] *Mass. Centinel*, December 23, 1786.

little medium of any kind circulated. "I go to church both parts of the day," confided William Pynchon to his diary. "Through the scarcity of cash, scarce a dollar is collected at Communion."[1]

No one can say whether the cry of scarcity of money had much foundation; at every industrial panic there is a demand for more money; people without money themselves believe that the effect is the cause and get hopelessly immeshed in the snares of argument. Naturally, amid all this industrial and financial disorder, the improvident suffered most severely, and they naturally raised a cry for more money. Men that had borrowed money or run into debt for goods when a day-laborer on the highways received £7 10s. a day might well wonder as to the possibility of paying their creditors when the wage of the common laborer had fallen to fifty cents.[2]

In addition to all this the Revolution had brought times of laxity and extravagance.[3] It was easy enough, of course, for the old squires to mourn the virtue of bygone days and to lament the inroad of recklessness and presumption—to immovable conservatives the old times are always the better—and yet the laments were in part justified. The war had loosed from the old-time restraint the lower

[1] *Diary of William Pynchon*, February 12, 1786, p. 231.
[2] Adams, *Hist. of Quincy*, 260, 261.
[3] Lincoln, quoted in Hart, *Contemporaries*, III., 191; **Am. Hist.** Assoc., *Report*, 1896, I., 740; *Boston Gazette*, July 31, 1786; *Mass. Centinel*, September 20, 1786.

elements of society and had raised up the ignorant to places they were not fit to fill.[1] Of this there are many evidences besides the complaining of the time. Much of the trouble, too, must be attributed to the general state of uneasiness, which was a moral rather than an economic result of the Revolution, to a feeling of envy for the rich and successful. Many were looking anxiously for the golden fruit of the tree of liberty, and they found it not. "That taxes," said Knox to Washington, "may be the ostensible cause is true, but that they are the true cause is as far remote from truth as light from darkness. The people who are the insurgents have never paid any or but very little taxes. But they see the weakness of government: they feel at once their own poverty compared with the opulent, and their own force, and they are determined to make use of the latter in order to remedy the former."[2]

The vicious, the restless, the ignorant, the foolish —and there were plenty of each class—were coming together to test the strength of the newly established government of Massachusetts. They did not determine in advance on breaking up the government, but they were restless and uneasy; they were advocating measures which if given free op-

[1] Adams, *Hist. of Quincy*, 265; Jameson, *Introd. to the Study of the States (Johns Hopkins University Studies*, IV., No. 5, 202), 21; Boston *Independent Chronicle*, December 15, 1786.
[2] Brooks, *Henry Knox*, 194.

portunity for development would have undermined government and liberty together. The cause of the trouble was declared by General Lincoln to be a want of industry, economy, and common honesty. It did not better matters that along with these dangerous malcontents were many honest citizens in real distress and in sore dismay and wonderment.[1]

Against the lawyers who took money for trying suits against the helpless debtors, or who made out the papers that cast the indigent into prison for debt, there was an especially bitter feeling; and from the lawyers the dislike was readily transferred to the courts themselves as a needless encumbrance on a free people. During the days of monetary inflation, when scrip was handed about in rolls or when debts could be paid according to the tender-act in enumerated articles rather than money, some creditors had shrewdly not pushed their debtors for payment; and when under more normal conditions suits were begun to collect money,[2] the shiftless, the improvident, and the unfortunate were in straits. They naturally detested lawyers and cherished no love for courts and judges. Some there were that found fault with the rich merchants of Boston, who, drinking costly wines and clad in imported stuffs, were the very vampires of the state. The wife and daughters of the governor, too,

---

[1] Hart, *Contemporaries*, III., 191.
[2] Minot, *Hist. of Insur. in Mass.*, 14; Lincoln, *Hist. of Worcester*, 131.

were living without work instead of toiling like common people; and money, moreover, stayed in Boston instead of being divided.[1] Of course there was no reasoning with men talking such rubbish; some were too simple to see their folly; some were shrewd enough to hope for gain; others, normally sober-minded and not without sense, listened to the clamor and followed wistfully in the train of the talkers.[2]

Even the law-abiding citizen began to wonder whether it would not be well to try paper money once again, whether remedies against the money-sharpers could not be found, whether it would not be wise to move the general court from Boston away from the contaminating influence of the well-to-do. Even in such a town as Quincy, where the hearts of the citizens were said to be "inflamed with true Patriotism," there were complaints of "numerous Grievances" and "intolerable Burthens," and the town's representative was instructed to favor the making of "Land a Tender for all debts at the Price it stood at when the debts were contracted," and to use his efforts to remove the legislature from Boston. The people wished the lawmakers to "crush or at least put a proper check . . . on that order of Gentlemen denominated Lawyers the completion of whos modern conduct appears to us to tend rather to the distruction than the preservation

[1] *Diary of William Pynchon*, September 18, 1786, p. 250.
[2] *Mass. Centinel*, December 9, 1786.

of the Commonwealth." [1] They also desired the
court of common pleas and general sessions of the
peace to "be removed in perpetuam rei Memoriam."

Extreme measures were now advocated. A convention of fifty towns in the county of Hampshire
(August, 1786),[2] after dwelling on the grievances of
the time, passed a series of resolutions complaining
of taxes, courts, lawyers, and scarcity of money,
and asking "to have emitted a bank of paper money,
subject to a depreciation," as legal tender in payment of all debts—a pleasant plan whereby it was
to be arranged, presumably, that the money should
decline by easy stages from par to nothing, in accordance with some predetermined requirements
of descent. A man might thus pay, perchance,
$4 for a pair of boots in January, $6 the next July,
$8 in December, until finally if he wished to buy
boots with scrip he must needs draw his money to
market in the farm wagon. The acme of this style
of reasoning was reached in a petition which declared that the advisable plan was to have a depreciation of a shilling per pound each year; thus
the money would "go out of circulation in the
term of twenty years." "By the quantity in circulation thus constantly lessening," said the pe-
titioners, " . . . the credit of the money will be sup-

---

[1] Adams, *Hist. of Quincy*, 264, 265.
[2] Minot, *Hist. of Insur. in Mass.*, 34–38; see also, for example, resolutions of Middlesex convention, Boston *Independent Chronicle*, October 19, 1786,

ported." [1] This is not far from saying that if the value of the money could only depreciate by agreement with sufficient rapidity its value would be maintained.

Fantastic as these recommendations were, they were but the prelude to radical acts. A mob took possession of the court-house at Northampton and prevented the sitting of the court. A similar occurrence took place at Worcester.[2] There were likewise uprisings at Taunton and other places. At Concord a band of merchants, headed by Job Shattuck and a man named Smith, paraded the streets in martial order and intimidated the judges into promising that no court should be held. Smith harangued the crowd of spectators, who were too wise or too timid to join the insurgents, declaring that "as Christ laid down his life to save the world," so he would lay down his life "to suppress the government from all triannical oppression." Those who would not fall into the ranks of the rebels were warned that after two hours they would "stand the monuments of God's sparing mercy." [3] When Job Shattuck took his part in the harangue and announced that the time had come to wipe out debts, some disrespectful auditor shouted out, "Well said, well said, Job, for I know you have bought two farms lately which you can never pay for." [4]

[1] Lunenberg Petition (MS.), in Mass. Archives, Senate Document No. 620, 2; quoted in Warren, *Shays's Rebellion* (MS.).

[2] Lincoln, *Hist. of Worcester*, 134.

[3] *Pa. Packet*, September 23, 1786.

[4] McMaster, *United States*, I., 308, 309.

There were next serious uprisings in the western part of the state. At Great Barrington the jails were broken open, the courts were prevented from sitting, and all but one of the judges compelled to sign a pledge that they would not act until the grievances of the people were redressed. Later in the year even greater outrages were perpetrated, law-abiding citizens were hounded out of town, houses were searched, citizens were fired on.[1]

The condition was now nothing short of civil war. Fortunately the governor, James Bowdoin, was no demagogue. He had already spoken in clear tones, and he was determined, if possible, to protect the courts and keep the peace. At Springfield bloodshed was narrowly avoided. The court was protected by the militia; but a mob of one thousand men with sundry arms and implements of war paraded the street under the leadership of Daniel Shays, a man of no great caliber, who had seen service in the continental army, and now looked for new fame as the leader of a popular uprising.

The situation was not materially improved by the acts and resolves of the general court, which now met at Boston. The governor was supported in his vigorous measures to sustain the courts and protect property; but there were members in the house who had much sympathy with the rioters and preferred soft words to strenuous action. A vote was

[1] Minot, *Hist. of Insur. in Mass.*, 44 – 50; Holland, *Hist. of Western Mass.*, I., 244–248; *Diary of William Pynchon*, 249.

passed granting pardon to all who within a given time would take the oath of allegiance.[1] An address was issued to the people, showing that the whole annual expense of the government averaged only £18,109, and did not amount to sixteen pence per ratable poll.[2] Certain stringent measures were enacted, and others for the relief of the people, but the tone of the legislature was not decisive; the rioting continued in various parts of the state, and after the adjournment of the legislature in November there was even more turbulence than before.

The time for promises and parleyings was, in fact, long since passed. Nothing would now tell but force, and Bowdoin was not loath to use it. A riot again occurred at Worcester,[3] and the court was once more prevented from holding its sessions. But when disturbances were threatened at Concord a company of cavalry was sent out against the rebels, and it captured the ringleaders, including the redoubtable Job Shattuck. Despite the cold of December weather and heavy snow, an army under Shays was gathering at Worcester and seemed to be threatening to attack Cambridge. When steps were taken to protect the city the rebels instead of advancing began a disorderly retreat. The cold

[1] *Acts and Laws of Mass.*, 1786–1787, chap. xv., November 15, 1786.

[2] Minot, *Hist. of Insur. in Mass.*, 68; *Boston Mag.*, III., 435.

[3] *Mass. Centinel*, November 29, 1786. See Bowdoin's speech of February 3, 1787, *ibid.*, February 7.

was intense,[1] the snow deep, there was a scarcity of provisions, and the insurgents suffered severely, some dying from exposure. This did not end the rebellion, however, and an army of four thousand four hundred men was now raised and put under the command of General Lincoln. So empty was the treasury that funds for the support of the troops had to be furnished by voluntary loans from wealthy citizens of Boston and other towns.[2]

The centre of the trouble was now shifted to Springfield, where an army of rebels commanded by Shays, Eli Parsons, and Luke Day was posted. Before Lincoln could reach the town an attack on the arsenal was beaten back by the militia under General Shepard.[3] On Lincoln's arrival Shays retreated with his forces in great disorder. Lincoln pursued relentlessly. Negotiations begun by the rebels for a time delayed him at Hadley; but discovering that negotiations were only a pretence and that Shays had moved on to Petersham, he set out from Hadley in pursuit, and, not deterred by cutting winds, deep snow, and bitter cold, his soldiers marched thirty miles in a single night and utterly routed the rebel army.[4] The most painful results of civil conflict followed. Little

[1] *Mass. Centinel*, December 13, 1786.
[2] Higginson to Knox, Amer. Hist. Assoc., *Report*, 1896, I., 744; Minot, *Hist. of Insur. in Mass.*, 93, 94.
[3] *Mass. Centinel*, January 31, 1787.
[4] See for this, letter of E. Whitney in Cutler, *Cutler*, I., 197-200; *Mass. Centinel*, February 3 and 7, 1787.

bands of the demoralized insurgents preyed on the country. Some of the rebels were intent on continuing the struggle, and Eli Parsons, deploring that he had not "the tongue of a ready writer," begged them not to give up and "see and hear of the yeomanry of this Commonwealth being parched, and cut to pieces by the cruel and merciless tools of tyrannical power."[1] But before spring the insurgents either were safe at home trying to look as if they had spent a placid winter in the quiet of their own chimney-corners, or had retreated across the border into neighboring states.

Thanks to the firm hand of James Bowdoin, to whose dignity, steadfastness, and right-mindedness much praise is due, the insurrection was at length suppressed. But let us not suppose that the people of Massachusetts, startled by grim-visaged war, hastened to pay honor to the man who had done so much to save and redeem the state. On the contrary, at the next election Bowdoin was badly defeated and John Hancock, a popular favorite, who loved nothing better than sunning himself in the smiles of the crowd, was elected governor. As a final outcome the rebels were not punished, and even Shays was allowed to retire into merited obscurity. Shays had not proved a successful leader; but probably Napoleon himself would have been at a loss to lead such a rabble of independent spirits. In later years he told of asking

[1] Minot, *Hist. of Insur. in Mass.*, 146, 147.

a man to stand guard. "No, I won't," was the
response. "Let that man; he is not so sick as I
be."[1]

While the rebellion was in progress Congress had
begun to raise troops, ostensibly to quell the Indians
on the frontier, really to assist Massachusetts if
necessary. But though "not only bound by the
confederation and good faith, but strongly prompted by friendship, affection, and sound policy," to
help the troubled state, and though the arsenal at
Springfield was the property of the Confederation,
Congress did not dare say that the troops were to
be used to restore order and support government
in Massachusetts. Moreover, in reaching its conclusion to raise troops, Congress thought it wise to
inscribe on its secret journals the statement that it
"would not hazard the perilous step of putting arms
into the hands of men whose fidelity must in some
degree depend on the faithful payment of their
wages, had not they the fullest confidence . . . of the
most liberal exertions of the money holders in the
state of Massachusetts and the other states in filling
the loans authorized by the resolve of this date."[2]
Here, certainly, was the faintest shadow of self-
respecting government—afraid to let it be known
that it intended to protect its own property or
assist in suppressing rebellion, afraid also to put

[1] Lincoln, *Hist. of Worcester*, 371.
[2] *Secret Journals of Congress*, I., 267 et seq., October 21, 1786;
see also Elliot, *Debates*, I., 94, 95.

arms in the hands of men lest the soldiers turn upon it and demand their pay. It dared to take the step of calling for troops only because it had been assured that "money holders" would take up a loan of $500,000 at six per cent., for the payment of which it pledged the hoped-for returns from a new requisition on the states.

Shays's rebellion merits attention, not because it was the only evidence of social disturbance, but because it was the conspicuous uprising that startled the thoughtful men of every state and made them wonder what the end of their great war for independence might prove to be. "There are combustibles in every State," wrote Washington, "which a spark might set fire to." [1] "I feel," he declared, ". . . infinitely more than I can express to you, for the disorders, which have arisen in these States. Good God! Who, besides a Tory, could have foreseen, or a Briton predicted them?" The rebellion, therefore, by disclosing the danger, helped to bring about a reaction, strengthen the hands of the conservatives, discredit extreme democratic tendencies, and aid the men that were seeking to give vigor to the Union. The reaction immensely helped the establishment of new institutions and the creation of a government capable of insuring "domestic tranquillity."

The paper - money craze, the tender - acts providing that produce rather than money could be

[1] Washington, *Writings* (Ford's ed.), XI., 103, 104.

offered in payment of debts, the opposition to
Congressional authority, the restlessness and uneasiness in the land, the mobs and riotings, the
desire of the poor to enjoy the goods of the rich,
the notion that debts should be cancelled, were all
a part of the war which did not lose its momentum
at Yorktown. Its impulse as a social upheaval, as
an expression of individualistic sentiment, went on.
And here again we see, too, not only the philosophy
that had been shouted by orators from the house-
tops, but the results of an early idealism from
which the cooler heads were now turning away, the
notion that men would naturally be good and would
instinctively be law-abiding, that government was
needed only for occasional restraint. But all these
mishaps were bringing men to their senses. "We
find that we are men," wrote Knox, "—actual men,
possessing all the turbulent passions belonging to
that animal, and that we must have a government proper and adequate for him." [1]

[1] Brooks, *Henry Knox*, 195.

CHAPTER XI

PROPOSALS TO ALTER THE ARTICLES OF CONFEDERATION

(1781–1786)

THE year 1786 was, as we have already seen, one of discouragement. The country was filled with the discontented, who had succeeded in the majority of states in getting possession of the government. The dangerous restlessness of the people, the absurd extravagances of Rhode Island, and, above all, the insurrection in Massachusetts cast deep gloom over conservative men. Congress, begging for power and money, placed solemnly before the people their choice of life or death as a nation; but there was no indication of willingness on the part of the states to give up money to save the country from disgrace.

Everywhere there was great cause for despondency: disorder within the states, plots and threatenings on the border, loud laments over commercial distress and heavy taxes, and, worst of all, a reckless disregard of political obligations. But in this year of despair there were some men who still worked for real government, and we may now turn our attention to the efforts to amend the Articles of

168

Confederation and to establish the necessary authority; we shall see that these efforts, reaching a climax in 1786, had in reality begun some years before.

Almost from the time of their adoption there had been dissatisfaction with the Articles and little hope of their success. No one saw the situation more clearly than Washington, who did not hesitate at the very outset to say that the affairs of the nation could not be well conducted by a Congress with only power of recommendation. As early as 1781 he declared that a mere nominal head would no longer do, and that a real controlling power and the right to regulate all matters of general concern should be given to Congress.[1] He saw with his accustomed simplicity and directness that the states could not be relied on to do what Congress asked, and he pointed out that the Articles provided no means of compelling states to furnish men and money, and that for want of such coercive power the war would necessarily be prolonged. Like others who were to work over this problem in the succeeding years, he wondered how the states could be forced to do their duty, but he was confident that some means must be found. Thus, even before the war was over, Washington had stated what was the most evident fact and the most trying problem of the anxious days of political reorganization.[2]

[1] Washington, *Writings* (Ford's ed.), IX., 135, 175, 176.
[2] Madison, *Papers* (Gilpin's ed.), I., 81 – 84; see also Bancroft, *Hist. of the Const.*, I., 17–23.

Hamilton was dissatisfied and disappointed. Months before the Articles were accepted by the last state, he wrote (September 3, 1780) to James Duane a remarkable letter, in which the young statesman, then but twenty-three years of age, showed a thorough appreciation of the situation, marked out with astonishing preciseness the defects in the Confederation, and indicated the necessary modifications. A "solid coercive union" he deemed then a necessity, and he proposed, if Congress did not assume the dictatorial power rightfully belonging to it, that a general convention should be summoned immediately.[1] Two years later he published in the public press a series of able articles exposing the frailty of the existing system; every man of information, he asserted, would acknowledge the inadequacy of the Confederation, and he urged the bestowal upon Congress of authority to levy taxes and regulate commerce. He wrote eloquently for a larger conception of national power and dignity. "There is something . . . diminutive and contemptible in the prospect of a number of petty States, with the appearance only of union, jarring, jealous, and perverse, without any determined direction, fluctuating and unhappy at home, weak and insignificant by their dissensions in the eyes of other nations."[2] Under Hamilton's influence, as early as 1782 the legislature of New York proposed a convention of the states to revise

[1] Hamilton, *Works* (Hamilton's ed.), I., 150 et seq.
[2] *Ibid.*, II., 201.

and amend the Articles of Confederation, and declared that the radical source of the existing em-
barrassments was the want of power in Congress;
but on this recommendation Congress took no action.

In the meantime Madison had been at work in
Congress for improvement of the Articles. As early
as March, 1781, he brought in a report from a committee which pointed to the fact that the states
had promised to observe the Articles, and by so doing impliedly vested in Congress the right to carry
them into effect against any state which might
refuse to abide by the determination of Congress.
That there might be no doubt of the existence of
this coercive power, the committee advised the adoption of an additional article expressly authorizing
Congress to employ the force of the United States to
compel the states to fulfil their federal engagements.[1]
Congress hesitated about adopting such radical
measures, but the matter was not allowed to drop
without further attention. In August a new special
committee, of which Randolph was chairman, handed
in a carefully prepared report which declared that
the Articles needed execution in twenty-one different
particulars, and that seven additional powers should
be bestowed on Congress; among these seven was the
power " to distrain the property of a state delinquent
in its assigned proportion of men and money."[2]

Thus before the Articles had been in full operation

---

[1] Madison, *Papers* (Gilpin's ed.), I., 88–90.
[2] Bancroft, *Hist. of the Const.*, I., App., 286–288.

for half a year, if indeed one is justified in using such a strong word as operation, Congress was deliberating over the necessity of change. Of the revenue amendments proposed in 1781 and 1783, and of the amendment authorizing the passage of a navigation law which was proposed in 1784, we have already seen the fate; some states reluctantly granted the additional power, but the acquiescence of all the states could not be obtained. It seemed impossible to secure any valuable alteration of the old system by the process of pleading, remonstrance, and expostulation.

In 1786 the enlargement and improvement of the Confederation received consideration from a grand committee which proposed the addition of seven articles, and attempted especially to provide for the collection of taxes.[1] With this elaborate report Congress again did nothing; in fact, that sober body of deputies was getting to be worse than helpless; a good part of the time it could not even pass resolutions; and it was largely made up of decidedly second-rate men, who could not see an inch into the future. The whole fabric of the Confederation was creaking in every joint.

The propriety of calling a general convention had been widely discussed. In 1784 the plan was common talk among the members of Congress,[2] but no

---

[1] Bancroft, *Hist. of the Const.*, II., 374–377.
[2] Hunt, *Madison*, 108; Madison, *Writings* (Hunt's ed.), II., 99, 100.

definite action was taken; and in all probability the delegates could have reached no conclusion had they tried, for to leave politics aside and agree upon movements of deep interest often transcended their capacity. When in 1785 the general court of Massachusetts passed resolutions favoring a convention to revise the Confederation, the delegates from that state, with rare audacity, refused to lay the resolutions before Congress. They gave as one of their reasons their apprehension of danger from the Cincinnati and the likelihood that " such a measure would produce thro'out the Union, an exertion of the friends of an Aristocracy to Send members who would promote a change of Government." [1] When a man like Rufus King was using such absurd language as this, what prospect for a national convention or for real improvement of the Articles?

Experience, it is plain, had before 1786 taught the necessity of bestowing on some central authority the power to regulate commerce and the power to obtain revenue without merely begging for it. Every passing year since the adoption of the Articles had shown more clearly that these two powers should have been given to Congress, because without the latter Congress was impotent and ridiculous, and without the former it had no method of meeting the exactions of European nations. It was compelled to look on helplessly while the states working at cross-purposes were angrily trying to retaliate

[1] King, *Life and Corresp. of King*, I., 63 et seq.

against foreign restrictions, or at the next turn of the wheel of popular caprice were threatening their neighbors with commercial war. The necessity of bestowing such powers was clear, for the lesson had been sharply taught, and though of course it was not learned by the ignorant or the narrow-minded, it was obvious to the intelligent statesmen and men of affairs, who were not yet prepared to give up their country to civil war and ruin. At least this much of the great task of imperial organization had been made clear by the troublesome years of war and the no less anxious years of peace.

But there were plainly other troubles. Congress had been given power to make treaties, but this power could not be properly exercised; and our commissioners, confident and loyal as they were, could not negotiate with assurance or make equitable treaties as long as the states, feeling that they were quite as wise as Congress, were ready to disregard all foreign obligations when they chose. Our relations with Spain and England were fraught with danger. Surely, if commerce was to prosper, if the country was to hold up its head among the nations, the states must be under compulsion to perform their parts, to abide by the promises of Congress and not wantonly break the plighted faith of their representatives. In the formation of lasting political order in America some method must be discovered for securing the observance of treaties; without assurance of honesty any confederation

or any national system would be but sounding
brass.

This was clear, and thinking men went further;
they saw that, if America was to hold together, more
than mere promise and pledge was an absolute necessity. Not for treaties alone, but for other obligations as well, for the satisfactory exercise of the
powers given to Congress, there must be some sort
of compulsive authority. So plain was this that
even Richard Henry Lee doubted whether Congress
could ever get its money unless it could use force;[1]
and the wiser statesmen had come to believe in the
absolute need of coercion for the support of government. Jefferson, it is true, was blithely writing
from Paris that he liked a "little rebellion now and
then," that it was "like a storm in the atmosphere,"
and that perhaps, after all, the Indians, who had no
government, were in the best condition;[2]   but Jefferson had learned no recent lesson in the art of constructing government or in founding an imperial
system; his mind had not advanced much, if at all,
beyond the Declaration of Independence.   He was
still toying with liberty after it had degenerated
into license.

But Madison's mind, a mind of superior order, had
advanced; Washington was as clear-headed as ever;
Hamilton and Jay and other great statesmen of the
time were seeing things face to face.   Evidently

[1] Rowland, *George Mason*, II., 105.
[2] Jefferson, *Writings* (Ford's ed.), IV., 362, 370.

some radical change was needed, and there arose what was the most critical and perplexing problem of the period, the most difficult part in the enormously difficult task of constructing a satisfactory political organization for America.

I have already said that the proper distribution of separate powers between the central authority and the parts was absolutely necessary if the general system was to last; but the experiences of the Confederation had so plainly shown what powers were general and what were local that the task of adjustment and proportionment was by no means insurmountable and did not appeal to the men of the time as a task of great labor or trouble. But supposing that the cleverest adjustment of powers, the most accurate assignment of authority, was at last discovered, what security could there be that the states would regard the system, play their parts, and abide by their obligations? Could any method be found for making certain the observance of the Articles of Union, for making certain the power of the central authority to perform the duties bestowed upon it? Could this be done without destroying the states as political entities or reducing them to mere districts? That was a question that might well have confused the clearest brain of the time; no more delicate and intricate problem in practical politics and statecraft ever confronted a thinking people. If a system could be found which did not involve the destruction of the states, which preserved an equitable distribution of authority between the centre and the parts, the great problem of imperial organization had found a solution. If this could be done, America would make one of the greatest contributions ever made by a nation to the theory and practice of government, a contribution hardly second in importance to the principle of representation itself.

That nothing worth while could be accomplished unless there was coercive authority in the centre was to some of the men of the time, as we have said, perfectly plain. An interesting essay written by Noah Webster in 1785, though probably without influence in his day, shows how far the thought of the time had advanced: "There must be a supreme power at the head of the union, vested with authority to make laws that respect the states in general and to compel obedience to those laws. . . . The truth of this is taught by the principles of government, and confirmed by the experience of America. . . . So long as any individual state has power to defeat the measures of the other twelve, our pretended union is but a name and our Confederation, a cobweb." "A law without a penalty is mere *advice;* a magistrate, without the power of punishing, is a *cypher*."[1] These were strong words and full of sense, but it was apparent that the writer had not fully solved the problem; a mere provision for a national government of supreme authority was not enough.

[1] Noah Webster, *Sketches of American Policy,* 31, 32, 44.

In an interesting scheme for a general reorganization of the Confederation which was prepared by Pelatiah Webster, one of the clearest-headed writers of the day, we find once again the assertion that the states must surrender a portion of their sovereignty, and that the laws of the Union must carry in them "a force which extends to their effectual and final execution"; and we find also the naïve suggestion that in order to secure obedience to the laws of the central government, every person whatever, in either his public or his private character, disobeying the supreme authority should be summoned to appear before Congress and be punished.[1] Such a clumsy method of securing obedience to law seems whimsical enough; for Congress to call before it a governor or a member of a state legislature and punish him for violation of the law in an official capacity would of course have been impossible and absurd. But the proposition is an illuminating example of how men were seeking far and near a solution of the problems that oppressed them.

Madison, of course, thought this problem over carefully and saw the real difficulty. "An individual independence of the States," he wrote Randolph, "is utterly irreconcilable with the idea of an aggregate sovereignty. I think, at the same time, that a consolidation of the States into one simple republic is not less unattainable than it would be inexpedient. Let it be tried, then, whether any middle ground can

[1] Pelatiah Webster, *Political Essays*, 222, 223.

be taken, which will at once support a due suprem-
acy of the national authority, and leave in force the
local authorities so far as they can be subordinately
useful." He proposed, therefore, a system which
would work "without the intervention of the States,"
and declared that the national government should
have a veto on all acts of the state legislatures like
that exercised by the king of England over the
colonies; and he may also have thought, though this
is not quite plain, that the central authority should
have the right to overthrow the decisions of state
judges.[1] Thus far had men come in their effort to
build up in America a substantial organization
preserving local liberty and power, but expressing
also the general interests and the common life of
the nation.

In this dreary year of 1786, while men were writing and arguing, and the liberal-minded among them
were almost in despair, a movement which had results of unexpected magnitude was already under
way. It grew out of the need of some sort of understanding between Maryland and Virginia concerning the navigation of the Potomac; and back of the
plan of agreement and accommodation were Washington and Madison. As early as 1777 three commissioners had been appointed from each of the
two states. Nothing having been accomplished at
the first convention, Virginia, in 1784, again appointed commissioners, and in January, 1785, Maryland,

[1] Madison, *Writings* (Hunt's ed.), II., 337–339.

willing to co-operate, took like action. On the invitation of Washington, who was then greatly interested in projects for opening up routes of communication between the east and the west, five of the commissioners met in the spring of 1785 at Mount Vernon, drew up resolutions to be submitted to their states, and asked the co-operation of Pennsylvania in their plans. This report was accepted by each of the states, but Maryland was prepared to go further; she asked for a new conference on commercial questions and proposed the concurrence of Pennsylvania and Delaware.[1]

Those who were anxiously scanning the horizon saw hope in the suggestion; if two more states were to come into the conference they would "naturally pay the same compliment to their neighbours."[2] Madison, hard at work in the legislature, was ready to do what he could to further the movement; but he had to contend with a vehement anti-nationalist party, who were "bitter and illiberal against Congress . . . beyond example," and in their narrow dread of northern commercial power actually considered whether it would not be well to encourage British shipping in preference to that of the eastern states. When resolutions granting Congress authority to regulate commerce were brought before the legislature, they were long discussed, but were at length so hopelessly mutilated that friends of the measure

[1] Scharf, *Hist. of Md.*, II., 532.
[2] Madison, *Writings* (Hunt's ed.), II., 198.

lost interest in their passage; and on the last day of
the session another resolution, which had been lying
peacefully on the table, was taken up and passed
almost without opposition (January, 1786).[1] This
resolution appointed commissioners to meet such
commissioners as might be appointed by other states
to take into consideration the trade of the Union,
and "to consider how far a uniform system in their
commercial regulations may be necessary to their
common interest and their permanent harmony."
The commissioners, of whom, of course, Madison
was one, being instructed to make the necessary
arrangements, invited the other states to send delegates to a convention at Annapolis to be held the
first Monday in September, 1786.

During the summer before the meeting Madison
was doing what he could, but had not much hope.
"I almost despair of success,"[2] he wrote. And yet he
believed that something must be done quickly, for
delay added to the peril; the introduction of new
states might add new elements of uncertainty and
perhaps of discord, and there was, moreover, so
much selfishness and rascality abroad in the land
that any one looking about him might well have
feared that the game by which Philip managed the
confederacy of the Greeks would be played on the
American states.[3] "I saw eno'," Madison said,
"during the late Assembly of the influence of the

---

[1] Madison, *Writings* (Hunt's ed.), II., 218.   [2] *Ibid.*, 229.
[3] *Ibid.*, 229.

desperate circumstances of individuals on their public conduct to admonish me of the possibility of finding in the council of some one of the states fit instruments of foreign machinations."

The convention met at Annapolis, but delegations from only five states were in attendance. Evidently nothing could be done in the way of carrying out the express purpose of the meeting, and it was therefore decided to take another bold step forward and to hope for better results. A report, written by Hamilton, was unanimously adopted. It pointed to the critical situation of the states, which called for the exercise "of the united virtue and wisdom of all the members of the confederacy," and it proposed a convention of delegates from all the states to meet at Philadelphia the second Monday in May (1787) "to take into consideration the situation of the United States, to devise such further provisions as shall appear to them necessary to render the constitution of the federal government adequate to the exigencies of the Union; and to report such an act for that purpose to the United States in Congress assembled, as, when agreed to by them, and afterwards confirmed by the legislatures of every state, will effectually provide for the same." [1]

Although the commissioners declared that they could properly address only the states, "from motives of respect" they transmitted their report to Con-

[1] Elliot, *Debates*, I., 118.

gress as well as to the governments of all the states. Congress might have been expected to grasp at this opportunity for bettering national conditions, but it hesitated and demurred, and finally, February 21, without mentioning the request of the Annapolis convention, called a convention to meet at the time and place mentioned in the report of the commissioners, "for the sole and express purpose of revising the articles of confederation," and to report such alterations as should "render the federal constitution adequate to the exigencies of government, and the preservation of the union." [1]

For the men who had been looking for the establishment of respectable institutions the winter was full of activity and interest. In the end twelve states appointed delegates to the convention, Rhode Island alone holding aloof. But the wisest men in the land were not very hopeful of results. Jay pointed out that the great trouble was not merely "want of knowledge," and that "reason and public spirit" required the aid of virtue. Washington lamented the factious spirit of the state politicians and, above all, the "thirst for power, and the bantling—I had like to have said MONSTER—sovereignty," which had taken fast hold on the states.[2]

[1] *Journals of Congress*, February 21, 1787.
[2] Jay, *Corresp. and Public Papers*, III., 239, 244.

CHAPTER XII

PLAN FOR A NATIONAL GOVERNMENT
(1787)

AS the delegates chosen to the convention began coming together in Philadelphia in May, it was apparent that the crisis had produced an assembly of capable men; many of them had already won distinction; most of them had had experience in political affairs. They represented on the whole the conservative elements of the nation, who were dismayed by the appearance of discord and lawlessness, and who appreciated the national danger. They were more than practical politicians; they were men of education as well as of experience; about half of them had had college education; many of them were learned in law and history.

Washington and Franklin, the most famous members, were without the advantages of university training; but they had the wisdom which is not gleaned from books or absorbed from teachers— rare judgment, wide knowledge of men, profound insight into human motives, remarkable sanity, and a capacity for generous appreciation of the sentiments of their fellows. Franklin did not play a very conspicuous part in the convention, but his kindly humor and his national spirit were of value. Washington had hoped that he would be excused from attending; his friends persuaded him to come, however, and no one better realized the gravity of the movement—he saw the best men of the country chosen as delegates; the convention was the end for which earnest men had long been toiling; if it failed, what hope of reformation or the saving of national credit and reputation? "My wish is," he wrote, "that the convention may adopt no temporizing expedients, but probe the defects of the constitution to the bottom, and provide a radical cure, whether they are agreed to or not." [1] He did not take an active part in the debates of the convention; there is no evidence of his having spoken more than once; but by sheer weight of character he did what much volubility and streams of sonorous language could not have accomplished.

Of the more active members of the convention Madison deserves chief consideration. We have already seen how anxious he was to better the federal government; he had been waging continuous warfare against the paper-money men and the forces of disorganization within his state. He prepared carefully for the work of the convention: he bought and read books; he studied the confederacies of the ancient world and the combinations of modern states; he noted carefully the characteristics of each

[1] Washington, *Writings* (Ford's ed.), XI., 134.

and dwelt on the ideas that were pertinent to American problems. He saw that the Amphictyonic Council could employ the "whole force of Greece against such as refused to execute its decrees." In the Lycian League he found that "the number of votes allotted to each member was proportioned to its pecuniary contributions." [1] Before the convention met he draughted an indictment of the vices of the political system of the United States. The first and most significant of the faults of the Confederation was the failure of the states to comply with the constitutional requisitions. This he declared to be exemplified in every confederacy and fatal to the objects of the American Union. The other vices he enumerated serve to show how clearly Madison saw the situation and what he deemed the task of the convention: encroachments by the states on the federal authority; violations of the law of nations and of treaties; trespasses of the states on one another's rights; want of concert in matters of common interest; absence of a guaranty for state constitutions and laws against domestic violence; no sanction to the laws and no coercive powers in the central government; ratification of the Articles by the legislatures and not by the people; multiplicity, mutability, and injustice of state laws. "A sanction," he declared, "is essential to the idea of law, as coercion is to that of Government [2] For want of real power

---

[1] Madison, *Writings* (Hunt's ed.), II., 369, 372.
[2] *Ibid.*, 361–369.

the Confederation had been a failure; the confidence which the framers of the Articles had shown in the good faith of the state legislatures only did honor to the "enthusiastic virtue of the compilers" of the instrument.

By such careful methods of study and by accurate thinking Madison had fitted himself to take a leading part in the convention's work. Quiet and unobtrusive, his knowledge gave him an advantage over more eloquent members. "In the management of every great question," wrote a delegate from Georgia, "he evidently took the lead in the Convention. . . . From a spirit of industry and application which he possesses in a most eminent degree, he always comes forward the best informed Man of any point in debate." [1]

The Pennsylvania delegation included several men of unusual talent. Robert Morris took no share in the public discussions, but he had done much and learned much in the days of trouble, and he appreciated the need of real government. Gouverneur Morris, one of the enthusiastic, daring young men of the day, was a brilliant and effective debater and a speaker of unusual power; alert, dogmatic, caustic, and positive, he occasionally repelled rather than convinced his opponents; but he toiled for a national system and was filled with real patriotic spirit. The felicitous wording of the Constitution in its final form [2]

---

[1] Pierce's notes, in *Amer. Hist. Review*, III., 331.
[2] Letter of Madison in Sparks, *Gouverneur Morris*, I., 284.

is due to Morris's command of simple and forcible English. From Pennsylvania came also James Wilson, a Scotchman by birth, educated at a university in North Britain, learned in the law, a student of history and political theory. No one saw more clearly the central point of the great problem before the convention; no one labored more steadily, or was able, casting all details aside, to grasp more firmly the most essential and significant principles. He shared with Madison the honor of leadership during the first half of the convention's work, planning and toiling and speaking for the recognition of national life in the establishment of a national government.

New York sent two men of mediocre attainments, Lansing and Yates, who feared for the safety of state ascendancy. The third member of the delegation was Alexander Hamilton. He had for years been working for a stronger central government, and he understood the situation well, but he was embarrassed by his colleagues, who could always cast the vote of the state against his wishes; and he was now so insistent upon authority, so out of patience with feeble government, that for the moment at least his ideas were extreme and inapplicable. He was young, enthusiastic, self-satisfied, and clear-headed, and rather "a convincing Speaker" than "a blazing Orator." [1]

From Connecticut came three men of the first

[1] Pierce's notes, in *Amer. Hist. Review*, III., 327.

rank, William Samuel Johnson, Oliver Ellsworth, and Roger Sherman. Johnson, just elected president of Columbia College, had been a member of Congress, and had a broad view of the situation. Ellsworth was a lawyer of reputation and had at an early age been made a judge of the superior court of his state. Sherman had started life as a shoemaker, had entered into the political struggles of the Revolution, and had held many positions of trust and honor. His simple honesty, his sound sense, and his straightforward thinking made him a man on whom others relied. The two most prominent delegates from Massachusetts were Elbridge Gerry and Rufus King. Both had been members of Congress. Both were young men of talent. Gerry played a curious rôle in the convention, and has not left a reputation for either just discrimination or wise judgment. King, an eloquent and polished speaker, a man of exceptional personal charm, had for some time been opposed to radical action in altering the Confederation; but he had come to see the danger of delay, and was now ready to act with Wilson and Madison as one of the most effective nationalists in the convention.

In the New Jersey delegation was William Paterson, a lawyer like many of the rest, a man of good ability and of undoubted rectitude of purpose. He was not, however, broad-minded, when compared with the best men about him, and he did not, as we now see, appreciate the magnitude of the problem or really know the condition of the country. From Delaware came John Dickinson, who had won undying reputation as the "penman of the Revolution." One of the ablest lawyers and most scholarly men of his day, honest, right-minded, and earnest, he did not always have the faculty of looking at things simply or without misgivings and hesitations. The most conspicuous delegate from Maryland was Luther Martin, a learned lawyer, an implacable and irritating opponent, a prolix and wearisome speaker.[1] The delegates from South Carolina, John Rutledge, Charles Cotesworth Pinckney, Charles Pinckney, and Pierce Butler, were men of strength. The youngest of them all, Charles Pinckney, then under thirty years of age, had already been a member of Congress and had taken a deep interest in the reformation of the Confederation.[2] His experience in public affairs had taught him the need of a thorough change in the organization of the Union.

The second Monday in May was the day set for the convention, but when the time came only a few delegates had assembled. Rhode Island, in placid self-assurance, had not appointed any delegates, and had no intention of doing so. New Hampshire did not appoint till June.[3] At the beginning, therefore, the most that could be expected was representation from eleven states. These early days, when the

[1] Pierce's notes, in *Amer. Hist. Review*, III., 330; P. L. Ford, *Essays on the Constitution*, 183.

[2] *Amer. Hist. Review*, IX., 738.   [3] Elliot, *Debates*, I., 126.

delegates on the ground were waiting for a quorum, were not without their value. The more earnest advocates of strong government had a chance to talk over the situation. There was prevalent among the delegates that first assembled a desire for radical action. Some of them had clearly in mind a total alteration of the existing system—they proposed to establish "a great national council or parliament" consisting of two branches; to base this council on proportional representation of the states; to grant it full legislative authority; to bestow upon it unrestricted power of vetoing state laws; and to create an executive office and a judicial system.[1] The Pennsylvania delegates proposed to Virginia that the large states should at the outset unite in refusing the small states an equal vote in the convention, "as unreasonable, and as enabling the small States to negative every good system of government." The Virginia representatives, fearing that such an effort would beget fatal altercations, did not favor the project, but proposed that the smaller states should be prevailed on in the course of the debates to yield their equality.[2] This was the beginning of the large-state or national party of the convention.

On May 25 enough states were represented to allow the organization of the convention. Washington was unanimously chosen president. It was

---

[1] Rowland, *George Mason*, II., 101.
[2] Madison, *Writings* (Hunt's ed.), III., 7, *n*.

determined that the discussions should be carried on in profound secrecy, and that nothing spoken in the house should be printed or otherwise made public without permission. We are, therefore, dependent for our knowledge of those immortal debates in part on the formal journal; in part on the occasional letters that were sent by the delegates to their friends; in part on the hasty notes that were written down by Yates, King, and a few other delegates; but chiefly on the careful reports prepared by the methodical Madison. Knowing the importance of the assembly, Madison took a seat near the front, listened with attention to the speeches, and laboriously wrote down brief and luminous condensations of them.

The delegates from Virginia, doubtless again guided by Madison's indefatigable temper, met daily before the convention assembled,[1] and drew up a plan of a constitution, which was introduced by Randolph on May 29.[2] In an able speech he spoke of the defects of the Confederation, the prospect of anarchy, and the remedy in the establishment of effective government which could defend itself against encroachment and be superior to the state constitutions. The Virginia resolutions deserve careful consideration because they were taken as the basis of the convention's work, and formed the foundation of the new Constitution.

They declared that the Articles of Confederation

[1] Rowland, *George Mason*, II., 101.
[2] Madison, *Writings* (Hunt's ed.), III., 15.

should be corrected and enlarged, and that to accomplish that object the right of suffrage in the national legislature should be proportioned either to the quotas of contribution or to the number of free inhabitants; that there should be a legislature of two branches, the members of the first branch to be chosen by the people of the several states and to be ineligible to office under either the United States or any state during their term of service. The members of the second branch were to be elected by those of the first, and were likewise to be ineligible to office under either the United States or any state. Each branch was to have the right to originate bills. The national legislature was to have all the powers vested in the Congress of the Confederation, and in addition other powers which the states were incompetent to exercise. A national executive was to be established, and a national judiciary with a limited jurisdiction including the right to try suits in which foreigners were interested, which concerned the national revenue, or which involved the "national peace and harmony," as well as all cases of impeachment. Provision was made for the admission of new states, for the guaranty of a republican government to the states, for amendment "of the Articles of Union." It was expressly provided also that the alterations proposed to the existing Confederation should be submitted to state constituent assemblies or conventions expressly chosen to consider them in the various states.

Evidently the Virginia plan was not a mere "temporizing expedient." It contemplated the establishment of a national government and the formation of a real constitution. Apparently the new government was to have powers of legislation and not merely of recommendation. There was, moreover, some provision for the maintenance of authority, a remedy offered for the old difficulty. The plan provided that the officials of every state should "be bound by oath to support the articles of Union"; that the national legislature should have power to call forth the militia against any member "failing to fulfil its duty"; and that it should likewise be empowered to negative all laws contravening in its opinion the Articles of Union. Such was the remedy offered—the moral obligation of an oath, the force of neighboring states, the veto in the hands of the central government. Something better than this must be discovered before the convention solved its most trying problem.

When Randolph had finished, Charles Pinckney introduced a plan[1] of his own, confessing that it was based on the same principles as Randolph's.[2] It also proposed a legislature of two branches, executive and judicial departments, and a negative on the acts of the states. This plan was not discussed in detail before the convention, but it had considerable influence in determining the contents of the Con-

[1] Madison, *Writings* (Hunt's ed.), III., 22.
[2] Elliot, *Debates*, I., 391.

stitution.[1] It should be noticed that the plan commonly printed in the *Journal*[2] of the convention
and in Madison's notes is not the real plan Pinckney
presented; as it stands in the *Journal* it has deceived
thousands of persons, who have been struck with
the remarkable resemblance between the plan there
printed and the finished Constitution, a resemblance
accounted for by the fact that when the *Journal*
was being printed, in 1818, Pinckney sent in as a
copy of his plan, not his original propositions at all,
but a paper which marked an advanced stage of the
convention's work.[3]

The fundamental proposition presented to the
convention by the Virginia plan was next put forward sharply in a series of resolutions which were
offered by Randolph on the suggestion of Gouverneur Morris: the eager young statesman from Pennsylvania could not wait for any gradual elaboration
of a plan or principle of government. These resolutions showed clearly the intent of the leaders of
the large-state party: (1) "that a union of the States
merely federal will not accomplish the objects proposed by the articles of Confederation"; (2) "that
no treaty or treaties among the whole or part of the
States, as individual Sovereignties, would be sufficient"; (3) "that a *national* Government ought to

[1] *Amer. Hist. Review*, IX., 736.
[2] Elliot, *Debates* I., 145; Madison, *Writings* (Hunt's ed.), III.,
23; *Journal of the Constitutional Convention* (Scott's ed.), 64.
[3] Amer. Hist. Assoc., *Report*, 1902, I., 112.

be established consisting of a *supreme* Legislative, Executive and Judiciary." [1]   Of these resolutions the first two were passed by without much discussion. The third, which went to the gist of the question before the convention, was agreed to, New York being divided and Connecticut voting no.

Morris, in the course of the debate, explained the distinction between a federal and a national or supreme government, "the former being a mere compact resting on the good faith of the parties; the latter having a compleat and *compulsive* operation." Mason declared the Confederation deficient in not providing for coercion and punishment against delinquent states, but argued cogently that punishment could not in the nature of things be visited on states, and that consequently a government was needed that could directly operate on men and punish only those whose guilt required it.[2]   There was thus brought clearly before the convention the cardinal and central proposition of the Virginia members which the men of national enthusiasm in the convention were hastening to support—a government over men, a rejection of the old theory of states united in a perpetual league of inefficient friendship. By the adoption of this resolution the convention in reality set upon the work, not of patching up the old Confederation, but, by a peaceful revolution, of putting aside the old impotent system altogether.

[1] Madison, *Writings* (Hunt's ed.), III., 37.   [2] *Ibid.*, 39.

In the resolution thus first adopted as the expression of the general intention of the convention, the word "national" was used, as in other resolutions of the Virginia plan. Later in the history of the convention this word was stricken out wherever it appeared, and from this fact it has been plausibly argued that the framers of the Constitution abandoned their intention of establishing a national government. The elision of the word had, in fact, no such significance, for the resolution to omit the word was unanimously adopted at a time (June 20) when the men desiring a national government were in control of the convention; the reason alleged for the omission was not that the purpose of establishing a national government was given up; the men chiefly desiring a national government were evidently not intent on the word, if their object was accomplished; the word was used and the fact dwelt on in debate after the omission of the word from the resolutions. In short, the erasure is of no significance except for the fact that in years to come it gave some ground for argument and assertion.

When the proposition for the establishment of proportional representation came up, Madison explained that while there might have been reason for "equality of suffrage when the Union was a federal one among sovereign States," [1] there was no sense in continuing that method of representation when a national government was established. But this line

[1] Madison, *Writings* (Hunt's ed.), III., 44.

of argument was not quite satisfactory to some of the delegates: Delaware had willingly enough voted for a national government, but when it came to voting for proportional representation, that was another matter; she did not intend to yield her equal share of political influence. The delegates from that state reminded the convention that they were restrained by their commission from assenting to any change in the rule of suffrage, and, if such a change were insisted on, might feel bound to leave and go home.[1] Morris was not unwilling to force a decision on the question in spite of Delaware's protest; but the question was at length postponed.

Thus began the controversy over proportional representation, the bitter controversy of the convention. It was not new. It had its roots in the envy and local jealousies that had for ten years and more been showing themselves as the bane of continental politics. When the question as to the manner of voting under the Articles of Confederation was under consideration,[2] there had been the same difference of opinion, and the little states had maintained their right to an equal share in the suffrage. The landless states, like Maryland, New Jersey, and Delaware, had in the past feared the strength of their bigger neighbors, and this same unreasonable but natural fear, aided by a zeal for the maintenance

[1] Madison, *Writings* (Hunt's ed.), III., 43.
[2] Elliot, *Debates*, I., 74, 75.

of their political importance, constituted the greatest difficulty the convention had now to meet.   Men
that were not on principle averse to the establishment of a national government were decidedly opposed to a surrender of the political influence of
their constituents.[1]

For a time after the first appearance of this om-
inous question all went smoothly.   Men differed,
but differed amicably.   It was quickly decided to
have a legislature of two branches, but there were
differences of opinion as to the method of electing
the members to the legislature.   Here evidences of
a reaction against popular government disclosed
themselves; the excesses of the mobs had startled
the New-Englanders.[2]   Sherman opposed the election by the people, declaring that they should have as
little to do with government as possible, while Gerry
maintained that the evils of the country flowed from
an excess of democracy.   "The people do not want
virtue," he said, "but are the dupes of pretended
patriots."   Mason admitted that the country had
been too democratic, but he thought there was
danger of going to the other extreme; and he argued
strongly for an election of the first branch of the legislature by the people.   He was ably supported by
Wilson and Madison.   Wilson declared that he "was
for raising the federal pyramid to a considerable alti-
tude," and therefore "wished to give it as broad a

[1] Madison, *Writings* (Hunt's ed.), III., **166, *n.***
[2] Grayson's statement, *ibid.*, **36.**

basis as possible."[1]   In spite of these differences of opinion a conclusion was soon reached in favor of popular election of the first branch.[2]   Although the question came up again for debate,[3] on this point the convention had no serious troubles.   But to reach a conclusion as to the method of electing the members of the second branch was evidently out of the question at that time, and the matter was postponed, to be discussed more than once again in the weeks that followed.

[1] Madison, *Writings* (Hunt's ed.), III., 46–48.
[2] Elliot, *Debates*, I., 152.   [3] June 6.

CHAPTER XIII

SHALL THE CONFEDERATION BE PATCHED UP?

(1787)

THE consideration of the Virginia plan went rapidly forward in the early days of the convention. The discussions were in the committee of the whole house, and there was so much agreement that there seemed good reason for hoping that within a short time all the essential features of the new Constitution could be decided on. The convention was in the hands of the large-state men, and opposition to their general plans was not as yet crystallized. For the time being the critical proposition, the suggestion of proportional representation, was postponed.

Without discussion it was resolved that each branch of the legislature should have the right to originate laws, and that all powers belonging to the Congress of the Confederation should be transferred to the new government. The proposal to give the central authority legislative power in "cases to which the separate states are incompetent"[1] met with some objection, for the fear naturally arose that the states would be robbed of

[1] Elliot, *Debates*, I., 153; Madison, *Writings* (Hunt's ed.), III., 53.

201

their essential powers. Madison and Randolph declared their preference for definite and enumerated powers; but for the time being the resolution in the general form was adopted. Without opposition it was resolved to bestow on the national legislature the right to negative all laws contravening in its opinion the Articles of Union or any treaties subsisting under the authority of the Union. The adoption of such a resolution (May 31), before the convention had been at work a week, shows the settled purposes of the men controlling its deliberations, their determination to remedy the chief fault of the Confederation, and also the advantage they had in the early days over the localists, who were as yet without organization.

There also arose even before June 1 the critical proposition to grant the national legislature the right "to call forth the force of the Union against any member . . . failing to fulfil its duty under the articles thereof." Madison, the real author of the Virginia plan,[1] which was meeting such favor, was eager for effective government but he doubted the practicability, justice, and efficacy of force, "when applied to people collectively and not individually." "The use of force against a State, would look more like a declaration of war, than an infliction of punishment."[2] He hoped that a better system could be

[1] Madison, *Writings* (Hunt's ed.), II., 338. Abbreviations are not literally followed in my quotations from this edition.
[2] *Ibid.*, III., 56.

found, and on his motion the resolution was for a
time put by. Plainly the delegates had not yet quite
freed themselves from the old notion of the Confederation; they did not yet see the significance
of their task or just where the Virginia plan was
leading them. Some saw that government must
act on men, but even the full force of this was not
yet clear.

So rapidly did the work of the convention go
forward that by June 5 a large portion of the
Virginia plan had been adopted in committee.
True, as we have seen, some of the really critical
questions were postponed and many of the resolutions as adopted were very general in terms;
nevertheless, the main features of the new order
were coming into sight—a government with executive, legislative, and judicial branches, possessed
of wide general authority. There was, obviously,
a determination on the part of the leaders to frame
a system which would not be burdened by the
failings of the distracted Confederation. The states
must be preserved; but they must not be allowed
to disregard their obligations. It was evident, too,
that the nationalists were not to be easily discouraged. When the resolution recommending conventions for the adoption of the Constitution was
under discussion, Wilson spoke in plain terms; he
hoped that a disposition on the part of a plurality
of states to organize "anew on better principles"
would not be allowed "to be defeated by the in-

considerate or selfish opposition of a few States."
This remark was intended as a warning to New
Jersey and Delaware,[1] who were apparently giving
signs of uneasiness and disaffection. It is an evidence that the leaders of the convention feared
the obstinate objection to some essential portion of
their plan.

On June 6 arose again the question of choosing
the members of the first branch of the legislature;
and in the ensuing discussion certain fundamental
ideas were brought forward. Once more distrust
of democracy disclosed itself. Charles Pinckney
wished an election by state legislatures, since the
people were unfit for the work. "In Massachusetts," said Gerry, "the worst men get into the
Legislature. Several members of that Body had
lately been convicted of infamous crimes."[2] Wilson,
on the other hand, contended that the government
ought to possess not only the force but the mind or
sense of the people at large; the opposition to be expected to the new system would not come from the
citizens of the states but from their governments.
"The State officers were to be the losers of power."
Mason too believed, as before, in popular election.
"Under the existing Confederacy," he said, "Congress represent the *States* and not the *people* of
the States: their acts operate on the *States*, not
on the individuals. The case will be changed in
the new plan of Government. The people will be

[1] Madison, *Writings* (Hunt's ed.), III., 96.   [2] *Ibid.*, 100.

represented; they ought therefore to choose the Representatives." [1] Dickinson thought it essential that one branch of the legislature should be drawn immediately from the people and the other chosen by the state legislatures.[2] After due discussion, the convention refused to alter its decision in favor of popular election for the first branch.

The next day (June 7) it was resolved that the second branch should be chosen, as Mr. Dickinson wished, by the state legislatures. In the course of the discussion serious questions came to the surface, for some of the large-state men saw that an election by state legislatures meant either a surrender of proportional representation or a very large and cumbersome second branch, inasmuch as each state would need to have at least one member. They had hoped for some method of election disregarding state boundaries. Notwithstanding the efforts of Madison and Wilson, the resolution received the unanimous vote of the states.[3]

Before June 1, as we have seen, a resolution had been adopted providing that the national legislature should have the right to veto all state laws contravening the treaties or the Articles of Union. Pinckney was dissatisfied with this; it did not go far enough for him, and he advocated granting authority to veto all laws that should be judged improper. The proposition was seriously debated,

---

[1] Madison, *Writings* (Hunt's ed.), III., 101.   [2] *Ibid.*, 105.
[3] *Ibid.*, 115, 120; Elliot, *Debates*, I., 165.

and was favored by Madison, who "could not but regard an indefinite power to negative legislative acts of the States as absolutely necessary to a perfect System."[1] Evidently the leaders did not yet see fairly and without obscurity the principles of the system they must work out. They had not yet followed to its end the logic of their own propositions. They did not see how difficult, not to say impossible, it would be to make the negative an effective means of union and order. To give the national legislature such a power to veto laws contravening the Constitution was to lay the foundation for bitter antagonism and probable strife; for such a method of correction implied friction between governments, continual affronts to state pride. But to carry out Pinckney's plan and to give the right to veto all laws deemed improper, whether contravening the Constitution or not, was not only to bestow on the central legislature dangerous authority, but to establish a relation resting not so much on law as on judgment, desire, and caprice. Those who were anxious to solve the great problem of the time and to discover suitable restraint for the states were as yet too much influenced by their remembrance of the British colonial administration.[2] They did not yet see face to face the legal system which they were to work out in their debates, a system based partly on colonial institutions and partly on principles of English law

[1] Madison, *Writings* (Hunt's ed.), III., 121.   [3] *Ibid.*

which were to be applied to wide purposes of imperial organization for the first time in the New World.

We may for the time being delay a consideration of how they solved the question. Clearly a free and unrestrained negative on all state laws would not do. Pinckney's motion was rejected.[1] The convention, however, held to the idea of giving Congress the power to negative unconstitutional state laws. Whether Congress was to have the right to coerce a state was as yet undecided. We must remember that these two propositions—a veto and coercion—were at first the favorite solutions for the most difficult part of the problem of imperial organization.

Two weeks had passed without serious difficulty, but on June 9 the resolution referring to proportional representation came up again. Here was the danger-point: the small-state men were gathering strength and getting ready for action. Evidently they would not surrender the equal representation of the states without a battle, and perhaps no argument could make them yield. To yield meant to give up, so it seemed to them, not only the sovereignty but the dignity and safety of their states. The convention was soon sharply divided. The delegates from Massachusetts, Pennsylvania, Virginia, North Carolina, South Carolina, and Georgia wished representation in proportion

[1] Madison, *Writings* (Hunt's ed.), III., 127.

to their importance, partly because they desired for their respective states greater political influence, partly because they feared, however slight the reason, that the small states would vote away their money. But it is plain, too, that the leaders of this party were in reality a national party, ready and anxious to discard the principle and underlying notion of the Confederation. They were desirous of establishing a national government, and yet to retain the states as useful parts of the new system. As the days went by, under the guidance of Madison, Wilson, and King they saw fully all that was involved, the foundation of a real government with powers of legislation and execution.

The small-state men, representing Connecticut, New York, New Jersey, Delaware, and Maryland, were controlled by various motives. Some were determined to maintain the principle of the Confederation, to preserve a union of states possessed of equal political rights, to continue the existence of the so-called sovereignty of the individual members. They wished rather to patch up the old than to create a new system. And yet even these men were willing to grant additional authority to Congress, and even to bestow the right to coerce a delinquent state, for all men of sense had learned that mere promises were futile. Others, although not averse to a national government,[1] were fearful, with the old-

[1] E.g., see Madison, *Writings* (Hunt's ed.), 116, 125, 166, 322.

time fear, that the larger states would devour the small. In part their contention was not for principle but for power.

However mixed their motives, they were in earnest. Martin was prepared to weary the convention with long harangues. Paterson of New Jersey, the impetuous Bedford of Delaware, Lansing and Yates of New York, were unyielding. They were, moreover, helped by Dickinson, Sherman, and Ellsworth, no one of whom was narrow-minded or deeply prejudiced against a national government, but all of whom were determined not to surrender to the large states the power in the new system in proportion to their population or wealth. Even through the obscurity of the dry abstracts of the speeches, as we read them in Madison's notes, we can get some glimpse of the excitement, the bitter intensity of the next six weeks of debate; for the question at issue was vital, the real life of the nation was at stake, and men spoke with vehement earnestness.

As soon as the question was fairly before the convention, Paterson attacked proportional representation. He alluded to the hint thrown out by Wilson that the large states might form a union of their own if the others refused to concur, and reminded the convention that the small states could not be compelled to accept disagreeable conditions. "New Jersey," he declared, "will never confederate on the plan before the Committee. She would be swallowed up. He had rather submit to a monarch, to a despot, than to such a fate. He would not only oppose the plan here but on his return home do every thing in his power to defeat it there. . . . A confederacy," he said, "supposes sovereignty in the members composing it and sovereignty supposes equality."[1] Wilson answered him boldly. He was not afraid of the defection of the small states. "Are not the Citizens of Pennsylvania equal to those of New Jersey?" he asked. "Does it require one hundred and fifty of the former to balance fifty of the latter? . . . If the small States will not confederate on this plan, Pennsylvania and he presumed some other States, would not confederate on any other. We have been told that each State being sovereign, all are equal. So each man is naturally a sovereign over himself, and all men are therefore naturally equal. Can he retain this equality when he becomes a member of Civil Government? He can not. As little can a Sovereign State, when it becomes a member of a federal government. If New Jersey will not part with her sovereignty it is vain to talk of Government."[2]

The small-state men were at first no match for their opponents. Apparently they were not yet organized or prepared to play their strongest card, which was nothing more and nothing less than to

[1] Madison, *Writings* (Hunt's ed.), III., 133, 134.
[2] *Ibid.*, 135.

present, as alternatives, either a defeat of proportional representation or disruption of the convention. On June 11, therefore, the convention being not yet three weeks old, the motion was carried in favor of "equitable" rather than equal representation. For proportional representation in the first branch the vote stood seven to three. Connecticut voted with the large-state party, and the vote of Maryland was divided. For proportional representation in the second branch, the vote was only six to five, because on this point the small-state men were in accord. Dickinson and Sherman had already advocated equal representation in the second branch, and the latter now declared that on that one point the small states would never yield.[1] It remained to be seen whether in spite of such opposition the large-state men could retain their advantage. On their side was strength of argument and national patriotism; on the other, persistence, local pride, and the threat to break up the convention.

If one could judge from the records of the convention alone, he would be obliged to think that up to the middle of June the national party was convinced of its complete victory; it had certainly carried through its programme with remarkable success. The committee of the whole reported (June 13) that it had gone through the propositions proposed by Randolph and was prepared to submit its results. Practically the whole of the Virginia plan

[1] Madison, *Writings* (Hunt's ed.), III., 112, 144.

had been adopted; all its radical features had been preserved, except the provision for the coercion of states, concerning which there was disagreement even among the large-state leaders. Nineteen resolutions had been accepted, providing for a national government based on the people of the United States.[1] It is probable, however, that Madison, Wilson, and their followers were not so confident of ultimate victory as the records on the secretary's books might seem to warrant; a determined spirit of opposition had disclosed itself in debate, and we can well imagine how sharply the party differences must have shown themselves in the arguments that were going on with decorum and secrecy at the inns and coffee-houses of placid old Philadelphia. As a matter of fact, the great battle of the convention was hardly as yet begun.

When the committee of the whole had completed its work on the Randolph resolutions, Paterson asked for further time for considering it, and for the preparation of a plan "purely federal" in its principles—in other words, a plan retaining the treaty features of the old Confederation, not proposing the establishment of a really national government. The next day he laid before the convention the New Jersey plan, the work, in fact, of the small-state party, whose eagerness and obstinacy "began now," as Madison tells us, "to produce serious anxiety for the result of the Convention." "You see," confided

[1] Madison, *Writings* (Hunt's ed.), III., 160–164.

Dickinson to Madison, "the consequence of pushing things too far. Some of the members from the small States wish for two branches in the General Legis-- lature, and are friends to a good National Government; but we would sooner submit to foreign power, than submit to be deprived of an equality of suffrage in both branches of the legislature, and thereby be thrown under the domination of the large States." [1] It was like Dickinson to be afraid to push things too far, but there is no doubt that the danger was serious.

The New Jersey plan proposed a revision and improvement of the Confederation. To Congress was to be given the right to levy duties on imports and to regulate trade, to make requisitions on the states for funds, and in case of non-payment "to direct the collection." The scheme provided for a plural executive, and for a judiciary in addition to the old Congress, for the admission of new states, for uniform naturalization, and for the extradition of criminals fleeing from one state to another.[2] All this looked much like a mere amendment of the Articles, and that was doubtless what was intended; but it should be noticed that even the framers of the small-state plan were well aware that amendments and alterations which left Congress dependent on the capri-

[1] Madison, *Writings* (Hunt's ed.), III., 166, *n.*
[2] *Ibid.*, 166 – 170, 178; Amer. Hist. Assoc., *Report*, 1902, I., 133–143; *Amer. Hist. Review*, IX., 310–340; Elliot, *Debates*, I., 175–177.

cious acquiescence of promising states would be of little avail, and that they consequently made provision not only for directing the collection of taxes, but for compelling obedience to the laws and treaties of the United States: "If any State, or any body of men in any State shall oppose or prevent the carrying into execution such acts or treaties, the federal Executive shall be authorized to call forth the power of the Confederated States, or so much thereof as may be necessary to enforce and compel an Obedience to such Acts, or an observance of such Treaties."

These were cogent phrases. Would their adoption have transformed the old Articles from a "rope of sand" into bands of steel? Probably not; the device of coercion was clumsy at the best, and was put forth by men who, anxiously clinging to the notion of state sovereignty, or, at least, to the equality of the states, still saw clearly that force was a necessity. Possibly, one may argue theoretically, their adoption would really have transmuted the old Confederation into something stronger, something more like a state than a bundle of states; but in fact the provision for coercion of states was logically more consistent with the establishment of a confederation than of a government. Such arguments, however, go for little except to show how even those most solicitous for the states recognized the need of force; and we may be sure that if the new Constitution did not, when finished, provide for coercion of states, such an omission was not due to the notion that state pledges and local good - humor could be relied on, but because a more effective and sagacious plan was the outcome of the debates.

One other provision of the small-state plan challenges our attention, for it was an early phrasing of a momentous idea, the full drift of which probably no one in the convention yet fully comprehended. All acts of Congress that were made in pursuance of its powers, and all treaties made and ratified under the authority of the United States, were declared to "be the supreme law of the respective States so far forth as those Acts or Treaties shall relate to the said States or their Citizens"; and the courts of the several states were to be bound by such acts and treaties in their decisions, "any thing in the respective laws of the Individual States to the Contrary notwithstanding." It does not appear that Paterson or any of the others was aware that in one essential particular they had discovered the most valuable single principle that had yet been presented, but we shall see that as the days went by this proposition of the small states was not forgotten.

The discussion of the Paterson plan began with great earnestness. The plan of Mr. Paterson, said Lansing, of New York, "sustains the sovereignty of the respective States, that of Mr. Randolph destroys it"; one plan he declared was federal, the other national.[1] Paterson made the leading speech in

[1] Madison, *Writings* (Hunt's ed.), III., 171; Yates's minutes, in Elliot, *Debates*, I., 411.

favor of his propositions, contending that the powers of the convention were limited to a revision of the old Articles, that "an equal Sovereignty" was the basis of a confederation, and if the idea of state sovereignty was to be given up, the only logical plan was "that of throwing the States into Hotchpot."[1] He here discussed the idea of erasing state boundaries, a scheme which he and his colleague, Brearley, seem actually to have had in serious contemplation. Evidently he could see no middle ground between state sovereignty and the total extinction of the states. Happily, wiser counsels prevailed even among the most enthusiastic nationalists.

Wilson answered Paterson in an able speech. He did not fear the antagonism of the people. "He could not persuade himself that the State Governments and Sovereignties were so much the idols of the people, nor a National Government so obnoxious to them, as some supposed. Why should a National Government be unpopular? Has it less dignity? will each Citizen enjoy under it less liberty or protection? Will a Citizen of *Deleware* be degraded by becoming a Citizen of the *United States?* Where do the people look at present for relief from the evils of which they complain? Is it from an internal reform of their Governments? no, Sir. It is from the National Councils that relief is expected."[2]

---

[1] Madison, *Writings* (Hunt's ed.), III., 173–175; Madison, *Papers* (Gilpin's ed.), II., 869–871.

[2] Madison, *Writings* (Hunt's ed.), III., 176.

The difficulty was well summed up by Charles C. Pinckney, who doubtless saw that it was not so much theoretical state sovereignty that influenced most of the small - state men as a modicum of state pride mixed with a good alloy of old-time jealousy and a nameless dread of some unknown evil. "The whole comes to this," said Pinckney. "Give New Jersey an equal vote, and she will dismiss her scruples, and concur in the National system."[1]

Randolph, never in his life appearing to better advantage, now spoke with rare wisdom and precision (June 17). He spurned the notion that the convention was to be mildly obedient to letters of instruction. He "was not scrupulous on the point of power. When the Salvation of the Republic was at stake, it would be treason to our trust, not to propose what we found necessary. . . . The true question is whether we shall adhere to the federal plan, or introduce the national plan. The insufficiency of the former has been fully displayed by the trial already made. There are but two modes, by which the end of a General Government can be attained: the first is by coercion as proposed by Mr. Paterson's plan; the second, by real legislation as proposed by the other plan." He declared that coercion was "*impracticable, expensive, cruel to individuals.*" "We must resort therefore to a National *Legislation over individuals*, for which Congress are unfit." "A National Government

[1] Madison, *Writings* (Hunt's ed.), III., 179.

alone, properly constituted," he asserted, "will answer the purpose"; and he begged his hearers to remember that the present was the last moment for establishing one. "After this select experiment, the people will yield to despair."[1]

Up to that time Hamilton had been silent, though it was not his practice to spare words or be chary of opinions. Probably he was embarrassed by the fact that he was outvoted by his colleagues from New York. Perhaps he was for the time pessimistic and curious rather than deeply impressed. But he now broke silence, and with a long speech presented in outline his notion of government, of which little need be said. His propositions were extreme, for he freely declared "that the British Government was the best in the world: and that he doubted much whether any thing short of it would do in America." In popular governments, however modified, Hamilton had little faith; they were "but *pork still, with a little change of the sauce.*"[2] The House of Lords he declared was "a most noble institution," forming a "permanent barrier against every pernicious innovation," such a barrier as no mere elective senate could ever be. The New Jersey plan was utterly untenable, but he saw great difficulty in establishing a good national government on the Virginia plan.[3]

[1] Madison, *Writings* (Hunt's ed.), III., 179–181.
[2] *Ibid.*, 190; Yates's minutes, in Elliot, *Debates*, I., 423.
[3] Elliot, *Debates*, I., 417.

According to his own ideas the national legislature should have authority to pass all laws whatsoever, subject to a veto in the hands of the executive. Members of the Senate and the executive were to be elected by electors, and to hold office during good behavior. The supreme judicial authority was to be vested in judges holding office during good behavior. Laws of the states contrary to the Constitution of the United States were to be utterly void; and, to prevent the passage of such laws, state governors, appointed by the general government, were to have the right to veto all laws about to be passed in their respective states. From our present point of view, we see that these propositions had few merits, and that Hamilton either failed to grasp the idea or was out of sympathy with the cardinal thought of the new Constitution, which, under the influence of Randolph, Wilson, Madison, and King, was gradually unfolding. Toward the close of the convention Hamilton gave to Madison a paper which he said described the plan he should have liked to see adopted.[1]

Hamilton's general scheme was not seriously considered, but the debate continued on Paterson's plan. Madison fairly riddled it with objections which showed its failure to meet the exigencies of the moment; and it was at length determined, by a vote of seven to three, to adhere to Randolph's plan as preferable to Paterson's.[2] Maryland's vote was

[1] Madison, *Writings* (Hunt's ed.), III., 197.
[2] Elliot, *Debates*, I., 180.

divided. Connecticut voted with the majority. The delegates from that state were still desirous of protecting its interests by some method of equal representation, but nevertheless were unwilling to put up with the makeshift proposition. Thus far (June 19) the national party was clearly in the lead, and there was no longer much danger that their whole plan would be overthrown; but there was danger that the convention would be broken up or the plan spoiled by vicious alterations.

CHAPTER XIV

THE GREAT COMPROMISE

(1787)

WHEN the Virginia plan, as modified in the committee of the whole, was formally taken up by the house (June 19) it had been under consideration for three weeks. Each clause was now debated anew, and another opportunity was given for discussion on every portion of the plan. Old differences reappeared. Evidently the small-state party was not yet utterly routed; evidently long weeks of debate still remained before adjournment.

On the consideration of the first resolution, which had been adopted in committee May 30, an interesting discussion arose. Wilson said that by a national government he did not mean one that would swallow up the states. Hamilton again advocated the bestowal of indefinite authority on the national government: "If it were limited at all, the rivalship of the States would gradually subvert it."[1] King declared that the states had never, properly speaking, been sovereign. "They did not possess the peculiar features of sovereignty, they could not

---

[1] Madison, *Writings* (Hunt's ed.), III., 221.

make war, nor peace, nor alliances, nor treaties. Considering them as political Beings, they were dumb, for they could not speak to any foreign Sovereign whatever. They were deaf, for they could not hear any propositions from such Sovereign. They had not even the organs or faculties of defence or offence, for they could not of themselves raise troops, or equip vessels, for war. On the other side, if the Union of the States comprises the idea of a confederation, it comprises that also of consolidation. A Union of the States is a Union of the men composing them, from whence a *national* character results to the whole. . . . If the States therefore retained some portion of their sovereignty, they had certainly divested themselves of essential portions of it." [1]

It may be that the reader will say that King was wrong and that the states were sovereign. Possibly they were; so much depends on what the much-abused word sovereign signifies. In the development of modern metaphysics, a development applied in America to practical politics, has come the announcement that it is impossible to divide sovereignty or for a true state to be divested of "portions" of sovereignty. However that may be—for to discuss metaphysical sovereignty is to get lost in mazes of intangible argument and of more impalpable assertion—King was bent on bringing out clearly the necessity of establishing a national gov-

[1] Madison, *Writings* (Hunt's ed.), III., 221.

ernment and of preserving the states as real political entities—a difficult task, it is true—but on the
proper working out of this middle ground, on the
proper balancing of the national power and local interest, depended the success of the convention and
the foundation of a new political order, which
should be neither a thoroughly consolidated state
on the one hand nor a mere group of states on the
other.

It was at this time that the word "national" was
stricken from the Randolph plan (June 20),[1] and
surely it is unnecessary to assert that the unanimous
consent for such erasure was not obtained because
men had given up the hope of establishing a national
government; for the change was made when those
in favor of the Randolph plan and opposed to the
Paterson movement had won in the convention by a
vote of more than two to one.   Ellsworth had asked
that the word be erased, so that the resolution would
run: "that the Government of the United States
ought to consist of a supreme Legislative, Executive and Judiciary."   This change, he said, would
give "the proper title, 'the United States.'"   He
wished the plan "to go forth as an amendment of
the articles of the Confederation, since under this idea
the authority of the Legislatures could ratify it."
Randolph, in reply, "did not object to the change of
expression, but apprised the gentleman who wished
for it that he did not admit it for the reasons as-

[1] Madison, *Writings* (Hunt's ed.), III., 226.

signed; particularly that of getting rid of a reference to the people for ratification." [1]

When the question arose, as it did on the second of Randolph's resolutions, as to whether or not there should be two branches of the legislature, the discussion once more went to the nature of the plan. Lansing contended that the true question "was, whether the Convention would adhere to or depart from the foundation of the present Confederacy." He was answered by Mason, who did not expect, he said, that this point would be reagitated. On two points he declared the mind of the American people was settled: first, in an attachment to republican government; and second, in an attachment to more than one branch in the legislature. Coercion of states, such as Paterson's plan contemplated, he could think of only with horror; solicitous for the establishment of a national government, he would, nevertheless, not consent to the abolition of the states. As the debate continued, it must have been apparent that the defenders of the Randolph scheme had much the advantage in argument, if not in assertion. The fear that the new government would endanger the liberties of the people and encroach upon the rights of the states was frankly met. Madison and Wilson, who had had sorry experiences as members of the impotent Congress, insisted that the real

[1] Madison, *Writings* (Hunt's ed.), III., 226; see especially Martin's letter, in Elliot, *Debates*, I., 362; Bancroft, *Hist. of the Const.*, II., 51.

peril was gradual disorganization, because of the selfishness and petty pride of the individual states. "A Citizen of Delaware," said Madison, "was not more free than a Citizen of Virginia: nor would either be more free than a Citizen of America."[1]

The situation was clearly seen by Johnson of Connecticut, an able, serene man of good sense, who was willing to look at the whole subject fairly and debate it without passion. The New Jersey plan, he said, preserves the states; the Virginia plan professes not to destroy them, but is "charged with such a tendency." One man alone[2] boldly advocates the abolition of the states. "Mr. Wilson and the gentleman from Virginia," he said, "who also were adversaries of the plan of New Jersey held a different language. They wished to leave the States in possession of a considerable, though a subordinate jurisdiction." Could this arrangement be made? That was the question; evidently that was what was troubling the Connecticut delegation. Could the power be divided between state and nation, and the plan be so carefully adjusted that the states would be secure in the portions of sovereignty they retained? Could such a division be made secure and permanent unless each state were given a "distinct and equal vote for the purpose of defending" itself "in the general Councils"?[3] Plainly Johnson

---

[1] Madison, *Writings* (Hunt's ed.), III., 243.
[2] Hamilton.
[3] Madison, *Writings* (Hunt's ed.), III., 239, 240.

was sincerely anxious for information, and his fair-minded question seemed to indicate that, if the states should be provided with means of self-defence, Connecticut would not vote against a national government. On the motion to establish a legislature with two branches, the votes stood seven to three, with Maryland divided.[1]

On this question Connecticut voted with the large states, and her delegates apparently saw their rôle clearly: they would not oppose a good national government, but they would work for a recognition of the states. Strong men these were, with wide experience and breadth of view, and they feared that unless the states were given distinct political power they would be absorbed or lose their significance altogether under the weight of a centralized national authority. Sherman, perhaps the most influential of them all, would not be likely to yield his chief purpose; calm, deliberate, quietly argumentative, he was as persistent as pursuing fate, and, if willing to yield a little here and there, it was only that he might get as much of his own way as sweet temper and plodding patience could secure.

We can pass rapidly over the debates of the next few days, for in general only matters of secondary importance were discussed. The vexed question of representation was still to be balloted upon. For, although the large-state men had as yet won decisively on every significant ballot, and might

[1] Elliot, *Debates*, I., 184.

well have thought their opponents hopelessly beaten, the small - state partisans, some of them now much excited, were in no mood to give up the fight.

Near the end of June, after the convention had been in session over a month, the resolution for proportional representation, which had been adopted in the committee of the whole, came before the convention. The small-state men were now ready for a supreme effort. Martin made a long and wearisome address, contending with deep earnestness that the power of the general government ought to be kept within narrow limits, that it was meant to preserve the state governments and not to control individuals. "The corner-stone of a federal government is equality of votes."[1] "I would rather confederate," he exclaimed, "with any single state than submit to the Virginia plan."[2] All the discussion seemed to lead to nothing, and Franklin solemnly proposed "imploring the assistance of Heaven." "I have lived, Sir, a long time," he said, "and the longer I live, the more convincing proofs I see of this truth—*that God Governs in the affairs of men.*" He advocated the opening of the morning sessions with prayer.[3] Some of the delegates thought that such action would arouse suspicion of dissension in the convention, and the motion was not adopted.

Men argued about the question of state sovereignty

---

[1] Yates's minutes, in Elliot, *Debates*, I., 454.
[2] *Ibid.*, 457.   [3] Madison, *Writings* (Hunt's ed.), III., 310.

and perhaps knew in a measure what they were talking about; but they seemed for a time no nearer the solution of the controversy. For some, like Martin, contended that the states were sovereign, and others, like Madison and Wilson and Hamilton and King, did not believe that the states by separating from Great Britain became separated from one another. A bootless discussion, and one that would interest us less were it not that in the days to come the question of state sovereignty and sundry metaphysical subtilties rose like a cloud of darkening locusts.

The debate continued with the fundamental problem inextricably connected with the question of representation still unsettled. Strong speeches were made. But the national party argued in vain and pointed to the dangers that all could see. Were the small states anxious for liberty? Then let them unite and not stand aloof in awe of their more powerful neighbors. If no union resulted on just principles, if the states watched one another in jealous dread, each would soon seek to render itself secure by a standing army, and America would soon be burdened by military expenses and sustained by despotic government. "Constant apprehension of war," said Madison, "has the same tendency to render the head too large for the body. . . . The means of defence against foreign danger, have been always the instruments of tyranny at home."[1]

[1] Madison, *Writings* (Hunt's ed.), III., 317.

The old argument was forcibly repeated by Hamilton:[1] the small states might perhaps lose their equality, but their citizens would not thus lose their freedom. But the truth was, as Hamilton keenly said, this was "a contest for power, not for liberty." The small states were solicitous for power, but were ostensibly anxious for liberty. At length the vote came (June 29), and again the national men were in the lead. Massachusetts, Pennsylvania, Virginia, North Carolina, South Carolina, and Georgia voted in favor of proportional representation in the first branch of the legislature. Connecticut, New York, New Jersey, and Delaware voted for equal representation. Maryland was divided, for the truculent Martin could not control the vote of his state.

As soon as the vote was declared, the Connecticut men demanded a decision as to the make-up of the second branch of the legislature.[2] Ellsworth began by saying that on the whole he was not sorry that the convention had determined to have unequal representation in the first branch of the legislature; such a decision furnished a ground for compromise by giving the states equal representation in the second branch. He described the Union as partly federal and partly national, and asked that in the make-up of the government this substantial fact find recognition. To the notion that there

---

[1] Madison, *Writings* (Hunt's ed.), III., 319.
[2] Johnson and Ellsworth, *ibid.*, 322.

was real danger of the combination of the large against the small states he still steadfastly clung. With this bold demand from the Connecticut men for equal representation in the Senate, the convention reached its most critical stage; it was "on the verge of dissolution, scarce held together by the strength of a hair."[1]

The early days of July were full of excitement. Despite continued defeats, the small-state men were more determined than ever, for, although those desiring merely to patch up the Confederation were beaten beyond hope of recovery, and though the convention was evidently determined to establish a national government, they still hoped for recognition of the states, and in this contest were guided by real leaders. The large-state men were equally determined. Wilson hoped that men were too wise to "abandon a Country to which they were bound by so many strong and endearing ties. But should the deplored event happen, it would neither stagger his sentiments nor his duty. If the minority of the people of America refuse to coalesce with the majority on just and proper principles, if a separation must take place, it could never happen on better grounds."[2] Some of the delegates were on the verge of losing their unsteady tempers, and Bedford, of Delaware, stepped fairly over the margin and challenged the large states to do their worst:

[1] Martin's letters, in Elliot, *Debates*, I., 358.
[2] Madison, *Writings* (Hunt's ed.), III., 327.

"We have been told with a dictatorial air that this is the last moment for a fair trial in favor of a Good Government. It will be the last indeed if the propositions reported from the Committee go forth to the people. He was under no apprehensions," he declared. "The Large States dare not dissolve the Confederation. If they do the small ones will find some foreign ally of more honor and good faith, who will take them by the hand and do them justice."[1]

Even from the meagre notes of Madison we can see something of the excitement, the feeling only half suppressed, the grim determination of those trying days. We can imagine the hurried conferences of the different factions and the long, secret conferences of the different partisans at their lodgings. Wilson, Madison, and King made great speeches and spoke clear sense, but to little purpose. It did no good to point out the fact that there was no real antagonism of interest between the big states and the little ones, and that a government designed to counteract an imaginary danger was based on a fanciful foundation. The real antithesis lay between the north and the south, and men like Madison saw the fact and emphasized it. But the small - state men would have none of it. In some way they succeeded in reasoning that if proportional representation were adopted in both houses the government would be aristocratic or

[1] Madison, *Writings* (Hunt's ed.), III., 340.

become so. "Are the people of the three large States more aristocratic than those of the small ones?" asked Wilson. "Whence then the danger of aristocracy from their influence? It is all a mere illusion of names. . . . Is a real and fair majority, the natural hot-bed of aristocracy?"[1]

The difficulty of establishing proportional representation presented, however, one real difficulty. If the people of each state were to be given the right to elect one senator, the number of members in the second branch would be too large. Ninety or a hundred senators seemed altogether too large a number; for the delegates had in mind the small upper houses of the state legislatures or the small councils that had existed in colonial times, and they probably supposed that the Senate was to have more than merely legislative functions. To elect senators without reference to state lines also presented difficulties, and perhaps needlessly injured the self-esteem of the smallest states, like Delaware, whose impetuous representative on the floor of the convention had been asserting the sovereignty of her forty thousand souls. As a compromise, Wilson proposed a senator for every one hundred thousand inhabitants, with the proviso that each state should have at least one.[2]

In this suggestion some of the national party were willing to acquiesce; but it did little to soothe the

---

[1] Madison, *Writings* (Hunt's ed.), III., 328, 329, 333.
[2] *Ibid.*, 335.

feelings of the localists. King in an eloquent speech pleaded for agreement; "his feelings were more harrowed and his fears more agitated for his Country than he could express."; and this he conceived " to be the last opportunity of providing for its liberty and happiness." "When a just government founded on a fair representation of the *people* of America was within" reach, he was amazed that men should renounce their blessings from an attachment "to the ideal freedom and importance of *States*." King's fervor was wasted. "When assertion is given for proof," said Dayton, of New Jersey, an ardent statesman of twenty-six years, "and terror substituted for argument, he presumed they would have no effect however eloquently spoken. . . . He considered the system on the table as a novelty, an amphibious monster." [1]

On July 2 the question as to the constitution of the second branch came to a vote. Hitherto on the critical questions the vote of Maryland was divided and not counted; but now, in the absence of his colleagues, Martin cast the vote of the state for equal state representation. On the other hand, the delegation from Georgia, thus far acting with the larger states, was divided; Baldwin, a Connecticut man and a graduate and former tutor of Yale College, possibly influenced by men from his native state, voted for equal representation. The states, therefore, were evenly divided—five to five; Georgia's

[1] Madison, *Writings* (Hunt's ed.), III., 338.

course was uncertain, but she could no longer be counted on for the full purposes of the large-state leaders.[1] What was to be done?

General Pinckney moved the appointment of a grand committee of a member from each state, and the proposition met with favor. "We are now at a full stop," said Sherman, "and nobody . . . meant that we should break up without doing something." Wilson and Madison strongly protested that their Congressional experience had taught them the uselessness of grand committees.[2] Perhaps they already saw the battle going against them; certainly fears of defeat were well founded. One would fain know the political manœuvring that preceded the election of the committee. The moment that it was chosen, the large-state party was beaten in its effort to have proportional representation in both houses; for not one of the really strong men of the nationalists was chosen. From Massachusetts came not clear-minded King, but Gerry; from Pennsylvania, not vigorous Wilson, but accommodating Franklin; from Virginia, not the broad-minded Madison, but Mason, who was now lukewarm and was to change into an avowed enemy of the Constitution he had helped to frame. On the other hand, the committee contained Ellsworth, Yates, Paterson, the irrepressible Bedford of Delaware, the obstinate Martin of Maryland,

[1] *Literary Diary of Ezra Stiles*, III., 291; Elliot, *Debates*, I., 193.
[2] Madison, *Writings* (Hunt's ed.), III., 344, 349, 350.

Baldwin of Georgia, by whose vote Georgia had for the moment been lost from the ranks of the large-state party, and Davie of North Carolina, who had already given signs of indecision.[1] The eleventh member was Rutledge of South Carolina.

The work of the committee could end in nothing but a report surrendering proportional representation in the second branch. On July 5 it recommended the resolution of proportional representation for the first branch of the legislature, and that all bills for fixing salaries, or for raising or appropriating money, should originate in that branch, but that in the second branch each state should have an equal vote.[2]

[1] Madison, *Writings* (Hunt's ed.), III., 334.
[2] *Ibid.*, 352; Elliot, *Debates*, I., 194.

CHAPTER XV

THE LAW OF THE LAND

(1787)

THE compromise report of the grand committee on representation did not immediately allay excitement and ill-feeling. The large-state men strongly objected, and some of the small-state men were not altogether satisfied.[1] Lansing and Yates now left the convention, giving up hope that its labors would be satisfactory to them, as it had taken upon itself to do more than revise the Confederation, and had gone ahead to establish a "consolidated government."[2] They thought that they had no right to take part in a proceeding that would result in depriving "the state government of its most essential rights of sovereignty."[3] Hamilton had for some time been absent, and he did not return till the middle of August; and even then, in the absence of the majority of the delegates, was unable to cast the vote of the state.

Portions of the compromise were long discussed, and a peaceful settlement seemed for a time as

[1] King, *Life and Corresp. of King*, I., 614.
[2] Elliot, *Debates*, I., 480.   [3] *Ibid.*

236

distant as ever. Gouverneur Morris, who had returned a few days before, after a long absence from the convention, attacked the report and pleaded with the members to avoid narrowness and to accept broad and patriotic views. "He came here," he said, "as a Representative of America; he flattered himself he came here in some degree as a Representative of the whole human race; for the whole human race will be affected by the proceedings of this Convention. He wished gentlemen to extend their views beyond the present moment of time; beyond the narrow limits of place from which they derive their political origin. If he were to believe some things which he had heard, he should suppose that we were assembled to truck and bargain for our particular States." These were noble words, and did honor to the man that spoke them. He saw with clear vision that the failure of the convention meant discredit to America, meant a distracted, perhaps a warring nation. "This country must be united," he exclaimed. "If persuasion does not unite it, the sword will. . . . State attachments, and State importance have been the bane of this Country. We can not annihilate; but we may perhaps take out the teeth of the serpents."[1] No sounder truth was spoken in the course of the convention's work.

The small-state men that were prating of sovereignty might well listen; the sovereignty of assumption,

---

[1] Madison, *Writings* (Hunt's ed.), III., 357-359.

the sovereignty of legal fiction, could not hold out against the force of fact, and the controlling fact was that the country must be united. And yet these eloquent words had little effect. Bedford half apologized for his previous threats, but found some consolation for his own warmth in Morris's reference to the sword: "To hear such language without emotion, would be to renounce the feelings of a man and the duty of a Citizen." [1]

Though the stalwart members of the national party still fought lustily for a union based on truth and not on fiction, there was a growing desire to reach agreement. Gerry, of Massachusetts, whose whole orbit it is difficult to trace, could now see no hope of proportional representation in both branches and was getting ready to yield. King protested strongly against his colleague's defection. The proposed government, he said, was to be "substantially and formally, a General and National Government over the people of America"; there would never be a case in which it would "act as a federal Government on the States and not on the individual Citizens." [2] The rule of representation in both branches, therefore, should be the same. But Strong, of Massachusetts, was also wavering: "If no Accommodation takes place, the Union itself must soon be dissolved." [3] The small-state men, on the other hand, were as determined as ever. On July 16, after the

[1] Madison, *Writings* (Hunt's ed.), III., 360.
[2] *Ibid.*, 429.   [3] *Ibid.*, 431.

convention had been in session nearly two months, the vote was cast in favor of equal representation in the second chamber. This time Massachusetts was divided, and North Carolina left the ranks of the large - state party. The vote stood five to four;[1] one state was divided, and three were at that time without representation on the floor.

The large - state men were loath to give up the contest. The strongest among them had seen the impotency of Congress, where narrow jealousy and petty state politics had played so conspicuous a rôle. Some of them had objected for years to the real injustice of the equal representation that had been in vogue from the beginning; and in organizing a national government they had grounds for hoping that a plan agreeable neither to reason nor to justice would be abandoned. The next morning after the eventful vote a caucus of the large-state party was held before the convention assembled. Some of the small-state men were in attendance. Should the compromise be acquiesced in, or should the large-state party, relying on the justice of their cause, persist in their opposition and proceed by themselves to frame a constitution?[2] No conclusion could be reached, and when the convention assembled most of the men were in their places and the work went on.

In this way the great cause of disagreement was put aside. Much still remained to be done, re-

[1] Madison, *Writings* (Hunt's ed.), III., 438.   [2] *Ibid.*, 443.

quiring wisdom, patience, and thoughtful statesmanship; but from this time forward men could differ
without losing their tempers. The small-state men
ceased to interfere with the work of the convention.
Bedford soon left, or, at least, ceased speaking in the
convention. Paterson ere long disappeared from
sight. Nothing more was heard of Brearley for
over a month. Lansing and Yates had already
gone home in disgust. The resolute Martin remained till near the end of the session, and then
went home to denounce the large-state party and
their success in the establishment of a national
government. Ellsworth, Sherman, and Dickinson,
who had been all along not ill-disposed to a national
government if the security of the states was assured, remained to be of much service in working
out the details of the Constitution.

The large-state party was much cast down, but
there was no real occasion; they had themselves
seen that there was no reason for expecting actual
diversity of interest between the big and the little
states, and there was no real fear that the Senate
would become another impotent Congress repro-
ducing the imbecility of the Confederation. The
time was not far distant when the citizens of the
states themselves would be divided into political
parties on national issues, and forget in a measure
the old-time state antagonisms. It was, moreover,
moved in the convention, only a short time after
this critical vote on the great compromise was taken,

that the members of the second branch should vote per capita and not by states;[1] and notwithstanding the objection from Martin that this meant a departure from the idea of representation of the states, the motion was carried. Long as the small-state men had fought for equal representation, the party desiring a continuance of the Confederation and not the establishment of a national government were beaten; those were successful who, not objecting to a national government, wished in one of its members a means of restraint to protect the states in case of attack. If any one has the idea that the particularists believed they had succeeded in preventing the convention from forming a national government, he may well read Lansing and Yates's letter to the governor of New York,[2] Luther Martin's "Genuine Information,"[3] the writings of Richard Henry Lee[4] or of George Clinton.[5] The friends of the convention's work, in their defence, felt compelled to insist on the idea that the Constitution provided for a system only partly national.

Before decision was reached on the great compromise, a few fundamental ideas had been hammered out in debate. Little by little the principle had been made clear that in all the arrangements of the new order the state and the national governments should be kept free from interference. This

---

[1] Madison, *Writings* (Hunt's ed.), IV., 45; Elliot, *Debates*, I., 215.
[2] Elliot, *Debates*, I., 480–482.   [3] *Ibid.*, 344–389.
[4] Ford, *Pamphlets on the Constitution*, 277–325.
[5] Ford, *Essays on the Constitution*, 248.

thought had found vague expression in the early days, but was brought out more clearly in later discussions. Those who knew the unwholesome rivalries of the Confederation had been taught that a government as such has its own pride and foibles, its own self-love; and that if the new government was to succeed, it must not depend on execution by state officials but be able to work its will without reference to the governments of the states, unaffected, indeed, by the presence of the states. In some measure this idea was involved in the proposition to establish a general government; but a general government could have been established on a different principle, its machinery in contact with the machinery of the states. Such confederacies have in our day been set up in Switzerland and Germany.

In working out this idea of separation, there came out clearly certain foundation principles, which were most remarkable and far-reaching, the essentials of a system of imperial government new to the world: the general government was to legislate for men and not for states; it was to rest directly on its own citizens; it was to legislate directly and immediately for them. Over each citizen there were to be two governments. In a powerful speech, as early as June 25, Wilson explained the significance of the proposed system. He spoke of the "twofold relation in which the people would stand," first as citizens of the general government, and second as citizens of their particular states. "The General Government was meant for them in the first capacity: the State Governments in the second. Both Governments were derived from the people—both meant for the people—both therefore ought to be regulated on the same principles. The same train of ideas which belonged to the relation of the Citizens to their State Governments were applicable to their relation to the General Government and in forming the latter, we ought to proceed, by abstracting as much as possible from the idea of the State Governments. With respect to the province and object of the General Government they should be considered as having no existence." [1] Wilson put forth this argument in opposition to the notion of election of senators by state legislatures. It is true that that method of election was finally adopted; but in the scheme worked out by the convention this was almost the only variation from the principle that he was advocating.

This new political idea, which Wilson thus clearly explained, did not involve the establishment of a national government which was to be superior to the state governments. There was evidently to be a distribution of political authority, and each government in its peculiar sphere was to exercise power, not one over the other, but directly and without mediation on its own citizens. Strange, perhaps,

[1] Madison, *Writings* (Hunt's ed.), III., 279; see also King, *Life and Corresp. of King*, I., 607.

that these simple thoughts were so often to be forgotten, if indeed they were fully understood, by combative statesmen of the future. But stranger still was the clear vision, the power of sober thought, which enabled the leaders of the convention to learn so well the teaching of the eleven distracted years since America had declared her independence. For these principles of political activity were new in the world's history, and these men were engaged in solving a problem of imperial organization in the presence of which the statesmen of England had shown neither comprehension nor insight.

This notion of the relationship of government to the individual was so clearly worked out that the delegates began to see that if the principle were fully applied there was no need of the coercion of states. Each of the three plans presented had in one form or another proposed coercion of delinquent states.[1] But the notion of using force against a state became more and more objectionable, and it was seen that there was no need of coercing states if individuals could be reached directly.

Soon after the convention adjourned, Madison, in writing to Jefferson, gave the reason for omitting from the Constitution a provision authorizing the central government to call forth the force of the Union against a delinquent state: it was omitted

[1] Madison, *Writings* (Hunt's ed.), III., 19, 170; A. C. McLaughlin, "Sketch of Pinckney's Plan for a Constitution," in *Amer. Hist. Review*, IX., 746.

because a much more reasonable and efficacious plan
was devised. "It was generally agreed," he wrote,
"that the objects of the Union could not be secured
by any system founded on the principle of a confederation of Sovereign States. A *voluntary* observance of the federal law by all the members could
never be hoped for. A *compulsive* one could
evidently never be reduced to practice, and if it
could, involved equal calamities to the innocent
and the guilty, the necessity of a military force,
both obnoxious and dangerous, and, in general, a
scene resembling much more a civil war than the administration of a regular Government. Hence was
embraced the alternative of a Government which,
instead of operating on the States, should operate
without their intervention on the individuals composing them; and hence the change in the principle
and proportion of representation."[1] In other words,
to coerce states is to make war—justifiable under
an agreement between sovereign states, but out of
place when a government is acting on its citizens.
A government enforces law. Of course, in the enforcement of law, troops may be needed, and the
Constitution therefore gave authority for calling
forth the militia to execute the laws of the Union,
suppress insurrections, and repel invasion.

Both the Virginia and the Pinckney plans[2] proposed that the central authority should have the

---

[1] Madison, *Letters* (ed. of 1865), I., 344.
[2] *Amer. Hist. Review*, IX., 744.

right to negative state laws, and, as we have already seen, this principle was at first adopted by the convention in committee of the whole. Many of the members felt that only by granting such a power to the central authority could there be any assurance that the states would do their duty and play their part in the new order. But this, like the right to coerce, was abandoned. The whole principle of the veto was contradictory to the theory, the underlying notion of the Constitution, as it took form and meaning in the minds of its makers; there could logically be no law—that is, no state act really legal—if it contravened the Constitution and if the Constitution itself be law. Sherman saw this most surely. "Such a power," he said, referring to the veto in the hands of the national authorities, "involves a wrong principle, to wit, that a law of a State contrary to the articles of the Union would if not negatived, be valid, and operative." [1]

We have seen that the rejected New Jersey plan contained a provision concerning the binding effect of the laws of the Union. After the resolution for granting the right to veto had been voted down, Luther Martin brought forward the old proposition of the New Jersey plan, and it was unanimously adopted. [2] On the basis of this proposition was built up the central clause of the Constitution, which was to enable the new system to work smoothly and

[1] Madison, *Writings* (Hunt's ed.), III., 449; see also 447.
[2] *Ibid.*, 449.

without administrative friction, was to provide a restraint upon the states, to maintain the dignity of the central government, and to preserve a complicated and delicate political system by peaceful and judicial processes. In its finished form, as it stands in the Constitution, this clause reads: "This Constitution, and the Laws of the United States which shall be made in Pursuance thereof; and all Treaties made, or which shall be made, under the Authority of the United States, shall be the supreme Law of the Land; and the Judges in every State shall be bound thereby, any Thing in the Constitution or Laws of any State to the Contrary notwithstanding."

This clause may be called the central clause of the Constitution, because without it the whole system would be unwieldy, if not impracticable. Draw out this particular bolt, and the machinery falls to pieces. In these words the Constitution is plainly made not merely a declaration, a manifesto, dependent for its life and usefulness on the passing will of statesmen or of people, but a fundamental law, enforceable like any other law in courts. For the first time in history, courts are called upon by the simple processes of administering justice, in cases where private right or personal injury is involved, to uphold the structure of the body politic and the principles of the Constitution. In this clause, moreover, the salient and characteristic fact of the whole American constitutional system was made manifest, the fact that, in accordance with the theory of organization, the people make the law, and all acts of legislation must be in conformity with this law. For the most telling word is not "supreme" but "law." And thus the men at Philadelphia were, in theory, completing the historical process that had been working out in English history since the meeting of the barons with John Lackland at Runnymede. The long effort to establish a government of law and not of men was reaching its logical conclusion in an effort to make the government itself dependent on fundamental law.

We should notice chiefly that this principle was of especial value in solving the perplexing problem of the time. If the states had voluntarily and with good-humor lived up to their obligations under the old system, all might have gone well. But they would not. Under the Constitution, therefore, the new government was to act by its own laws on its own citizens; and in addition the states were to be placed in a distinctly legal relationship, and were to be bound to recognize their duties as legal duties; the Constitution was to be the law of the land, enforceable in state courts, to be applied by state judges, to be appealed to by state citizens asking their own judges for justice. The states were not to be ordered by the central government to erase acts from their statute-books, or directed to do this or not to do that; they might pass illegal acts, but their own judges in the quiet of their own court-rooms, at the instance of private suitors asking for their rights, were to be called on to disregard all state acts contrary to the law of the land. Had the convention, instead of finding this admirable idea, bestowed on the central authority the right to veto laws, untold friction would have resulted; it is difficult to see how the Constitution could have lasted a decade.

The Constitution was to be binding as law on state officers and to be applied by state judges; it was likewise, of course, to bind the central government in all of its branches. If the national government overstepped its authority, it also should be restrained by the courts, by the refusal of judges to recognize invalid enactments or illegal official action. Concerning the advisability of establishing a federal judiciary there was from the beginning of the convention's work a general agreement;[1] but as to the structure and functions of the department there was much difference of opinion. Provision for the system at length reached satisfactory form; a separate and distinct department of government, one supreme court and such inferior courts as Congress might establish, the judges to hold office during good behavior, the court to have a wide jurisdiction.

Here again we must especially remark the power, the duty, of the federal courts to recognize the Constitution as law, and thus with the state courts to preserve the Constitution, to maintain the distribu-

[1] Virginia plan, in Madison, *Writings* (Hunt's ed.), III., 19; New Jersey plan, *ibid.*, 169; Pinckney plan, in *Amer. Hist. Review*, IX. 745.

tion of power between state and nation, and to enforce its obligations. With regard to state courts, the Constitution contented itself with saying that the Constitution as law was to be binding on state judges; in prescribing the jurisdiction of the federal courts there was in addition the statement that they were to have cognizance of cases "arising under this Constitution." Possibly the framers did not consciously intend by these words expressly to declare that the federal courts would have the right in all cases to declare a law of Congress void because exceeding Constitutional limits. As to that it is hard to speak with absolute assurance. Certainly the Constitution was by this clause recognized and proclaimed as law, and we may at least assert that by force of logic, if not because of the full conscious purpose of the members of the convention, this power was bestowed—the power to declare of no effect an act of Congress contrary to the law of the land.[1]

The delegates at Philadelphia must have known that the new state constitutions were regarded as law by the state courts. When the Federal Convention assembled, the nature of a written constitution, emanating from an authority outside the government, had already been made manifest by several judicial decisions. In New Jersey, as early as 1780, the court refused, in the case of Holmes *vs.* Walton, to regard as valid an unconstitutional act of the

[1] Brinton Coxe, *Judicial Power and Unconstitutional Legislation*, especially pt. iv.

legislature.[1] Two years later a similar doctrine
was laid down in Virginia, and in 1786, as we have
already seen, the Rhode Island court announced
the same principle. Just as the convention was
assembling at Philadelphia, the superior court of
North Carolina distinctly asserted that the legislature could not by passing any act " repeal or alter
the constitution, because if they could do this, they
would at the same instant of time, destroy their own
existence as a legislature, and dissolve the government thereby established." [2]

The preservation of the Constitution, the maintenance of the authority, laws, and treaties of the
national government, was of the deepest importance
to the delegates at Philadelphia; but they did not
establish a special tribunal, as a body of censors, or a
special court to declare state or national acts void.
All that was necessary was to see that the Constitution was made law and had the qualities of a fundamental law. It would then be the duty, not of the
supreme court alone, but of all state and national
courts, to recognize it as law and to apply it in controversies coming before them. This, then, was a
great discovery, and not less great because it required no novel and unfamiliar machinery, no principle altogether new and strange. The courts, act-

[1] Austin Scott, "Holmes *vs.* Walton," in *Amer. Hist. Review*,
IV., 456.
[2] Coxe, *Judicial Power*, 221, 251; Thayer, *Cases on Constitutional Law*, pt. i., 55–80; McRee, *Life and Corresp. of Iredell*,
II., 169, 170, 172.

ing as courts have always acted in distributing justice to litigants, were to declare the law and decide cases accordingly, by the well-known methods of English and American jurisprudence; they were simply expected in all controversies to apply, when need be, the Constitution as the supreme law of the land.

CHAPTER XVI

FURTHER COMPROMISES AND THE CONCLUSION OF THE CONVENTION'S WORK

(1787)

WHILE these fundamental problems were being settled, others scarcely less important were also discussed. Of course to determine the extent of the new government's power, or, rather, the number of its powers, occupied much time and proved a matter of difficulty. The task was "to draw a line of demarkation which would give to the General Government every power requisite for general purposes, and leave to the States every power which might be most beneficially administered by them." [1] To draw this line with accuracy was as desirable as it was difficult; on the preciseness with which the distribution was made depended, in no small degree, the permanence and effectiveness of the new order.

The resolutions on this subject, as first adopted, were general in their terms, providing that the national legislature ought to have the powers of the old Congress and the right to legislate in all cases

---

[1] Madison, *Letters*, I., 344.

beyond the competence of the individual states.[1] But these general words were in time abandoned for definite statements; a number of distinct powers were specifically granted to the national government; it was empowered to coin money, to establish post-offices, to borrow money, to establish a uniform rule of naturalization, to define and punish piracy on the high seas, to declare war, to raise and support armies, to provide and maintain a navy, to perform certain other duties of a general character, and "to make all Laws which shall be necessary and proper for carrying into Execution the foregoing Powers." In thus assigning powers to the national government, the convention carried out the principle of distributing authority between two different kinds of government, of which each was to have its own sphere of political activity.

Whenever the question of representation arose, difficulties disclosed themselves, partly because of the varied character of the states, partly because the delegates naturally looked after the political interests of their constituents. Though it was decided that there should be proportional representation in the lower house, to agree on the general basis of representation was not easy. If the number of representatives was made to depend on the population alone, the result, some of the delegates believed, would be disastrous; for they greatly feared the increasing influence of the western states

[1] Elliot, *Debates*, I., 181.

that might soon be formed beyond the mountains. Jealousies between the north and south, moreover, came to light and caused anxiety. The northern men could see no propriety in counting slaves in the basis of representation; on the other hand, the southern delegates, especially those from South Carolina and Georgia, were determined that their slaves should be counted. The southern states believed, too, that they were gradually outstripping the north in wealth and population, and that that fact should be taken into account in the assignment of representation and in the plans for a gradual increase. "The people and strength of America," said Butler, of South Carolina, "are evidently bearing Southwardly and Southwestwardly." [1] After the New York delegates had left, and before the appearance of the New Hampshire men, there were only four states north of Mason and Dixon's line on the floor of the convention, while there were six southern states. It was possible, therefore, for the southern states, if they chose, to decide all questions of representation to suit themselves.

Had all the members believed that men, as such, were entitled to representation, the problem would still have been perplexing; but democratic doctrine had not yet advanced so far. The delegates believed that society existed for the preservation of property,[2] and that the wealth of the respective

[1] Madison, *Writings* (Hunt's ed.), III., 423; see also *ibid.*, 405.
[2] *Ibid.*, 363, 364, 366, 367.

states should therefore be taken into account in preparing any scheme of representation.

At the very time when the despised Congress at New York was framing the Ordinance of 1787, the delegates at Philadelphia were soberly discussing the propriety of discriminating against the growing population of the Mississippi Valley. That states should grow up in the west could not be prevented; but perhaps the Constitution might be so framed as to insure their permanent political inferiority. Strange that men who had fought through the war should have entertained toward the new land something of that exalted notion of superiority which lay at the bottom of English incapacity in her dealings with her colonies! Men like Gerry[1] and the hard-fighting Morris had no patience with the frontier, forgetting that, but a few years before, Pennsylvania was a wilderness, and that to the imagination of Europeans of their own day Americans were little above the savage. Morris declared that "the Busy haunts of men not the remote wilderness, was the proper school of political Talents. If the Western people get the power into their hands they will ruin the Atlantic interests. The Back members are always most averse to the best measures."[2] Gerry was supported by King in a motion that "to secure the liberties of the States already confederated," the number of rep-

---

[1] Madison, *Writings* (Hunt's ed.), III., 425.
[2] *Ibid.*, 401, 402; see also 382.

resentatives sent to the first branch of the national legislature by the new states should never exceed the number sent by the old.[1]

Fortunately, such narrowness did not prevail, though Massachusetts, Connecticut, Delaware, and Maryland voted for the motion; for there were some men who could read America aright and knew that her growth and prosperity waited only on justice. "Ought we to sacrifice," asked Mason, "what we know to be right in itself, lest it should prove favorable to States which are not yet in existence?"[2] "The majority of people," said Wilson, in a spirit more becoming the democratic nineteenth century than his own day, "wherever found ought in all questions to govern the minority. If the interior Country should acquire this majority, it will not only have the right, but will avail itself of it whether we will or no. This jealousy misled the policy of Great Britain with regard to America."[3]

The northern men did not say much against the general system of slavery, but they doubted the propriety of counting the slaves in the basis of representation. The whole matter was complicated: to agree that slaves as human beings were entitled to the suffrage and to choose delegates to Congress was of course beyond reason, and no such argument was indulged in; but if members in any community were an indication of its wealth, and if government

[1] Madison, *Writings* (Hunt's ed.), III., 425.
[2] *Ibid.*, 395.   [3] *Ibid.*, 423.

was supported by wealth and existed to protect property, there might be some ground for demanding that the whole population, black and white alike, should determine the number of representatives from any state. The delegates from South Carolina insisted that all the slaves should be counted,[1] and were supported, when a vote was taken, by Delaware and Georgia.[2] Williamson, of North Carolina, advocated the counting of three-fifths of the slaves, but at first this motion was defeated.[3] Doubtless this proposition was brought forward by Williamson because, four years before, Congress had proposed that in determining the amount to be paid by the respective states three-fifths of the slaves should be counted.

After this subject of the proper basis of representation had been for some time discussed by the convention, with little apparent prospect of reaching a conclusion, Gouverneur Morris moved to add to the clause empowering the legislature to vary the representation according to the principle of wealth and numbers a "proviso that taxation shall be in proportion to Representation."[4] This motion was made when the propriety of limiting the political influence of the west and the question as to whether slaves should be counted were both undetermined. It was, in fact, a two-edged sword, but it was neces-

---

[1] Madison, *Writings* (Hunt's ed.), III., 397.
[2] Elliot, *Debates*, I., 199.   [3] *Ibid.*, 200.
[4] Madison, *Writings* (Hunt's ed.), III., 409.

sary to grasp it by the blade.   If the boisterous west were to be given representation in accordance with numbers, the new states, though relatively poor, must pay taxes according to population; if the southern men demanded that their slaves be count- ed for representation on the ground that they created wealth, they must agree to pay taxes ac- cordingly.   South Carolina readily agreed to this as just, but asked, nevertheless, that all her slaves be enumerated.   From the logic of the situation, in fact, there could not be much objection to Morris's proposition; but a practical difficulty was brought out by Mason, who pointed out that the new government might be embarrassed by the applica- tion of that principle; for Congress might be driven to the plan of requisitions, inasmuch as customs dues and like levies could not be thus proportioned. The resolution was therefore altered and made to apply to direct taxation only.[1]   In this form the principle was adopted; direct taxes and representa- tion alike were to be proportioned to population.

This decision, however, did not entirely end the trouble.   Davie, of North Carolina, said it was high time "to speak out"; North Carolina, he said, would never enter the Union on any terms that did not provide for counting at least three-fifths of the slaves.   "If the Eastern States meant therefore to exclude them altogether the business was at an

[1] Elliot, *Debates*, I., 202; Madison, *Writings* (Hunt's ed.), III., 411.

end." It was not the extreme southern states alone that demanded some recognition of the black population; even Randolph, lamenting "that such a species of property existed," urged strongly "that express security ought to be provided for including slaves in the ratio of Representation."[1] The three-fifths proposition, supported by the fact that the old Congress had already hit upon the fraction as indicative of a comparative productive power, seemed a reasonable compromise, and was at length adopted.[2]

Of course the plan was not acceptable to all, but some conclusion had to be reached, and men had to accept unwelcome results. Wilson, for example, though apparently voting for this compromise, saw too clearly and too simply to avoid its difficulties; his clear head was perplexed with the same questions that were to bother men in the coming generations. "Are they admitted as Citizens?" he asked in the course of the debate; "then why are they not admitted on an equality with White Citizens? are they admitted as property? then why is not other property admitted into the computation?" He admitted that such difficulties "must be overruled by the necessity of compromise."[3]

The diversity of interest between the northern and the southern states was not shown very plainly in the early debates, especially during the time when

[1] Madison, *Writings* (Hunt's ed.), III., 411, 413.
[2] Elliot, *Debates*, I., 202, 203.
[3] Madison, *Writings* (Hunt's ed.), III., 407.

the states south of the Potomac were co-operating with Massachusetts and Pennsylvania to establish a national Constitution based on popular representation.   At a later time, however, there arose sharp differences of opinion, and the sectional opposition stood out with dangerous distinctness.   Butler went so far as to declare that he considered the interests of the southern and eastern states "to be as different as the interests of Russia and Turkey."[1] This diversity showed itself chiefly in connection with two questions: should Congress regulate commerce freely and pass a navigation act if it chose? should the states be allowed to import slaves?

The history of a generation had plainly taught that some general regulation of commerce was a necessity.   In the days before the war Americans and Englishmen had much dispute as to the right of Parliament to regulate trade, but the old Congress itself had declared its willingness, "from the necessity of the case,"[2] if not from law, to accept such regulatory acts if passed in good faith by the mother-country.   The disorder and confusion of the years after the announcement of independence ought to have brought home to all the folly of relying, for a proper management of commercial relations, on the caprice of the individual states.   Every man that

[1] Madison, *Writings* (Hunt's ed.), IV., 329.
[2] Declaration and resolves of the First Continental Congress, October 14, 1774; *Journals of the Continental Congress* (Ford's ed.), I., 68.

had learned anything from experience had learned this lesson pretty thoroughly, and the convention did not long hesitate to bestow on Congress the general right to regulate commerce. But the old jealousies were not all cleared away; some of them, indeed, were very much alive, and the southern delegates were fearful that the unrestricted right to pass navigation laws would be used to their detriment and to the advantage of the commercial states of the east. "The Southern States," said Mason, "are the *minority* in both Houses. Is it to be expected that they will deliver themselves bound hand and foot to the Eastern States, and enable them to exclaim, in the words of Cromwell on a certain occasion—' the lord hath delivered them into our hands'?"[1] As for the eastern states, on the other hand, Gorham asserted that they had no motive for union but a commercial one.

Concerning the slave-trade, too, there was much difference of opinion. The New England men were divided, the leading men from the middle states, including Virginia, Maryland, and Delaware, were outspoken in their opposition to the traffic and unsparing in their condemnation of slavery. The southern states insisted on their right to import slaves. Charles Pinckney declared that if the southern states were let alone they would probably of themselves stop importation, but the attempt to take away the right would produce serious ob-

[1] Madison, *Writings* (Hunt's ed.), IV., 273, 329.

jections to the Constitution.   With the same breath,
however, he declared that if slavery were wrong
it was justified by the example of all the world:
" In all ages one half of mankind have been slaves."[1]
C. C. Pinckney asserted that South Carolina and
Georgia could not do without slaves, and if Congress
were given the power to prohibit the slave - trade,
such action would be an exclusion of South Carolina
from the Union.   Williamson, of North Carolina, expressed himself in the same way; and Rutledge asserted that the three southern states would " never
be such fools as to give up so important an interest."

With deep feeling, with force of sincere conviction, the men from Maryland and Virginia answered the temporizing argument from the states of
the farther south.   Luther Martin, with a breadth
of national feeling one might not have expected,
said that " slaves weakened one part of the Union
which the other parts were bound to protect," and
that to have a clause in the Constitution permitting
the importation of slaves was inconsistent with the
principles of the Revolution and dishonorable to the
American character.[2]   Madison thought it wrong
to admit into the Constitution " the idea that there
could be property in men."[3]

The strongest denunciation of the system came
from George Mason, of Virginia.   He called on the
convention to give the general government the

---

[1] Madison, *Writings* (Hunt's ed.), IV., 268.
[2] *Ibid.*, 264.   [3] *Ibid.*, 306.

right to prevent the increase of slavery. He reminded his hearers that the west was already calling for slaves to develop the new lands of the interior, and would fill that country with black men if they could be brought through South Carolina and Georgia. "Slavery discourages arts and manufactures," he declared, with great earnestness. "The poor despise labor when performed by slaves. . . . They produce the most pernicious effect on manners. Every master of slaves is born a petty tyrant. They bring the judgment of heaven on a Country. As nations can not be rewarded or punished in the next world they must be in this. By an inevitable chain of causes and effects providence punishes national sins, by national calamities." He was sorry that the merchants of the northeast "had from a lust of gain embarked in this nefarious traffic."[1] Strong as these words were, spoken with sincerity by a man who was himself a slave-holder, a proprietor of one of the stately domains south of the Potomac, where white masters with large retinues of blacks lived in a sort of rude magnificence, his warning was prophetic but not convincing. The men of the far south would not listen, and, it may be added, some of the New-Englanders[2] were not deeply interested in the proposal to prohibit what Mason had called the "nefarious traffic."

[1] Madison, *Writings* (Hunt's ed.), IV., 266.
[2] *Ibid.*, 265, 267.

The difficulty of the problem was great: if Congress were given power to exclude slaves, at least two states would refuse to accept the Constitution; on the other hand, as Randolph pointed out, if Congress were forbidden to prohibit the importation, the clause "would revolt the Quakers, the Methodists, and many others" in the northern states. With a hope of finding some means of escape, a committee was appointed, and to it was referred both the problem as to whether the slave-trade should be prohibited and as to what limitation, if any, should be placed on the power of Congress to pass navigation acts.[1] The result was a compromise which was embodied in the Constitution. Congress was to be allowed to pass a navigation act under its general power to regulate commerce; but the importation of such "persons" as the several states then existing should think fit to admit was not to be prohibited before the year 1808. Congress might, however, levy a tax or duty not exceeding $10 "for each person."[2]

Thus, for the time being, the question was settled; but Mason's eloquent words were to prove prophetic; the young west, south of the Ohio, was to be burdened by slaves. And, though the rivalry between the agricultural south and the commercial east might for a moment be obscured by compromise, it was not easy to reconcile interests that were in

[1] Madison, *Writings* (Hunt's ed.), IV., 272, 273.
[2] *Ibid.*, 292, 303, 306.

apparent, if not in real, economic conflict. This rivalry had already shown itself in the problems of the Confederation; it was to serve as one chief reason for pa ty antagonism in the next two decades, to be the source of serious opposition to the general government forty years after the convention had finished its work, to furnish fuel for flames of sectional hatred long after every member of the convention was in his grave, and to underlie the political strife and recrimination that ended in civil war. This rivalry or this misunderstanding should be borne in mind in interpreting the history of the first hundred years under the new government.

Of all the problems of the convention not one caused greater perplexity than determining the powers of the president and the method of his election.[1] This fact should not surprise us if we stop to consider how difficult the task of providing for an executive head of a nation, who should have dignity and authority and yet be not overpowerful; who should work harmoniously with the other branches of government, and yet not be the creature of the legislature or of either chamber; who should be so hemmed about by republican restrictions as not to affright the populace when the veil was lifted from the work of their delegates.

The convention was bent on carrying into effect

[1] Wilson in the Pa. convention, in Elliot, *Debates*, II., 511; see also Madison, *Writings* (Hunt's ed.), IV., 367.

the principle that the three departments of government should be separate and independent.[1] With more or less accuracy that principle had already found its formulation in state constitutions, but to apply it to the national government was, nevertheless, not easy, chiefly, perhaps, because there was difficulty in discovering a suitable method of choosing the president. In fact the convention had on its hands a delicate task; it must hit on a method of adjusting the departments so nicely and yet with such strength that each could maintain itself for years to come, while the government performed its functions smoothly, safely, and efficiently. The result was, as we know, the establishment of what publicists now call the presidential form of government, one of the two great and successful forms of popular national government now in use in the civilized world. We need not wonder, then, that the problem was perplexing almost beyond compare, and that the delegates debated long and passed many resolutions, only to rescind them again.

On twenty-one different days the general subject of executive office was under discussion; and on the method of election alone over thirty distinct votes were taken.[2] If the executive were to be chosen by Congress, or by either branch, there was a likelihood

[1] Madison, *Writings* (Hunt's ed,), IV., 7.
[2] Farrand, "Compromises of the Constitution," in *Amer. Hist. Review*, IX., 486.

that he would be yielding and dependent in his relations with those to whom he owed his position. To trust the main body of the people seemed impossible. How could the common man judge who was fit to be president of the United States? To give the right to the legislatures of the states had its most obvious dangers. Moreover, any plan which took into consideration the size of the respective states gave the large states an advantage over their smaller neighbors. Here, in other words, came up the old antagonism; here in the effort to decide the most difficult and delicate of questions, and to adjust a complex piece of political mechanism, the delegates were harassed by an imaginary antithesis between big and little states and by temporary or trivial considerations.

After long consultation a committee was appointed, which reported (September 4) in favor of having the president chosen by electors, a plan that had been several times discussed. Each state was to appoint, in such manner as its legislature might direct, a number of electors equal to the whole number of its senators and representatives in Congress. Each elector was to vote for two persons, the one receiving the highest number, if a majority, to be president, the one receiving the next highest to be vice-president. This method gave an evident advantage to the large states, but the report of the committee also provided that, in case the electors should not by their votes give a majority to any one person, the choice of president from the five highest on the list should devolve upon the Senate; likewise the Senate should choose one of two receiving a majority and an equal number of votes.   By this plan it was supposed the election, in the first in- stance, would devolve on persons qualified to have opinions and express them, and yet would not mag- nify the authority of any official body in the states or of either house of Congress.   In this way also the power of the large states was in a measure recognized, for the larger the state the greater the number of electors.   The plan, moreover, was not without its advantages for the small states, since the alternative choice might devolve on the Senate, where the states were equally represented; and the delegates seemed actually to have believed that the electors in many, if not in the majority of cases, would not be in sufficient agreement to give any person a majority.[1]

This power of ultimate choice would, however, greatly increase the influence of the Senate, which had enough without it, and this was a real objection. Wilson, not generally fearful of authority, pointed to the Senate's power over appointments and the making of treaties and its right to try impeach- ments.   "According to the plan as it now stands," he said, "the President will not be the man of the people as he ought to be, but the minion of the Senate. He cannot even appoint a tide-waiter without the

[1] Madison, *Writings* (Hunt's ed.), IV., 374, 383.

Senate."[1] Apparently influenced by such considerations as these, the right to select the president, in case the electors failed to choose, was transferred from the Senate to the House of Representatives, with the proviso that in the House each state should have one vote. Of the ignorance of the fathers concerning political parties, this naïve compromise with all its complexities stands as a golden example. It did not occur to them that in a few years men from New Hampshire to Georgia would be deciding on candidates for party purposes, that the party reins would reach into the remotest corner of the land, and that before long these electors would be but men of straw, mere pieces of machinery, to register the will of the people or their political masters.

As the convention neared the end of its labors its perplexities did not diminish. The summer had gone and the early days of September passed, and yet, after four months of toil and of remarkable patience, the delegates found themselves dissatisfied. No one seemed wholly content, and those who labored most earnestly could only say that the instrument before them was the result of their best efforts and ought to be adopted by the people. They might all have said, with Touchstone, "An ill-favored thing, Sir, but mine own." Franklin urged unanimity of action, even if the Constitution did not suit everybody in all its parts. "The older I grow," he said, "the more apt

[1] Madison, *Writings* (Hunt's ed.), IV., 381. Cf. 382.

I am to doubt my own judgment," and he pleasantly told of "a certain french lady"—perhaps one of the many who had listened to his own wisdom in his conquering days in France—who in a dispute with her sister said, "I don't know how it happens, Sister but I meet with nobody but myself, that is always in the right—*Il n'y a que moi qui a toujours raison.*" [1]

Franklin's pleasantry was of possible service, but it did not win all the discontented. The new Constitution must go forth to be criticised by some who had helped to make it. Most of the delegates, it is true, were ready to sign the finished instrument and advocate adoption, although not entirely satisfied. Even Hamilton, who had not taken an important part and who openly expressed his dislike of the system, was ready to acquiesce, declaring that it was impossible "to deliberate between anarchy and Convulsion on one side, and the chance of good"[2] on the other.

But some of the delegates were not so reasonable. Martin, who had stayed till near the end, went home to attack the Constitution with his customary vehemence. Mason remained to the end, but, vigorously protesting against the powers of Congress by a mere majority to pass navigation acts, a power which "would enable a few rich merchants"

---

[1] Madison, *Writings* (Hunt's ed.), IV., 473. A similar expression is quoted in *The Letters of Horace Walpole* (Cunningham's ed.), IV., 415, where it is attributed to the Duchess de La Ferté.

[2] Madison, *Writings* (Hunt's ed.), IV., 478.

of the northern cities to monopolize the staples of the southern states,[1] refused to accept the Constitution or to advocate its adoption. Randolph and Gerry also protested and declined to sign. Altogether seventy-three delegates had been appointed to the convention. Of these, fifty-five were at one time or another in attendance; but only thirty-nine signed the finished instrument. Of the twelve regular members, not counting Martin, who were not in attendance at the end and did not sign, seven are known to have approved of the Constitution and three are known to have disapproved.[2]

For the purpose of sending out the Constitution supported by apparent unanimity, and also if possible to win the hesitant, Franklin proposed as a form of ratification by the convention, "Done in Convention by the unanimous consent of *the States* present."[3] This equivocal expression was adopted and the work of the convention finished on September 17. Incomplete and inadequate as the men believed it to be, there was hope in its lines, and the best among them could honestly ask the people to establish the work of their hands.

The document to which the framers attached their names with mingled hopes and misgivings that September day in the old state - house in Philadelphia has come to be looked on as one of the great

[1] Madison, *Writings* (Hunt's ed.), IV., 469.
[2] Amer. Hist. Assoc., *Report*, 1902, 157.
[3] Madison, *Writings* (Hunt's ed.), IV., 475.

documents of the world's history; it is now the fundamental law of the oldest republic on earth; the government which it established has outlived dynasties and seen ancient governments totter; it has stood without destruction while England was abandoning her old-time aristocratic government, while France was making and remaking a series of constitutions, while Italy was unified and the German people were founding a national organization, while the pope himself was deprived of his ancient temporal authority, while Spain, who at one time claimed nearly the whole of the New World, was losing her dominions and shrinking back into the old limits of the Iberian peninsula.

The Constitution has sometimes been spoken of as if it were in all respects the creature of the men at Philadelphia, or as if it were, as Mr. Gladstone once said, "the most wonderful work ever struck off at a given time by the brain and purpose of man." [1] That in one sense the Constitution was made in four months' time is true; in four months a series of articles and sections were pieced together. In another sense it is not true; time made the American Constitution as it has made others of any moment. An artificial constitution, not the product of a people's life, can never have vitality, strength, or usefulness. The delegates at Philadelphia did not sit brooding over the chaos of the Confederation to

---

[1] "Kin beyond Sea," in *North Am. Review*, CXXVII., 185; *Gleanings of Past Years*, I., 212.

bring forth by their fiat a new government. The idea that they created institutions out of nothingness loses sight of the manner and the conditions of their work. Neither is it true that they copied European institutions, borrowing scraps here and there to patch up a system suited to their tastes. Some of them were students of law, familiar with Vattel, Locke, Montesquieu, and Blackstone. Some of them had read history to a purpose, and could cite the failures of past confederacies or draw illustrations from the experiences of European states. But there is no evidence of borrowing or of slavish copying; for, while they were students and readers of history and knew that their own little experience was not the sum of knowledge, they were practical political workers, had for years studied the problems of forming governments, and had been acquainted with the great process of making state constitutions. The men of the generation that declared independence and formed new states were steeped in political theory as their great-grandfathers had been in theology, and for years they were engaged in the difficult process of adapting old institutions to new ideas, framing governments and laws that suited the economic, social, and moral conditions which the New World had produced.

We might, therefore, expect to find from these experienced craftsmen, not a document hurriedly patched together, nor one taken in part from distant ages or strange climes, but an American document, in its entirety new, but made up of parts that had found their places in the state organizations. If we look, then, for the origin of the Constitution, we find much of it in the failures of the Confederation, in the tribulations of eleven confused years when the nation was without a proper government and when distress and disorder and incompetence were showing the way to success; and much of it, too, in the state constitutions which had been drawn up by men familiar with colonial governments and administration. This old-fashioned colonial practice was not thrown aside when independence was declared, any more than a man throws aside his body or his brains when he emerges from boyhood to manhood. The work of constitution-making for the states was a work of adaptation, of enlargement, of emphasis, not of creation; it registered growth.

And thus it may be said that colonial history made the Constitution. Even in the division of authority between the states and the national government we see a readjustment of the old practical relationship between colonies and mother-country, a readjustment which was based in part on the imperfections of the old system but carried out the teachings of the Revolution. Even the essentially American notion, the notion that government is the agent of the people and must not transcend the law set by the people, was an outgrowth of the free society of a new world, had found its expression in the theory of the Revolution, and had arisen in a country in which from time immemorial there had been no government possessed of all political power. And this only means, of course, that the Constitution of the United States took its root in the history of England; it was not borrowed by conscious imitation from England, it was a product of the forces of English history; but it was shaped by American necessities, was framed by men who could learn lessons and use the material the tide of history washed to their feet.

CHAPTER XVII

THE CONSTITUTION BEFORE THE PEOPLE
(1787–1788)

WHEN the Constitution was finished it was submitted to Congress, then in session at New
York. A letter signed by Washington as president
of the convention was likewise sent to Congress.
He spoke of the difficulties that had confronted the
delegates, of the necessity of a generous consideration for common interests, and of the Constitution
as the result of a spirit of amity, mutual deference,
and concession.[1] The members of Congress did not
give the new plan an enthusiastic welcome. Richard
Henry Lee was ready for immediate attack, and he
was supported by Dane, of Massachusetts, and
Melancthon Smith, of New York. At first tech-
nical objections were raised, and then a demand was
made for certain radical amendments before the
transmission of the Constitution to the states. It
soon appeared, however, that such a course would
be inexpedient, and at length, without a word of
favorable comment, eleven states being present,
it was unanimously voted that the Constitution

[1] *Journals of Congress*, September 28, 1787.

should "be transmitted to the several legislatures in order to be submitted to a Convention of Delegates chosen in each state by the people thereof, in conformity to the resolves of the Convention." [1]

No one could tell what its fate would be. At first there were evidences of almost enthusiastic approval from the main body of the people.[2] Nervous patriots like Patrick Henry or surly localists like Richard Henry Lee needed time to impress on the multitude the enormity of the convention's misdeeds. Randolph reported to Madison that Baltimore was resounding "with friendship for the new Constitution," that in Alexandria the people were enthusiastic, and that every town in Virginia was resounding with applause.[3] Madison found New York City favorable, and heard encouraging reports from the eastern states.[4] New Jersey also appeared to be zealous. Gouverneur Morris wrote to Washington: "Jersey is so near unanimity in her favorable opinion, that we may count with certainty on something more than votes, should the state of affairs hereafter require the application of pointed arguments."[5] Thus in the early days there was good reason for hope of a speedy victory.

In truth, the Constitution had many foes to meet. There was a little band of irreconcilables who could

---

[1] *Journals of Congress*, September 28, 1787; Madison, *Papers* (Gilpin's ed.), II., 643–646, 650.
[2] *Ibid.*, 646–660.   [3] Conway, *Edmund Randolph*, 95.
[4] Elliot, *Debates*, V., 567; Madison, *Letters* (ed. of 1865), I., 355.
[5] Elliot, *Debates*, I., 505.

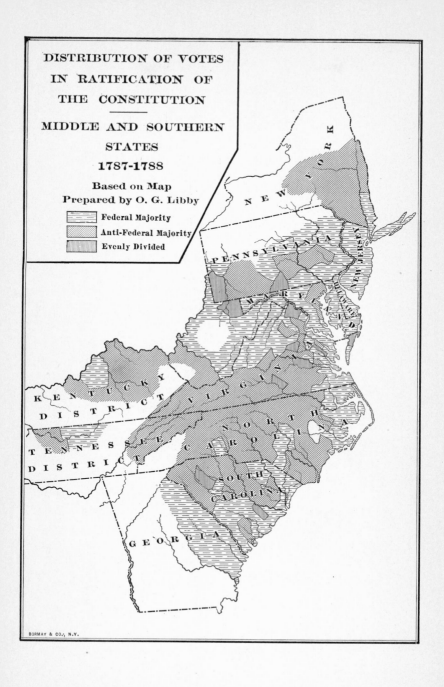

DISTRIBUTION OF VOTES
IN RATIFICATION OF
THE CONSTITUTION

MIDDLE AND SOUTHERN
STATES
1787-1788

Based on Map
Prepared by O. G. Libby

Federal Majority
Anti-Federal Majority
Evenly Divided

BORMAY & CO., N.Y.

see no good in making the central authority efficient, who had always opposed the extension of
national authority, and knew not how else to act.
There were men of wide influence, like Samuel Adams,
who had said so much about liberty that they were
not conversant with the arguments for government.
There were those who had already begun to cher-
ish sectional antagonism, fearing the development
of the west, or disliking the growing power of
commercial New England.   There were the paper-
money men and the discontented needy, who saw in
the Constitution a prohibition of bills of credit and
of laws impairing the obligations of contracts—a
party which had just been successful in controlling
the legislatures of seven states.   There were those
who had been indignant at the proposition to close
the Mississippi and were in no mood to see federal
power increased and the full right to make treaties
bestowed on the central government.   There was
the body of the people who for a generation had
listened to the enchanting oratory of liberty and
could be easily aroused to dread.   There were those
who, living away from the busy sources of trade,
saw no need of a central government with wide power
of taxation and authority to regulate commerce.
No one of these elements was dangerous alone, but
together they constituted a party of opposition
which was aided, of course, by the big body of
hesitants who at such times pause and shake their
heads and wonder if it would not be best to let well

enough alone. Fortunately, to leave bad enough alone was the alternative, and every day was sure to bring a few thoughtful reluctants to the support of the new Constitution.

As the days went by, difficulties disclosed themselves. The Federalists, as the supporters of the Constitution called themselves, to indicate that they were for union and a federal government, and their opponents for disunion, were evidently strong in the central states.[1] But in New York the country districts, under the guidance of Clinton and the state office - holders, were rallying to defeat ratification. In Massachusetts there was grave uncertainty. Virginia had among her counsellors not only Lee, but Mason and Patrick Henry, two powerful men, whose energy might yet be sufficient to defeat national union in the state of Madison and Washington. Recognizing the influence of Henry, Washington, on his return to Virginia, sent Henry and one or two others a copy of the Constitution, and delicately yet forcibly suggested the need of adoption. "From a variety of concurring accounts," he said, "it appears to me, that the political concerns of this country are in a manner suspended by a thread, and that the convention has been looked up to, by the reflecting part of the community, with a solicitude which is hardly to be conceived; and, if nothing had been agreed on by that body, anarchy would soon have ensued, the seeds being deeply sown in every

[1] Elliot, *Debates*, V., 569.

soil."[1]　Henry answered that he could not bring his "mind to accord with the proposed constitution."

In Pennsylvania there was undoubted enthusiasm for the new system, especially in Philadelphia and vicinity, and the Federalists without much difficulty passed through the legislature a resolution calling a convention.　Gouverneur Morris was partly right, however, in fearing the "cold and sour temper of the back counties" and the opposition of those who had "habituated themselves to live on the public" under the old system.[2]　Before the convention assembled, a torrent of newspaper articles and pamphlets supporting or defending the Constitution issued from the Pennsylvania press. The people were seriously in earnest.　There were papers by "Homespun" and "American Citizen" and "Turk" and "Tar and Feathers" and a score of others.　Turk thought he saw in the Constitution a resemblance "to that of our much admired Sublime Porte."　"Your President general," he said, "will greatly resemble in his powers the mighty Ahdul Ahmed, our august Sultan—the senate will be his divan—your standing army will come in the place of our janizaries—your judges unchecked by vile juries may with great propriety be styled cadis."　There was a heavy bit of satire signed by "John Humble, Secretary," and purporting to be the address of the "low-born" to their fellow-

[1] Washington, *Writings* (Ford's ed.), XI., 165.
[2] Elliot, *Debates*, I., 506.

slaves throughout the United States; in other words, to "all the people of the United States, except 600 or thereabouts,"—those who were well-born. The low-born multitude professed themselves ready to allow the well-born to establish the divine Constitution which had just been laid before them. Another writer, gifted with powers of prophecy, depicted the condition of the Union in case the new Constitution was rejected. Such items as this, he said, would appear in the public press: "On the 30th ult., his Excellency, David Shays, Esq., took possession of the government of Massachusetts. The execution of —— ——, Esq., the late tyrannical governor, was to take place the next day." [1]

On the other side an "American Citizen" argued that the ludicrous papers signed by "Turk" and "Gaul" and "Briton" were but cunning tricks to make the readers believe that the opposition came from foreigners, a "thread-bare piece of political jockeyism," when in reality British and foreign agents everywhere were "bellowing forth" the praises of the proposed Constitution.[2] A great deal of solemn nonsense was printed and some sound sense. From Pelatiah Webster and a few like him who could think with directness came vigorous arguments for the Constitution. The ablest single presentation of the whole subject was made by James Wilson in a speech before a mass-meeting

[1] McMaster and Stone, *Pa. and Fed. Const.*, 121, 159, 173.
[2] *Ibid.*, 164.

gathered at the Philadelphia state-house. The opponents of the Constitution, however, could not be silenced by argument, for in mere power to pour out words they surpassed the Federal leaders. Wilson was answered by being called "Jimmy" and "James de Caledonia."

The Pennsylvania state convention met November 21, 1787. The Federalists were well led by Wilson and Thomas McKean; the Anti-Federalists by Robert Whitehill, John Smilie, and William Findley. The debates were able: the Anti-Federalists were sometimes bitter, but they argued with strength and acumen till overborne by superior numbers. They attacked the Constitution because it did not have a bill of rights and because it endangered the existence of the states, or because, as they said, it established "a consolidated government."[1] These were the chief objections; but the infrequency of elections, the danger of an established aristocracy, the want of a proper guaranty of jury trial in the federal courts,[2] and, in general, the exclusive authority of Congress, were grounds of criticism and complaint. The Federalists asserted that a bill of rights was not an essential, and Benjamin Rush went so far as to say, "I consider it as an honor to the late convention, that this system has not been disgraced with a bill of rights." "Would it not be absurd," he said, "to frame a formal declaration

---

[1] McMaster and Stone, *Pa. and Fed. Const.*, 268.
[2] *Ibid.*, 368.

that our natural rights are acquired from our-selves?"[1]

The brunt of the contest fell on the shoulders of Wilson. Despite a quaint pedantry and a certain didactic manner that must have annoyed his opponents and wearied his friends, he spoke convincingly and with remarkable appreciation of the vitals of his subject. He dwelt on the essential nature of American institutions, emphasizing the fact that governments were now established by the people, who were the source of political authority. Borrowing his words from Montesquieu, he described the new political system as a "federal republic," a form of government which "consists in assembling distinct societies which are consolidated into a new body, capable of being increased by the addition of other members."[2]

Wilson's notion of the nature of the new order was well brought out by the term "federal liberty." "This, Sir, consists," he said, "in the aggregate of the civil liberty which is surrendered by each state to the national government; and the same principles that operate in the establishment of a single society, with respect to the rights reserved or resigned by the individuals that compose it, will justly apply in the case of a confederation of distinct and independent States." "This system, Sir, will at least make us a nation, and put it in the power of the

[1] McMaster and Stone, *Pa. and Fed. Const.*, 295.
[2] *Ibid.*, 221.

Union to act as such. We will be considered as
such by every nation in the world. We will regain
the confidence of our own citizens, and command
the respect of others." "I consider," he said again,
"the people of the United States as forming one
great community, and I consider the people of the
different States as forming communities again on a
lesser scale." [1] He called attention to the fact that
the work of the convention was new; there were, it
is true, groups of states known to history, but not
like the organization now proposed. "The United
Netherlands," he said, "are, indeed, an assemblage
of societies; but this assemblage constitutes *no new
one*, and therefore it does not correspond with the
full definition of a confederate republic." [2]

After three weeks of discussion the Anti-Federalists, hoping that delay might aid their cause, offered a series of fifteen amendments and proposed
adjournment that the people of the state might
have time for consideration. The Federalists resisted
all dilatory tactics and insisted on the immediate
adoption of the Constitution as it came from the
hands of its framers. The amendments were not
unreasonable; the resemblance between them and
the ten amendments afterward added to the Constitution is so striking that it has been suggested
that Madison used the proposition of the Pennsylvania minority when he drew up the amendments

[1] McMaster and Stone, *Pa. and Fed. Const.*, 227, 316, 415.
[2] Elliot, *Debates*, II., 422.
VOL. X.—20

in 1789 that were submitted to the states for adoption.[1]

The ratification of the Constitution by the Pennsylvania convention took place December 12 by a vote of forty-six to twenty-three.[2] There was rejoicing in Philadelphia. On the morrow a procession of dignitaries marched to the court-house, where the ratification was read to a great gathering. In proper Philadelphia fashion a dinner was held at Mr. Epple's tavern, at the seasonable hour of three in the afternoon, and "the remainder of the day was spent in mutual congratulations upon the happy prospect of enjoying, once more, order, justice and good government in the United States." Toasts were drunk to "The *People* of the United States,"[3] to the "virtuous minority of Rhode Island," and to other bodies equally deserving approval.

Delaware's convention met at Dover after the assembling of the Pennsylvania convention, but it reached an earlier conclusion, ratifying the Constitution by a unanimous vote December 7. New Jersey did not long delay. Its convention spent but a week in discussion and then without dissent voted for ratification (December 18). Thus three of the central states accepted the Constitution before the beginning of the new year. January 2 the convention of Georgia passed unanimously a res-

---

[1] McMaster and Stone, *Pa. and Fed. Const.*, 19, 421.
[2] Elliot, *Debates*, I., 319.
[3] McMaster and Stone, *Pa. and Fed. Const.*, 429.

olution for ratification. Among the eastern states, Connecticut acted promptly, ratifying (January 9) by a vote of one hundred and twenty-eight to forty.[1]

In Massachusetts, as in many other states, the first prospects for the adoption of the new Constitution were bright.[2] "The people of Boston," wrote Knox, "are in raptures with it as it is, but would have liked it still better had it been higher toned."[3] The reason for this apparent unanimity was probably the fact that the friends of the strong government were on the alert and were ready with arguments in favor of adoption. Opposition, however, soon developed, and ere long it was apparent that a hard struggle was at hand. Pamphlets and newspaper articles denouncing the Constitution as dangerous to the liberties of the people were widely circulated. Such pamphlets as Lee's *Letters of the Federal Farmer* and even George Mason's letter giving his reasons for refusing to sign the Constitution were scattered abroad. In a letter to the general court, which he is said to have prepared with the critical aid of Lee,[4] Gerry presented his objections to the Constitution: there was, he contended, no proper provision for representation; no suitable definition of the legislative powers of the new government; serious danger of an undue influence by the execu-

[1] *Journals of Congress* (ed. of 1823), IV., App., 46, 48, 49.
[2] Harding, *Fed. Const. in Mass.*, 16.
[3] Sparks, *Corresp. of the Rev.*, IV., 178.
[4] Bancroft, *Hist. of the Const.*, II., 230. For the letter, see Austin, *Elbridge Gerry*, II., 42–45.

tive and of oppression by the judiciary; no restraint on the powers of the president, with the advice of two-thirds of a quorum of the Senate, to make treaties. Like so many others, he found fault with the failure to append a bill of rights as a security for individual liberty. He strongly advised amendments before ratification. "The constitution proposed," he said, "has few, if any federal features, but is rather a system of national government."

Such were some of the more sober criticisms of the Constitution. Other writers objected to the annihilation of the Confederation, the surrender of annual elections, the power and structure of the Senate, the great and exclusive power of levying duties on imports and exports as well as collecting internal taxes, the power over the militia, the right of Congress to raise and support a standing army, the establishment of a supreme court superior to the courts of the states. "In short," said one of the least declamatory of the opponents, ". . . you must determine that the Constitution of your Commonwealth, which is instructive, beautiful and consistent in practice, . . . a Constitution which is especially calculated for your territory, and is made conformable to your genius, your habits, the mode of holding your estates, and your particular interests, shall be reduced in its powers to those of a City Corporation." [1]

[1] From *Amer. Herald*, October 29, 1787, quoted in Harding, *Fed. Const. in Mass.*, 25.

Arguments such as these, bearing as they did some show of reason and candor, were not the most difficult to meet and refute. Just recovering from the perils and anxieties of Shays's rebellion, Massachusetts was filled with uneasy spirits who were not prepared to consider any constitution on its merits. They were ready to break out into declamation, to appeal to class prejudices, and make much noise by the use of popular phrases whose cogency outweighed much calm discussion. Those who had followed the fortunes of Shays and Luke Day were wroth, indeed, at the sight of an instrument which forbade the states to issue paper money or impair the obligations of contracts, and which proposed to establish a powerful government that could collect taxes, establish federal courts, and put down insurrections. The Anti-Federalists came largely from the interior districts, from regions without capital or commerce, where paper money and tender - laws had found their chief support.[1] The old distrust of the upper classes and the "well-born," the hostility among the countrymen to the dwellers in Boston, the dislike of lawyers as instruments of injustice, all appear in the opposition to the Constitution. The advocates of adoption were declared by a vehement opponent to "consist generally, of the NOBLE order of C[incinnatu]s, holders of public securities, . . . B[an]k[er]s, and

[1] Libby, *Distribution of Vote on Federal Const.*, *1787 - 1788*, 12, 57.

L[aw]y[er]s: these with their train of dependents form the Aristocratick combination—the L[aw]y[e]r in particular, keep up an incessant declamation for its adoption, like greedy gudgeons they long to satiate their voracious stomacks with the golden bait."[1]

"It is a singular circumstance," wrote Knox, "that in Massachusetts, the property, the ability, and the virtue of the State, are almost solely in favor of the Constitution."[2] The clergymen, whose political influence was of real moment, the merchants and business men, the men of substance who had been startled by the recent popular extravagances, the sober-minded who could reason thoughtfully and were not easily driven by declamation, strongly favored the proposed government. The Anti-Federalists were challenged by a Boston newspaper to point out a man of independent sentiments, either merchant, trader, farmer, mechanic, lawyer, physician, or divine, who was not fully persuaded that on the adoption of the Constitution depended the peace, honor, and happiness of the land.[3]

The struggle in Massachusetts has for the student of history a profound interest. We see clearly the difficulty of establishing popular government, even under the best of circumstances—in a community where men were fairly well educated and had had practical experience in politics. The opposition to

[1] "A Federalist," in the *Boston Gazette*, November 26, 1787.
[2] *Debates and Proceedings*, 410; King, *Life and Corresp. of King*, I., 317.   [3] *Boston Gazette*, December 3, 1787.

the Constitution shows how hard it was to found a strong government at the end of a Revolution which had shaken the foundations of society. The conditions then disclosing themselves enable us to understand the political situation of the next generation, for party organizations were forming, and political prejudices and opinions were hardening in those days when the government of the new nation, peace, and domestic tranquillity were at stake. In watching the contest over the Constitution, we see the dangerous element of extreme democracy, vehement, suspicious, and talkative, which by its very strength confirmed the unbending conservatism of the substantial classes, the social and business leaders of the state, a conservatism which lasted for a generation and more. The substantial elements of society were gathering together preparing to support strong and efficient government; they were to fight off the development of democratic tendencies for many years to come; they were, in a reactionary spirit, to oppose the liberal and enlightened notions of the reasonable, patriotic, and progressive democracy that was soon to find its own organization, its own distinct purpose.

When the convention assembled, it was plain that the majority was opposed to ratification.[1] The Federalists found efficient leaders in King, Gorham, Strong, Fisher Ames, Parsons, and Bowdoin. The task was to meet prejudice and assertion with

---

[1] Knox to Washington, in *Debates and Proceedings*, 416.

patient argument, and to win over the remnant of silent delegates whose ears were still open to counsel.[1] The opponents of ratification demanded amendments in the nature of a bill of rights; they objected to the exclusive powers of Congress and to its wide power of taxation in particular; they found fault with the representation of slaves and with the right to introduce slaves for twenty years.[2] The problems of the Federal leaders were well described by King in a letter to Madison: "Our Convention proceeds slowly; an apprehension that the liberties of the people are in danger, and a distrust of men of property or education have a more powerful effect upon the minds of our opponents than any specific objections against the Constitution."[3]

There were two men in Massachusetts whose influence was much needed by the Federalists. Without them success was next to impossible. One was John Hancock. Though elected a delegate and chosen chairman of the convention, he did not at first attend the sessions, being detained at home by an attack of gout which some of his friends thought would disappear as soon as a majority was shown on either side of the difficult question.[4] Plans were

[1] Belknap Papers, pt. ii., in Mass. Hist. Soc., *Collections*, 5th series, III., 6.

[2] *Debates and Proceedings*, 208, 209; Elliot, *Debates*, II., 107.

[3] King, *Life and Corresp. of King*, I., 314.

[4] King, in Thatcher Papers, *Historical Magazine*, 2d series, VI., 266.

laid to secure his aid. He was given to understand
that the friends of Bowdoin would support him for
governor at the next election. He was also told
that his chances for election to the vice-presidency
were good, and that in case Virginia did not ratify
the Constitution he would naturally be chosen as
the first president of the new republic.[1]

The other man whose influence was needed was
the veteran politician Sam Adams. He was probably sincerely in doubt, for he did not lack decision
when he could read the stars aright. When the
Constitution first came into his hands he did not
like it. "I stumble at the threshold," he wrote
Lee in December. "I meet with a national government, instead of a federal union of sovereign states."[2]
The Federalists feared his opposition, for he had
already expressed his dissatisfaction;[3] but for some
reason, perhaps common political shrewdness, he
did not openly enter the lists of combatants, and
so when the friends of the Constitution began gathering their strength, and when the Boston tradesmen announced their desire for ratification, he was
ready to acquiesce without humiliation.

A letter from Washington, which probably had a
decided effect on the Massachusetts convention, was
now published in a Boston paper. "And clear I

---

[1] Harding, *Fed. Const. in Mass.*, 85–87, where evidence is
summarized; King, *Life and Corresp. of King*, I., 317, 319, 360;
The Writings of Laco, No. vii., 25, 28.

[2] Lee, *Richard Henry Lee*, II., 130.

[3] King, *Life and Corresp. of King*, I., 312.

am," he said, "if another Federal Convention is attempted, that the sentiments of the members will be more discordant. . . . I am fully persuaded . . . that it [the Constitution] or disunion is before us to chuse from. If the first is our election, a constitutional door is opened for amendments, and may be adopted in a peaceable manner, without tumult or disorder." [1] To those, then, who demanded a new convention or the adoption of amendments before ratification, the wiser plan was offered of adopting the Constitution and then asking for desired amendments.

After the convention had been in session about three weeks, Hancock took his place, and under the skilful coaching of the Federal leaders prepared to play his part. He offered a conciliatory proposition, proposing immediate ratification of the Constitution and the recommendation of amendments which would quiet the fear of the good people of Massachusetts. Adams looked with favor on this method of avoiding the difficulty, and moved the consideration [2] of Hancock's proposals. The victory of the Federalists was won. Even Nathaniel Barrell, who at the time of his election was "a flaming Antifederalite," announced his conversion. [3]

[1] Green's *Virginia Herald*, Fredericksburg, Va.; *Pennsylvania Packet*, January 11, 1788; *Massachusetts Centinel*, January 23, 1788.

[2] Elliot, *Debates*, II., 123.

[3] Thatcher Papers, in *Historical Magazine*, 2d series, VI., 271; Elliot, *Debates*, II., 159.

Several days of debate ensued, but when the final vote was taken, one hundred and eighty-seven voted for ratification and one hundred and sixty - eight against it.[1]

The amendments[2] which were asked for by the convention were intended to limit the powers of Congress and to assure the individual certain rights and privileges. The most important was the first, declaring that the Constitution should explicitly state that all powers not expressly delegated by the Constitution were reserved to the several states. The method of ratification had its influence in other states. Had the delegates been reduced to the alternative of rejecting the Constitution or accepting it without reasonable hope of amendment, their fears in some cases would have made rejection certain. But the conciliatory proposition met with favor. Of the seven states acting on the Constitution after Massachusetts, only one failed to accompany ratification with amendments recommended for subsequent adoption.

By February 7, six states had adopted the Constitution, but Federal success was not yet assured. Even Virginia and New York, two important states, might still refuse to ratify, and in others there was diligent opposition. In Maryland there was a sharp struggle. The Anti-Federalists, led by Martin and Samuel Chase, were vehement in their opposition, declaring the new Constitution, if adopted without

[1] Elliot, *Debates*, II., 181. [2] *Ibid.*, 177.

amendments, deadly to liberty. But the Federalists, controlling the convention and refusing to be enticed into fruitless discussion, remained at length "inflexibly silent,"[1] when their opponents demanded answers to their questions. The convention ratified the Constitution by a vote of sixty-three to eleven (April 26).[2]

When the Constitution came before the legislature of South Carolina in January, 1788, it was vigorously attacked and ably defended. Charles Pinckney took occasion to correct those who complained at the radical action of the makers of the Constitution who, being sent to add commercial and revenue powers to the authorities of the old Congress, had cast aside the Confederation and proposed a new system. Nothing can be more true, he said, than that the promoters of the Federal Convention had for their object the establishment of "a firm national government." The legislature finally voted to call a convention, and when the delegates came together they adopted the Constitution after a short discussion by a vote of over two to one.[3]

Eight states had now ratified the Constitution, and a determined effort was made to secure the ninth, so that it might at least be possible to organize the new government. New Hampshire gave both parties ground for hope. When the state

---

[1] Elliot, *Debates*, II., 549.
[2] *Docum. Hist. of the Const.*, II., **105**.
[3] Elliot, *Debates*, IV., 255, 340.

convention met in February, 1788, the Federalists found that if a vote were taken there would be a small majority for rejecting the Constitution, and it was therefore proposed to adjourn and meet again in June. The character of the convention was not the same when it reassembled. After four days of discussion the Constitution was ratified by a vote of fifty-seven to forty-seven.[1] The ninth state was secured at last. Before the result in New Hampshire was known in the south, Virginia, as we shall see, had met and passed the crisis.[2]

[1] Elliot, *Debates*, IV., 573; *Provincial and State Papers of New Hampshire*, X., 15, 19.
[2] Curtis, *Hist. of Const.*, II., 578, *n.*

CHAPTER XVIII

FOR BETTER OR FOR WORSE

(1788)

IN Virginia the contest was desperate. Only good fortune and hard work could bring success to the Federalists, for their opponents were ably led and were aided by local conditions. The source of the determined opposition is hard to trace. Oliver Ellsworth declared that it "wholly originated in two principles; the madness of Mason, and the enemity of the Lee faction to General Washington. Had the General not attended the convention nor given his sentiments respecting the constitution, the Lee party would undoubtedly have supported it, and Col. Mason would have vented his rage to his own negroes and to the winds." [1] In truth, however, there were other causes than personal pique and mean-minded jealousy: the spirit of local pride and the fear for personal liberty were easily aroused in Virginia; the western sections were already excited over the possibility of the surrender of American rights to Spain, while others were beginning to look

[1] "A Landholder" (Ellsworth), in Ford, *Essays on the Constitution*, 177

with suspicion on the commercial power of the New England states. Here, as elsewhere, the more thickly populated districts were favorable to the Constitution, and sectional conditions had their influence. In the eastern section four-fifths of the delegates that were chosen to the convention favored adoption; in the middle district, peopled by small farmers, three-fourths were opposed to adoption. The region somewhat farther west, also peopled by small farmers, who were chiefly Scotch - Irish and Germans from Pennsylvania, was almost a unit for adoption. On the other hand, nine-tenths of the delegates from the Kentucky region were Anti-Federalists.[1]

The leaders of both parties were able and untiring. Though Lee was not elected a member of the convention, he worked sedulously against adoption. Henry, at the head of the Anti-Federal delegates, exclaimed and expostulated in a turbulent stream of rhetoric. Mason, bitterly complaining over the establishment of a national government and over Congressional authority to regulate commerce, opposed the Constitution to the end with characteristic energy. Grayson also was in opposition, and Monroe, neglecting to follow the guidance of the wiser Madison, gave the Anti-Federalists such aid as he could.

Strong as these men were, they were met by their equals. Washington was not a member of the con-

[1] Libby, *Distribution of Vote on Federal Const.*, 34 et seq.

vention, but his unwavering support of the Constitution and his broad-minded utterances concerning the absolute necessity of union were of incalculable value. Randolph had by this time given up his uncertainty, and he spoke eloquently for adoption. John Marshall, a young man of thirty-two, with a clear head and an easy command of sound logic, was chosen to the convention and argued ably for the Constitution. Madison was the active leader of the Federalist forces, and he led them well; his temper was never ruffled nor his reason clouded. A careful study of Henry's brilliant oratory leaves one in wonder that day after day his fervid exclamations were answered with imperturbable calmness and placid good sense. Madison had none of the graces of oratory; he was small and unimpressive; his manner seemed at times to betoken irresolution; when he rose to speak, his voice was low, and he stood hat in hand as if he had just come in to give a passing word of counsel.[1] But he knew what he was talking about, he was prepared to speak, and he did not envelop his thought in ornamental rhetorical wrappings.

Henry began the contest in the convention by dramatically declaring that the conduct of the delegates to Philadelphia should be investigated. "Even from that illustrious man who saved us by his valor, I would have a reason for his conduct." "What

[1] Fisher Ames, *Works*, I., 35; Elliot, *Debates*, III., 86, 305, 395; Hunt, *Madison*, 151.

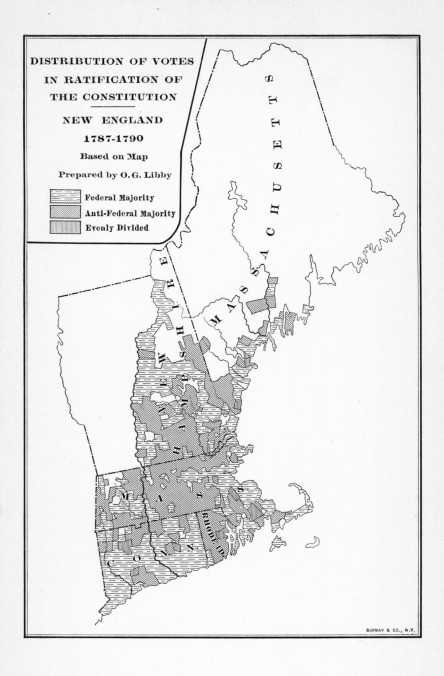

DISTRIBUTION OF VOTES
IN RATIFICATION OF
THE CONSTITUTION

NEW ENGLAND
1787-1790

Based on Map

Prepared by O. G. Libby

Federal Majority
Anti-Federal Majority
Evenly Divided

BORMAY & CO., N.Y.

right," he exclaimed, "had they to say, *We, the people?* . . . Who authorized them to speak the language of, *We, the people,* instead of, *We, the states?*" He declared that the Constitution established a consolidated government, and that the sovereignty of the states would be relinquished. Mason, too, asserted that "whether the Constitution be good or bad," the power to tax clearly showed that the new government was a national government: "The assumption of this power of laying direct taxes does, of itself, entirely change the confederation of the states into one consolidated government." [1]

To such declarations it was hard to give an explicit answer. Madison could only say that the new system was neither a thoroughly consolidated government nor a mere confederation: "It stands by itself. In some respects it is a government of a federal nature; in others, it is of a consolidated nature." Henry ridiculed this strange new government, "so new, it wants a name. I wish its other novelties were as harmless as this." [2] But his ridicule was misplaced; though we have lived over a hundred years under the Constitution, we should have difficulty in describing its system much more accurately than Madison then described it. It did not provide for a centralized state nor did it provide for a mere league of states. In the essays that Madison was

---

[1] Elliot, *Debates*, III., 22, 29, 44; see also 521, 522.
[2] *Ibid.*, 94, 160.

then writing for the press, seeking to allay the fears of the people for the security of the states, he made a similar assertion: "The proposed Constitution, therefore, even when tested by the rules laid down by its antagonists, is in strictness, neither a National nor a Federal Constitution; but a composition of both." [1] Another Federal member of the convention, Mr. Corbin, aptly called the new government "a representative federal republic, as contradistinguished from a confederacy." [2]

To obtain amendments as a condition of ratification or to secure the meeting of a second federal convention seems to have been Henry's purpose. But, indeed, there was little in the Constitution that suited him and his eager followers. In comparison with such a consolidated government, small confederacies, he declared, were little evils. The dangers of the new system were many and evident: the president would become a tyrant; America would be enslaved; there was no proper security for a safe basis of representation; Congress, by its power of taxation, would clutch the purse with one hand and wave the sword with the other; customs officers, for whom the American people cherished a hereditary hatred, would burden the people with their exactions. "I never will give up that darling word requisitions," exclaimed Henry, with dramatic pathos; "my country may give it up; a majority may

---

[1] *The Federalist*, No. xxxix. (Scott's ed.), 215.
[2] Elliot, *Debates*, III., 107.

wrest it from me, but I will never give it up till my grave."[1]

The clause giving Congress power to lay taxes to provide for the common defence and general welfare of the United States was termed the "sweeping clause";[2] it would in the end bestow all authority on the central government. There was great and serious danger lurking in the clause giving Congress exclusive power of legislation over a district ten miles square. "This ten miles square," said Mr. Mason, "may set at defiance the laws of the surrounding states, and may, like the custom of the superstitious days of our ancestors, become the sanctuary of the blackest crimes."[3] The treaty-making power was fraught with grave perils, and the Anti-Federalists, desiring to hold the vote of the Kentucky members, insisted that the closure of the Mississippi could more easily be brought about if the Constitution were adopted.[4]

These objections were met by the Federalists with good arguments. The "sweeping clause" was shown to contain no new powers, but to indicate only the purposes of taxation—to provide for the common defence and general welfare. Without exclusive legislation within ten miles square, Congress might be subjected to insult. As for the Mississippi, no reasonable treaty securing America rights of naviga-

---

[1] Elliot, *Debates*, III., 59, 60, 147, 148, 161.
[2] E.g., *ibid.*, 441–443.
[3] *Ibid.*, 431.   [4] *Ibid.*, 340, 501.

tion could be obtained under a weak and ineffective government.[1] The convention was urged to assure the success of the Constitution by ratifying as the ninth state; for, as we have said, New Hampshire's action was not yet known in Virginia.

The opponents of the Constitution objected to the clause allowing the importation of slaves for twenty years. "As much as I value a union of all the states," said Mason, "I would not admit the Southern States into the Union unless they agree to the discontinuance of this disgraceful trade." Yet he complained that Congress might, by taxation, bring about emancipation. Tyler pronounced the trade impolitic, iniquitous, and disgraceful. Henry, confessing that slavery was detested and declaring that it would rejoice his very soul if every one of his fellow-beings were set free, held up the fear that the northern states would free the slaves and declare "that every black man must fight."[2]

After a three weeks' session the convention was ready for a final vote. The Anti-Federalists debated to the end. The Federalists were willing that amendments to be adopted after ratification should be recommended; but Henry still asserted that there was no trouble about getting them adopted before ratification, and that subsequent amendments would but make matters worse. "The proposition of subsequent amendments is only to lull our ap-

[1] Elliot, *Debates*, III., 331, 433, 443.
[2] *Ibid.*, 452, 454, 590.

prehensions," he exclaimed. "Will gentlemen tell me that they are in earnest about these amendments? I am convinced they mean nothing serious."[1] When the vote came, eighty-nine delegates voted for ratification and seventy-nine against ratification (June 25, 1788).[2] The resolution was accompanied by a solemn statement that the powers granted under the Constitution, being derived from the people of the United States, might be resumed by them whenever the powers were perverted to their injury or oppression. A list of twenty articles constituting a bill of rights was added, beginning, of course, with the essential assertion "that there are certain natural rights, of which men, when they form a social compact, cannot deprive or divest their posterity."[3] Twenty other amendments were presented, and the convention in the name and behalf of the people of Virginia enjoined upon their representatives in Congress the duty of working for the adoption of all the amendments to the Constitution.

Difficult as was the task of the Federalists in Virginia and Massachusetts, still greater trouble faced them in New York, where the Anti-Federalists were led by George Clinton and formed a strong party of opposition. The city of New York and the immediate neighborhood were enthusiastically in favor of adoption; most of Long Island and a portion of the east bank of the Hudson were evenly

[1] Elliot, *Debates*, III., 649, 650.
[2] *Ibid.*, 654.　　　　[3] *Ibid.*, I., 327, III., 657.

divided; but the whole interior region was in opposition.[1] More than half the goods consumed in Connecticut, New Jersey, Vermont, and western Massachusetts were bought within the limits of New York and paid an import duty into its coffers. This fact caused many New-Yorkers to hesitate to surrender to the general government the power to levy certain duties, and it called forth obstinate and selfish opposition to the new Constitution.[2] The great landholders of the state, who were naturally jealous and conservative, were supported by the paper-money men and by the small band of office-holders, who feared that the state imposts would be lost[3] and their salaries reduced.

Some of these men were opposed not so much to the Constitution as to the federal impost.[4] The Federalists of the city and its vicinity were, however, very much in earnest and were not willing even to contemplate the organization of the new republic without New York; if Clinton and his followers were intent on holding aloof from the Union, what was to prevent the southern portion of the state from establishing an organization and ratifying the Constitution?[5]

Under the circumstances, to win the vote of New

[1] Libby, *Distribution of Vote on Federal Const.*, 18.
[2] McRee, *Life and Corresp. of Iredell*, II., 227, 228.
[3] Libby, *Distribution of Vote on Federal Const.*, 20, 26, 59.
[4] "A Landholder" (Ellsworth), in Ford, *Essays on the Constitution*, 176.
[5] *Pa. Gazette*, June 11, 1788, quoted in Libby, *Distribution of Vote on Federal Const.*, 19; *New Haven Gazette*, July 24, 1788, quoted, *ibid.*; Jay, *Corresp. and Public Papers*, III., 335.

York was difficult in the extreme. Hamilton proposed to Jay and Madison the publication of a series of papers in defence of the Constitution. They bore the title of "The Federalist," and appeared in the *Independent Journal*, the *Daily Advertiser*, the *Packet*, and other New York papers, over the name of "Publius." There is still some dispute as to the exact part taken by each member of this competent triumvirate.[1] Jay undoubtedly wrote but five of the essays; Madison seems to have been the author of twenty-nine, and Hamilton of fifty-one. Jay discussed the provisions of the Constitution affecting foreign affairs and the existing relations with foreign powers; Madison considered the foundations of government, the nature of confederacies and the examples of the past, the republican character of the new Constitution, the principle of separation of governmental powers, and representation under the new system. Hamilton commented on the need of union, on the danger of separation or the establishment of separate confederacies, on the glaring defects of the old Confederation, on the need of a government that could address itself immediately to the hopes and fears of individuals, on the functions of the executive and judicial departments, and on the necessity for the regulation of commerce.

[1] Bourne and Ford, in *Amer. Hist. Review*, II., 443, 675; see also introduction to editions of Dawson, Hamilton, Bourne, Ford, and Lodge.

All of these essays are written in a style simple, clear, and straightforward. Abstruse as are the topics discussed, there is no ambiguity, no faltering, no juggling after the manner of demagogues. Each proposition is presented by men who expected to be heard and wished to convince the listener. While every word spoken bears directly on the great issue at hand, there is no sign of littleness, no personal allusions, no narrowness of view; general principles are laid down with daring and assurance by men who were still young in years but had read widely and had studied human nature. "The Federalist" did not make much stir at the time, though some men were impressed by its power. And yet in the heat of this crisis these men were turning off with astonishing rapidity one of the greatest works ever written in the realm of political science. Perhaps America has as yet made no more signal contribution to learning or to literature.

When the New York convention assembled at Poughkeepsie in June, two-thirds of the delegates were hostile to the Constitution; and the task that confronted Hamilton, Jay, and Robert R. Livingston was a serious one. Lansing, Clinton, and Melancthon Smith led in the assault and were supported by their feebler followers. There was no disposition to defend the existing Confederation,[1] or to deny that the country needed peace and

---

[1] Elliot, *Debates*, II., 223, 358.

prosperity, but the Anti-Federalists were unwilling to accept the Constitution as a remedy.

For a time the chief object of attack was the system of representation, which was declared to be inadequate. Congress, it was said, would be corrupt and vicious; positions would be secured for life; the senators would become especially dangerous. "What will be their situation in a federal town?" exclaimed one delegate. "Nothing so unclean as state laws to enter there, surrounded, as they will be, by an impenetrable wall of adamant and gold, the wealth of the whole country flowing into it." Some one wanted to know what "wall" the speaker meant; "on which he turned, and replied, 'A wall of gold—of adamant, which will flow in from all parts of the continent.'" In spite of the amusement of the audience at his liquid wall of adamant, he went on to lament the luxurious life of congressmen within the sacred precincts of the federal city.[1] In general, of course, the arguments of the opposition were based on fear and suspicion, but there was not the narrow class jealousy that was manifested in Massachusetts, nor the flood of exuberant oratory that was poured out in Virginia. The union of the purse and sword, the extensive power of taxation granted to the national government, the weakness of the states, were all dwelt on at length as reasons for the rejection of the Constitution.

[1] Elliot, *Debates*, II., 287.

After the convention had been a week in session, news was brought that New Hampshire had ratified, and the establishment of the new Constitution was assured. On July 3 came the announcement that Virginia also had thrown in her lot with the majority. If New York rejected the Constitution, she was separated from the other states, and stood with Rhode Island and North Carolina. Such a fact must have acted as a powerful argument on the minds of the Anti-Federalists.

By this time different proposals, short of absolute rejection, were considered: to draw up and present amendments for adoption before ratification; to ratify and at the same time propose amendments with the declaration that, if the amendments should not be adopted within a certain time, the state would withdraw from the Union; and, lastly, to ratify and recommend amendments with the hope of their adoption. Hamilton, fearing that without material concession his opponents would win the day, wrote to Madison to inquire his opinion as to the propriety of a conditional ratification with "the *reservation* of a right to recede" if proper amendments were not made. "My opinion is," replied Madison, "that a reservation of a right to withdraw, if amendments be not decided on under the form of the Constitution within a certain time, is a *conditional* ratification; that it does not make New-York a member of the new Union, and consequently that she could not be received on that plan." [1]

Though Hamilton is said to have declared that the convention should never rise till the Constitution was adopted, to the end there seemed little hope of success.[2] He debated untiringly and with remarkable power and eloquence. At length the opposition began to give way, and Melancthon Smith himself, giving up his attempt to force conditional ratification, voted with the Federalists in favor of accepting the Constitution, "in full confidence" that certain amendments would be adopted. The final vote stood thirty for ratification and twenty-seven against it.[3] Before the vote was taken a resolution was unanimously passed favoring the preparation of a circular letter to the states recommending a second constitutional convention. The resolution, declared by Madison to be of "most pestilent tendency,"[4] was in reality a cheap price to pay for unconditional ratification. Counting New York, eleven states had adopted the Constitution, and, in spite of the demands of the politicians, the people were not ready to enter once again upon the troublesome task that was but just finished.

The circular letter, however, did for a time have some effect. In Virginia it fell on good ground,[5]

[1] Hamilton, *Works* (Hamilton's ed.), I., 464, 465.
[2] J. C. Hamilton, *Hist. of the Rep.*, III., 523.
[3] Elliot, *Debates*, II., 412, 413.
[4] Madison, *Letters*, I., 410.
[5] Henry, *Patrick Henry*, II., 409 et seq.

for the assembly, led by Henry, who was uneasy under defeat, was ready to do his bidding. A reply to the New York letter was drawn up, a circular to the states, and a memorial to Congress; the objections to the Constitution were said not to be founded on speculative theory, but deduced from the principles established by the melancholy example of other nations and of different ages. In Pennsylvania the Anti-Federalists, among whom Albert Gallatin now took a leading part, demanded a speedy revision by a general convention, but recommended the people of the state to acquiesce in the organization of the government.[1]

Two states lingered behind the others—Rhode Island, which was in no condition to do anything wise, and North Carolina, which lacked unity, was under the influence of frontier sentiment, and had not felt the pressure experienced by the commercial sections of the Union. The letter from New York probably affected the course of North Carolina, for the convention of that state came to no decision, the opponents of the Constitution refusing either to ratify or reject, and awaiting developments.

Rhode Island was still intent on showing her superiority over her neighbors; when the Constitution was received by the legislature, it voted to have the document printed and distributed, that the people might have "an opportunity of forming their

[1] Elliot, *Debates*, II., 544; McMaster and Stone, *Pa. and Fed. Const.*, 560.

sentiments" on the matter.[1] Some time afterward
the legislature solemnly enacted that on the fourth
Monday in March "all the freemen and freeholders" should convene in their several towns and
there deliberate upon the Constitution.[2] The town-
meetings were farcical: the Federalists as a rule
refused to vote, and the result was that 237 were
counted as voting for adoption and 2,708 in the
negative.[3] The Federalists were, however, not idle.
They formed a strong minority, and their ability
and strength were destined to win before long and
to wrest the state from the hands of the ignorant, suspicious, and bigoted men who had already
brought it into disrepute. Even in Rhode Island
the Federalists did not entirely despair. There was
still hope that the "inconsiderate people" would not
fill "up the measure of iniquity"; the belief prevailed
that the scales were "ready to drop from the eyes,
and the infatuation to be removed from the heart,"
of the state.[4]

We have now traced the establishment of the
supreme law of the new republic; we have seen how
the American people found adequate political organization, and closed, for a time at least, the great
political drama that began with the Stamp Act,
when England and America entered on the dispute

[1] Bates, *R. I. and the Union*, 162; Staples, *R. I. in the Continental Congress*, 584.
[2] *Ibid.*, 586.   [3] *Ibid.*, 589, 606.
[4] Washington, *Writings* (Ford's ed.), XI., 287.

as to the distribution of power and the principles
of government. There is no doubt that when the
Constitution was adopted its framers considered it
an experiment; but they hoped that it would last;
they planned for the far future. There is absolutely no evidence to support the notion that they believed they were simply entering into a new order of
things in which the states would have the right, as
before, to refuse obedience and to disregard obligations, or from which they could at any time quietly
retire when they believed the Union did not suit
their purposes. Everything points to the fact that
they intended to form a real government and a
permanent union; all the solemn debates in the
state conventions, all the heated arguments of the
Anti-Federalists, all the outcry against the establishment of a consolidated government, are absurd,
meaningless, if the people felt that they had the
legal right to go on just as before and leave the
Union when they saw fit. At times the Constitution
was spoken of as a compact, but this never meant
mere agreement equivalent to a treaty between
sovereign states. Compact was the most solemn
and serious word in the political vocabulary of the
men of that generation; society itself was founded on
compact, and government rested on the same foundation.[1] The words with which Massachusetts established her own constitution were almost exactly

[1] See for the whole subject, McLaughlin, "Social Compact and
Constitutional Construction," in *Amer. Hist. Review*, V., 467–490.

the same as those with which she established the
Constitution of the United States—which, in truth,
was also her own: "Acknowledging, with grateful
hearts, the goodness of the Supreme Ruler of the
universe in affording the people of the United States,
in the course of his providence, an opportunity,
deliberately and peaceably, without fraud or surprise, of entering into an explicit and solemn compact with each other, by assenting to and ratifying
a new Constitution."[1]

If one really wishes to know the sentiments of
the time, let him read the words of Ellsworth in
the Connecticut convention, for no one better than
he knew what was done and what the work of the
moment meant. "How contrary, then, to republican principles, how humiliating, is our present
situation! A single state can rise up, and put a
veto upon the most important public measures.
We have seen this actually take place. A single
state has controlled the general voice of the Union;
a minority, a very small minority, has governed us.
So far is this from being consistent with republican
principles, that it is, in effect, the worst species of
monarchy. Hence we see how necessary for the
Union is a coercive principle. No man pretends the
contrary; we all see and feel this necessity. The only
question is, Shall it be a coercion of law, or a coercion
of arms? . . . I am for coercion by law—that coercion which acts only upon delinquent individuals."[2]

[1] Elliot, *Debates*, II., 176.   [2] *Ibid.*, 197.

In the twelve years that followed the Declaration of Independence the American people had accomplished much. The war was carried to a successful conclusion; the settlements stretching along the Atlantic coast came into the possession of a wide territory extending over the mountains to the Mississippi; state constitutions, laying down broad principles of liberty and justice, were formed on lines of permanence; a new colonial system for the organization and government of the great west was formulated, a system that was to be of incalculable value in the process of occupying the continent and building up a mighty republic; new settlements that showed capacity for self - government and growth were made in the wilderness beyond the Alleghenies. And, finally, a federal Constitution was formed, having for its purpose the preservation of local rights, the establishment of national authority, the reconciliation of the particular interests and the general welfare. In solving the problem of imperial organization, America made a momentous contribution to the political knowledge of mankind.

With the adoption of the national Constitution the first period of the Constitutional history of the United States was closed. A suitable and appropriate national organization was now established. There remained questions to be answered by the coming decades: Was the system suited to the needs of an expanding people? Was the distribution of

authority between the national government and the
states so nicely adjusted that the complicated
political mechanism would stand the strain of local
interest and national growth? Would the people
who had founded a national government grow so
strongly in national spirit and patriotism that there
would be a real bond of affection and of mutual
good - will, supplementing and strengthening the
formal ties of the law?

CHAPTER XIX

CRITICAL ESSAY ON AUTHORITIES

THERE is no general bibliography covering the whole of the period treated in this volume; and it is quite impossible to mention here all the materials which the author has used in writing the foregoing pages. There are, however, several lists that will prove helpful to the student and investigator. Edward Channing and Albert Bushnell Hart, *Guide to the Study of American History* (1896), §§ 149–156, contains titles and references on the most significant features of the time. The more important books are critically annotated in J. N. Larned, *Literature of American History* (1902), 152–181. Justin Winsor, *Narrative and Critical History of America* (8 vols., 1889), VII., 233–236, 255–266, has a mass of detail, not brought down to the present time. A useful list of sources is in Paul L. Ford, *Bibliography and Reference List of the History and Literature relating to the Adoption of the Constitution of the United States* (1888). Some of the volumes treating of different phases of this period contain good bibliographical lists and will be mentioned in their appropriate places below; the foot-notes to Bancroft, Curtis, McMaster, and other general works will be found serviceable. A good list of helpful references is to be found in William E. Foster, *References to the Constitution of the United States* (1890). On the period of the Confederation many of the authorities are identical with those enumerated in C. H. Van Tyne, *The American Revolution*, chap. xviii.

GENERAL SECONDARY WORKS

The most important treatise on this period is George Bancroft, *History of the Formation of the Constitution of the*

United States of America (2 vols., 1882), text reprinted in volume VI. of *History of the United States*, "author's last revision" (6 vols., 1883–1885). The two volumes are fully equipped with foot-notes, and with appendixes containing valuable documents, some of which are nowhere else obtainable in print. The books are the product of great toil and conscientious effort, but the author's habit of altering quotations for literary effect is much to be deplored, as is his general method of arranging material. Too great an effort is often made to follow events chronologically where a topical treatment would add much to the clearness. Like the earlier volumes of his *History of the United States*, these are marred by the tone of exaltation with which it is almost impossible to write truthful history; and thus, although he narrates the facts honestly, the reader fails to get the right idea of the years of the Confederation. In spite of this, all students must acknowledge their gratitude to Bancroft's painstaking research and devotion to historical accuracy.

A full treatment of the period is in George Ticknor Curtis, *History of the Origin, Formation, and Adoption of the Constitution of the United States* (2 vols., 1854), reprinted unchanged, as vol. I. of his *Constitutional History of the United States* (2 vols., 1889 – 1896). These volumes are on the whole accurate, and are written apparently with painstaking effort, but without breadth of view. The statements of the text are not very carefully supported by references to authorities, and the somewhat complex and dry style leaves with the reader a feeling of dissatisfaction. John Fiske, *The Critical Period of American History, 1783–1789* (1888), is an exceedingly interesting and popular narrative. The author knew how to tell a story with inimitable skill. Although there are not many errors of fact in the book, and certain fundamental ideas are clearly brought out, as an authority the work is altogether without scientific standing, because it is little more than a remarkably skilful adaptation of a very few secondary authorities, showing almost no evidence of first - hand acquaintance with the sources. Even Bancroft's rearranged quotations have been taken in some cases without consulting the sources. It is not strong in its treatment of the industrial conditions of the period, and there is no evidence of any original thinking on the problem and work of the convention. The peace negotiations are described from the viewpoint of an uncritical admirer of Jay's policy.

Of the utmost importance for information on the life of the people is the first volume of John Bach McMaster, *History of the People of the United States from the Revolution to the Civil War* (5 vols., published, 1883–1900). An immense amount of valuable and suggestive material is drawn from the newspapers of the time, though no effort is made to discuss Constitutional history. Two good sketches are to be found in Winsor, *America*, VII., "The Confederation, 1781–1789," by Justin Winsor, and "The Constitution of the United States and Its History," by George Ticknor Curtis. Richard Hildreth, *History of the United States* (6 vols., 1849–1852; subsequent editions from same plates), in vol. IV., gives a short, clear, dry, and condensed account. Something is to be found in the first volume of James Schouler, *History of the United States under the Constitution* (6 vols., 1880–1899), and in Timothy Pitkin, *Political and Civil History of the United States* (2 vols., 1828). Hermann E. von Holst, *The Constitutional and Political History of the United States* (Lalor's transl., 8 vols., several editions, 1876–1892), gives a suggestive and philosophic discussion in volume I., chaps. i. and ii.

Of special service will be found the biographies of statesmen of the time, many of which contain considerable original material. William Jay, *The Life of John Jay, with Selections from His Correspondence and Miscellaneous Papers* (2 vols., 1833), and George Pellew, *John Jay* (1890), are helpful in studying diplomatic conditions. John C. Hamilton, *History of the Republic of the United States as Traced in the Writings of Alexander Hamilton and of His*

Cotemporaries (7 vols., 1857 – 1864, also later editions, unaltered), though written with bias, is useful. Valuable material will be found in Kate M. Rowland, *The Life of George Mason, 1725–1792, including His Speeches, Public Papers, and Correspondence* (2 vols., 1892). The best life of Madison in short form is Gaillard Hunt, *Life of James Madison* (1902), not a brilliant but a thoroughly scholarly book, written from the sources. A very able treatment of the period of the Confederation is William C. Rives, *History of the Life and Times of James Madison* (3 vols., 1859–1868). Among the biographers of greatest service on this period are William Wirt Henry, *Patrick Henry, Life, Correspondence, and Speeches* (3 vols., 1891), a work based on good material and containing much original matter; Moses Coit Tyler, *Patrick Henry* (1887), is somewhat eulogistic, but strong and entertaining; William V. Wells, *The Life and Public Services of Samuel Adams* (3 vols., 1865); James T. Austin, *The Life of Elbridge Gerry, with Contemporary Letters* (2 vols., 1828–1829); Charles J. Stillé, *The Life and Times of John Dickinson, 1732–1808* (1891, also in Historical Society of Pennsylvania, *Memoirs*, XIII.); Moncure D. Conway, *Omitted Chapters of History Disclosed in the Life and Papers of Edmund Randolph* (1888); Griffith J. McRee, *Life and Correspondence of James Iredell* (2 vols., 1857–1858), containing many original letters, some of considerable importance; Richard H. Lee, *Memoir of the Life of Richard Henry Lee and His Correspondence with the Most Distinguished Men in America and Europe* (2 vols., 1825), containing selected letters throwing insufficient light on the work and opinions of Lee; Thomas C. Amory, *Life of James Sullivan, with Selections from His Writings* (2 vols., 1859), giving some information concerning conditions in Massachusetts; Henry S. Randall, *Life of Thomas Jefferson* (3 vols., 1858), able, eulogistic, old-fashioned; John T. Morse, Jr., *Thomas Jefferson* (1883), *Benjamin Franklin* (1889), *John Adams* (1885); Sydney H. Gay, *James Madison* (1884); James Parton, *Life and Times of Benjamin Franklin* (2 vols., 1864); Henry Cabot Lodge, *Alexander Hamilton*

(1882), *George Washington* (2 vols., 1889), a hurried but readable sketch; John Marshall, *Life of Washington* (5 vols., 1804–1807, 2 vols., 1832), not particularly strong on the period of the Confederation; Theodore Roosevelt, *Gouverneur Morris* (1888).

GENERAL COLLECTIONS OF SOURCES

This period can be satisfactorily studied in its political and Constitutional aspects from collections of printed sources that are fairly accessible. *The Journals of Congress* and *The Secret Journals of Congress* are absolutely necessary. The *Journals* were printed in a number of editions, and it is unnecessary here to go into their complicated bibliography; see Paul L. Ford, "Some Materials for a Bibliography of the Official Publications of the Continental Congress" (Boston Public Library, *Bulletin*, VIII.–X.); Herbert M. Friedenwald, "Journals and Papers of the Continental Congress," with a bibliography (American Historical Association, *Annual Report*, 1896, I., 85–135). The Library of Congress has already issued one volume of a new edition of the *Journals*, edited by Worthington Chauncey Ford (1904–), which will supersede all previous editions. The originals are now in the Library of Congress.

The standard collection of material on the Constitutional conventions is Jonathan Elliot, *The Debates in the Several State Conventions, on the Adoption of the Federal Constitution* (5 vols., 2d ed., 1836–1845, also subsequent editions). Vol. I. contains a series of very important state papers, including the journal of the Philadelphia convention, valuable letters, and comments on the Constitution; vol. V. contains Madison's notes on the Federal Convention and on a few debates in the Congress of the Confederation. Albert Bushnell Hart, *American History Told by Contemporaries* (4 vols., 1897–1901), II., chap. xxxv., and III., pts. ii., iii., and iv., gives a few selected sources.

Hardly less in importance are the writings of the statesmen of the time. There are two editions of Washington's

works: *Writings of George Washington* (ed. by W. C. Ford,
14 vols., 1889–1893); *Writings of George Washington* (ed. by
Jared Sparks, 12 vols., 1834–1837), not so carefully edited
as the Ford edition. Madison's writings appear in three
forms: *The Writings of James Madison, Comprising His
Public Papers and His Private Correspondence*, etc. (ed.
by Gaillard Hunt, 5 vols. so far published, 1900–), the
most satisfactory collection of Madison's writings, carefully
edited, and containing much not to be found in the other
collections, which are fragmentary; *Letters and Other
Writings of Madison* (official ed., 4 vols., 1865); *The
Papers of James Madison . . . His Correspondence and
Reports of Debates During the Congress of the Confederation,
and His Reports of Debates . . . in the Federal Convention* (ed.
by Henry D. Gilpin, 3 vols., 1840). These volumes are of
inestimable value for tracing the work of the Continental
Congress and of the Federal Convention. Neither of the
two collections of Hamilton's writings is complete and
altogether satisfactory: *Complete Works of Alexander
Hamilton* (ed. by H. C. Lodge, 9 vols., 1885–1886); *The
Works of Alexander Hamilton, Comprising His Correspondence* (ed. by J. C. Hamilton, 7 vols., 1850–1851). The
so-called federal edition of the *Works* of Hamilton (also
edited by Lodge) is a reprint of the edition of 1885–1886
and without substantial alteration (12 vols., 1904). Of
Franklin's works, *The Complete Works of Benjamin Franklin*
(ed. by John Bigelow, 10 vols., 1887–1888) is the best yet
published; see also *The Works of Benjamin Franklin . . .
with Notes and a Life of the Author* (ed. by Jared Sparks,
10 vols., 1840–1850). A new set of Franklin's writings, in
ten volumes, edited by Albert Smythe, is in process of
collection and publication. For John Adams, *The Works
of John Adams . . . with a Life of the Author* (ed. by C. F.
Adams, 10 vols., 1850–1856), is a useful and entirely
satisfactory collection. *Writings of James Monroe* (ed.
by Stanislaus M. Hamilton, 7 vols., 1898–1903), throws
some light on the political events of the period as seen by
one of the inferior statesmen of the time. Especially useful

for all diplomatic matters is *The Correspondence and Public Papers of John Jay* (ed. by Henry P. Johnston, 4 vols., 1890–1893), furnishing us, however, with but a small part of Jay's voluminous correspondence. On the western question, and on the last days of the Confederation, aid may be had from Charles R. King, *The Life and Correspondence of Rufus King, Comprising His Letters, Private and Official, His Public Documents, and His Speeches* (6 vols., 1894–1900), full of original material, but with a great deal of secondary comment which is not especially helpful. The best edition of the works of Jefferson yet issued is *The Writings of Thomas Jefferson* (ed. by P. L. Ford, 10 vols., 1892–1899). An older edition is *The Writings of Thomas Jefferson: Being His Autobiography, Correspondence . . . and Other Writings* (ed. by H. A. Washington, 9 vols., 1853–1854). An edition in twenty volumes, which it is claimed will be more nearly complete than any previous edition, is in course of publication by the Thomas Jefferson Memorial Association (11 vols. so far published, 1903–1905).

THE TREATY OF PEACE

The most important sources are found in *The Revolutionary Diplomatic Correspondence of the United States* (ed. by Francis Wharton, 6 vols., 1889). The first volume is largely given up to comments by Mr. Wharton on the men and events of the period. He believes in the general trustworthiness of Vergennes, and sympathizes with Franklin in his attitude on the questions that arose at Paris. The volumes, containing long extracts from Adams's and Franklin's diaries and other like material, in addition to the regular formal diplomatic correspondence, leave little to be desired for understanding the main course of the negotiations. The last entry is under date of March 4, 1785. Wharton makes his position clear also in his *Digest of International Law* (3 vols., 1886), III., App. Useful also is *Diplomatic Correspondence of the American Revolution* (ed. by Jared Sparks, 12 vols., 1829–1830, also in

6 vols., 1857), a series which has the disadvantage of
Sparks's method of not copying materials with absolute
exactness.   Sparks is strongly of the opinion that Jay was
in error.   Essential for the appreciation of the general
diplomatic condition is Henri Doniol, *Histoire de la Participation de la France à l'Établissement des États-Unis
d'Amérique* (5 vols. and suppl., 1886–1900).   Doniol naturally believes that the Americans were unjust in their suspicions.   In addition to the sources already named, use must
be made of *The Correspondence and Public Papers of John
Jay* (Johnston's ed., II. and III.), and the works of Franklin
and Adams.   Edward Everett Hale and Edward E. Hale,
Jr., *Franklin in France* (2 vols., 1887–1888), gives much
source-material, most important being the letters of Oswald
and Oswald's so-called "Journal."   Strong defences of
Jay's position are to be found in "The Peace Negotiations
of 1782–1783," written by John Jay, a descendant of the
commissioner, in Winsor, *America*, VII.; and in George Pellew, *John Jay*.   Theodore Lyman, *The Diplomacy of the
United States* (2d ed., 2 vols., 1828), contains considerable
original material, but the treatment is on the whole now
antiquated.   Documents used by Bancroft are in Adolphe
de Circourt, *Histoire de l'Action Commune* . . . (3 vols.,
1876).   Of especial interest as giving a new view of the
plans and aims of France is F. J. Turner, "The Policy of
France toward the Mississippi Valley in the Period of Washington and Adams," in *American Historical Review*, X., 249–
279.   Professor Turner has collected evidence which may
indicate the aim of France during the Revolution to succeed Spain in the possession of the west.

For the English conditions, a most important source is
Edmond George Petty, Lord Fitzmaurice, *Life of William,
Earl of Shelburne* . . . *with Extracts from His Papers and
Correspondence* (3 vols., 1875–1876).   Use may also be made
of W. Bodham Donne, *The Correspondence of King George III.
with Lord North, 1768–1783* (2 vols., 1867); John Adolphus,
*History of England from the Accession to the Decease of George
III.* (7 vols., 1840–1845); W. E. H. Lecky, *History of Eng-*

land in the Eighteenth Century (8 vols., 1878–1890), IV.; Lord John Russell, *Life and Times of Charles James Fox* (3 vols., 1859–1866); George Thomas, Earl of Albemarle, *Memoirs of the Marquis of Rockingham* (2 vols., 1852).

FINANCIAL CONDITIONS OF THE CONFEDERATION

The investigator is chiefly dependent on the *Journals of Congress*, although much valuable material is also contained, for the earlier time, in Francis Wharton, *Diplomatic Correspondence*. A learned but arid and badly arranged work is William G. Sumner, *The Financier and the Finances of the American Revolution* (2 vols., 1891), filled with information, but absolutely unusable by the average reader. Very helpful is Charles J. Bullock, *Finances of the United States, 1775–1789, with Especial Reference to the Budget* (University of Wisconsin, *Bulletins, Economics, Political Science, and History Series*, I., No. 2, 1895); contains a good bibliography. Also Henry Phillips, *Historical Sketches of the Paper Currency of the American Colonies* (2 vols., 1865–1866). Some use may be made of Albert S. Bolles, *The Financial History of the United States* (3 vols., 1879–1886), I., 1774–1789; also Henry Bronson, "A Historical Account of Connecticut Currency, Continental Money, and the Finances of the Revolution" (New Haven Historical Society, *Papers*, I., 1865); E. P. Oberholtzer, *Robert Morris* (1903); Samuel Breck, *Historical Sketch of Continental Paper Money* (1843). For a short treatment, see Davis R. Dewey, *Financial History of the United States* (1903), chap. ii.

TROUBLES WITH THE ARMY

The subject is fully treated in chaps. viii. and ix. of Louis C. Hatch, *The Administration of the American Revolutionary Army* (*Harvard Historical Studies*, X., 1904), with bibliography. The Newburg addresses are in *Journals of Congress* under the date April 29, 1783. Besides the writ-

ings of the men of the time that have already been referred
to, use should be made of Francis S. Drake, *Life and Corre-
spondence of Henry Knox, Major-General in the American
Revolutionary Army* (1873); Noah Brooks, *Henry Knox, a
Soldier of the Revolution* (1900); Octavius Pickering and C. W.
Upham, *The Life of Timothy Pickering* (4 vols., 1867–1873);
B. J. Lossing, *The Life and Times of Philip Schuyler* (2 vols.,
1860–1873); Jared Sparks, *The Life of Gouverneur Morris,
with Selections from His Correspondence and Miscellaneous
Papers* (3 vols., 1832), containing valuable original material.

COMMERCIAL AND INDUSTRIAL CONDITIONS

Of immense service is John B. McMaster, *History of
the People of the United States*, I., though his facts are without arrangement except for graphic effect. William B.
Weeden, *Economic and Social History of New England,
1620–1789* (2 vols., 1890), is a necessity. A monograph by
Dr. Guy H. Roberts, *The Foreign Commerce of the United
States during the Confederation*, which I have been permitted
to see in manuscript, will be to the student of that topic,
when published, indispensable. In reaching the conclusions in the foregoing pages, many sorts of original
materials have been used, and reliance placed both on
facts and testimony. Special attention may be called to
"Letters of Stephen Higginson" and "Letters of Phineas
Bond" (American Historical Association, *Annual Report*,
1896, I., 513–659, 704–841); Jeremy Belknap, *History of
New Hampshire* (3 vols., 1784–1792, 2d ed., 1812); *Pennsylvania Archives*, 1783–1786; Jean Pierre Brissot de Warville, *New Travels in the United States* (2 vols., 2d ed.,
1794); François J. Chastellux, *Travels in North America,
1780–1782* (2 vols., 1787, 2d ed., 1828); *Literary Diary of
Ezra Stiles* (ed. by F. B. Dexter, 3 vols., 1901), III.; Isaac W.
Hammond, *New Hampshire Town Papers*, XIII. Of great
service are the writings of the statesmen, and the *Diplomatic Correspondence, 1783–1789*. Of service especially for
statistics are David Macpherson, *Annals of Commerce* (4

vols., 1805); Tench Coxe, *A View of the United States of America* (1794); Lord Sheffield, *Observations on the Commerce of the American States* (6th ed., 1784); Timothy Pitkin, *Statistical View of the Commerce of the United States* (1816); *American State Papers, Commerce and Navigation;* John Drayton, *A View of South-Carolina* (1802).

FOREIGN RELATIONS AFTER THE PEACE

On this topic, besides the authorities described above, we have full information in *The Diplomatic Correspondence of the United States, 1783–1789* (3 vols., 1837, also 7 vols., 1833–1834). This indispensable material suffers from being ill-arranged. In addition, use must be made of the writings of Adams, Franklin, Jefferson, and especially of Jay. The general reader may read Theodore Lyman, *The Diplomacy of the United States* (2 vols., 1828), I., chaps. iv.–viii.; William H. Trescot, *The Diplomatic History of the Administrations of Washington and Adams* (1857), chap. i.; and John W. Foster, *A Century of American Diplomacy* (1900), chap. iii. Good accounts of the trouble with Spain are found in Bancroft and McMaster. Use can be made of George Pellew's *Jay*. Valuable references to the subject are to be found in *Correspondence and Public Papers of Jay* (Johnston's ed.); *Writings of Madison* (Hunt's ed.); *Writings of Monroe* (S. M. Hamilton's ed.); *Writings of Jefferson* (P. L. Ford's ed.); W. W. Henry, *Patrick Henry;* and W. C. Ford, *The United States and Spain in 1790*, introduction. The conditions in the southwest are well treated by Charles E. A. Gayarré, *History of Louisiana* (in various editions, 4th ed., 4 vols., 1903). The conspiracy in Kentucky has been very well treated in Theodore Roosevelt, *Winning of the West*, and the various books on the history of Kentucky mentioned below. Special reference should be made to John Mason Brown, *The Political Beginnings of Kentucky* (Filson Club, *Publications*, No. 6, 1889), written for the purpose of exculpating the author's ancestor; and above all to Thomas M. Green,

*The Spanish Conspiracy: a Review of Early Spanish Move-
ments in the South-west, Containing Proofs of the Intrigues of
James Wilkinson and John Brown,* etc. (1891), written to
demonstrate that John Mason Brown was wrong in his
conclusions. General James Wilkinson, *Memoirs of My
Own Times* (3 vols., 1816), is an historical source com-
parable in authority to the writings of Benvenuto Cellini
or the lamented Baron Munchausen, but he gives some
account of his machinations. Conclusive proof of Wilkinson's rascality is to be found in William R. Shepherd,
"Wilkinson and the Beginnings of the Spanish Conspiracy"
(*American Historical Review*, IX., 490–506), and "Papers
Bearing on James Wilkinson's Relations with Spain, 1787–
1789" (*ibid.*, 748–766).

For our relations with England we have full material in
Diplomatic Correspondence, 1783–1789, and in the works of
John Adams and John Jay. As to the retention of the
western posts, see A. C. McLaughlin, "The Western Posts
and the British Debts" (American Historical Association,
Annual Report, 1894, 413–444). Our early relations with
the Barbary pirates are discussed in Eugene Schuyler,
American Diplomacy (1886).

WESTERN HISTORY

Theodore Roosevelt, *The Winning of the West* (4 vols.,
1889–1896), covers the period 1773–1807; a brilliant work
and on the whole trustworthy, though written in apparent
haste; a graphic picture of the life of the woodsmen and
their deeds in winning the Mississippi basin. For the
northwest, the best general treatment is Burke Aaron
Hinsdale, *The Old Northwest, the Beginnings of our Colonial
System* (2d ed., revised, 1899), a carefully prepared and
lucidly written volume with a good bibliography. Of more
doubtful utility is Justin Winsor, *The Westward Movement:
the Colonies and the Republic West of the Alleghanies, 1763–
1798* (1897), fully illustrated with maps. Covering the
period in a scholarly but uninteresting fashion, it contains

a vast amount of information. On the attitude of Maryland, see Herbert B. Adams, *Maryland's Influence upon Land Cessions to the United States* (*Johns Hopkins University Studies*, 3d series, III., No. 1., 1885). An excellent treatment of the Ordinance of 1787, with a good bibliography, is to be found in Jay A. Barrett, *Evolution of the Ordinance of 1787, with an Account of the Earlier Plans for the Government of the Northwest Territory* (*University of Nebraska Seminary Papers*, No. 1, 1891). On this subject see also James C. Welling, "The States'-Rights Conflict over the Public Lands" (American Historical Association, *Papers*, III., No. 2, p. 167); found also in Welling, *Addresses, Lectures, and Other Papers* (1903). John M. Merriam, "The Legislative History of the Ordinance of 1787" (American Antiquarian Society, *Proceedings*, new series, V., 303). John Marshall's report on the question of Connecticut title is in *American State Papers, Public Lands,* I., 94–98. See also chap. vii. of King, *Ohio, First Fruits of the Ordinance of 1787* (2d ed., 1903); Jacob P. Dunn, *Indiana* (1888), a very careful examination of the whole subject, including authorship; Thomas M. Cooley, *Michigan* (1885); William F. Poole, "Dr. Cutler and the Ordinance of 1787" (*North American Review*, CXXII., 229–265). Of special service are *Life, Journals, and Correspondence of Rev. Manasseh Cutler* (ed. by W. P. and Julia P. Cutler, 2 vols., 1888), containing much original material, including Cutler's journal. Use can be made of Pickering and Upham, *Life of Pickering;* Shosuke Sato, *History of the Land Question in the United States* (*Johns Hopkins University Studies,* 4th series, Nos. 7–9); George W. Knight, *History and Management of Land Grants for Education in the Northwest Territory* (American Historical Association, *Papers,* I., No. 3); Rowena Buell, *Memoirs of Rufus Putnam* (1903); W. H. Smith, *The St. Clair Papers* (2 vols., 1882). The early history of the northwest can be followed clearly only by reference to the *Journals of Congress.*

The history of the country south of the Ohio is well treated in a good many secondary authorities, notably

James Phelan, *History of Tennessee, the Making of a State* (1888); Nathaniel S. Shaler, *Kentucky* (1885); Lewis Collins, *History of Kentucky* (revised ed., 2 vols., 1874), a work containing a vast amount of information, not very attractive to the general reader; A. W. Putnam, *History of Middle Tennessee; or, Life and Times of Gen. James Robertson* (1859), containing much original material, but diffuse and wordy; James G. McG. Ramsey, *The Annals of Tennessee to the End of the Eighteenth Century* (1853), another storehouse of information, including documentary material of great assistance to the investigator; John Haywood, *Civil and Political History of Tennessee* (1823 and 1891), a work depending in a measure upon the narratives of frontiersmen, but, though to be used with care, of real service to the investigator. Most suggestive is Frederick J. Turner, "Western State-Making in the Revolutionary Era" (*American Historical Review*, I., 70–87, 251–269); it discusses the numerous efforts to make states in the transmontane region. See also George H. Alden, "The State of Franklin" (*American Historical Review*, VIII., 271–289), and "The Evolution of the American System of Forming and Admitting New States into the Union" (American Academy of Political and Social Science, *Annals*, XVIII., 469–479). The relations of the subject to the west during the Revolution appear in C. H. Van Tyne, *The American Revolution*, chap. xv.

PAPER MONEY

Information on this subject abounds in the writings of the leading men of the time, Washington, Madison, Jay, and others. Bibliography in Bullock, ut supra (*Wisconsin Bulletin*, 1895). W. Z. Ripley, *Financial History of Virginia, 1609–1776* (*Columbia Studies*, IV., No. 1, 1893), gives a few pages to this period, and a bibliography. Jeremy Belknap, *New Hampshire*, is also of use. On affairs in Rhode Island, see Samuel G. Arnold, *History of Rhode Island* (2 vols., 1859–1860); Brissot de Warville, *New*

Travels, 1794, see above); W. R. Staples, *Rhode Island in the Continental Congress* (1870); and F. G. Bates, *Rhode Island and the Formation of the Union* (*Columbia Studies*, X., No. 2, 1898), a careful study of the relations of Rhode Island to the federal government in the period of the Confederation. On the case of Trevett *vs.* Weeden, see James B. Thayer, *Cases on Constitutional Law* (2 vols., 1894–1895), I., 73–78; Brinton Coxe, *An Essay on Judicial Power and Unconstitutional Legislation* (1893); James M. Varnum, *The Case, Trevett against Weeden* (1787). Bancroft and Curtis have something to say of paper money, but of the general accounts the most helpful is found in McMaster, *History of the People of the United States*, I., chap. iii.

SHAYS'S REBELLION

Bibliography in Berkshire Athenæum, *Quarterly Bulletin* (October, 1903). The most useful source is George R. Minot, *The History of the Insurrections in Massachusetts, in the Year 1786, and the Rebellion Consequent Thereon* (1788; 2d ed., 1810), written by a man who took an active part in the affairs of his day. John S. Barry, *History of Massachusetts* (3 vols., 1855–1857), gives a clear account with abundant references. Some material is in Noah Brooks, *Henry Knox;* A. B. Hart, *American History Told by Contemporaries*, III., chap. ix. The town histories contain much valuable information. See Charles F. Adams, *History of Braintree . . . and . . . Quincy* (1891); J. G. Holland, *History of Western Massachusetts* (2 vols., 1855); William Lincoln, *History of Worcester* (1837). In the preparation of this chapter some helpful references have been received from an interesting monograph by Dr. Joseph P. Warren, on Shays's rebellion, which is to be published.

PROPOSALS TO AMEND THE ARTICLES OF CONFEDERATION

For the examination of this subject the *Journals of Congress* are a necessity. The most important original materials have, however, been gathered together in a little pamphlet, entitled, *Proposals to Amend the Articles of Confederation, 1781–1783* (*American History Leaflets*, No. 1, 1896). Resolutions and reports are also brought together in Jonathan Elliot, *Debates*, I., 85–116. For the Annapolis convention, especially helpful are William C. Rives, *Life of Madison;* J. Thomas Scharf, *History of Maryland* (3 vols., 1879); *The Writings of Madison* (Hunt's ed.), II.; Kate M. Rowland, *Life of George Mason*, II.

THE FEDERAL CONVENTION

The fullest discussions of the convention are those of Bancroft and Curtis; Hildreth, Fiske, McMaster, and other general writers all contain accounts more or less elaborate, and there is an arid, concise condensation in *Cambridge Modern History*, VII. (1903). The subject can be examined satisfactorily only in the original materials. Nearly all the information we have of the proceedings of the convention is contained in the official journal, in the minutes taken by Madison, Yates, King, Paterson, Pierce, and Hamilton, and in various letters written while the convention was in progress. The official journal is published in Elliot, *Debates*, I., and directly from the manuscript in the *Documentary History of the Constitution, 1786–1870* (5 vols., 1894–1905), I. Madison's notes, the chiefest source, have been variously published. The best edition is in *Writings of Madison* (Hunt's ed.), III., IV., the edition used by the writer of the present volume. Other editions are H. D. Gilpin, *The Papers of James Madison* (3 vols., 1840, 2d ed., 1841); Elliot, *Debates*, V., 109–565; Erastus H. Scott, erroneously entitled *Journal of the Federal Convention* (1893), a copy of Gilpin. An elaborate reproduction appears in the *Documentary History of the Constitution*, III. King's minutes are to be found in King, *Life and Correspondence of Rufus King*, I., 587–621; Yates's notes in Elliot, *Debates*, I., 389–479; Paterson's notes in *American Historical Review*, IX., 310–340; Alexander Hamilton's notes, *ibid.*, X., 97–109; Pierce's notes, *ibid.*, III., 310–334. The bibliography of the letters written by the leaders of the Philadelphia convention appears in J. Franklin Jameson, "Studies in the History of the Federal Convention of 1787" (American Historical Association, *Annual Report*, 1902, I.), which also contains very important treatment of the convention. Of service to the investigator is William M. Meigs, *Growth of the Constitution in the Federal Convention of 1787* (1900). Luther Martin's "Letter," or "Genuine Information," is in Elliot, *Debates*, I., 344–389. On "the law of the land" and powers of the judiciary, see Brinton Coxe, *Essay on Judicial Power*, etc. (1893); William M. Meigs, "The Relation of the Judiciary to the Constitution" (*American Law Review*, 1885, 175–203); J. B. Thayer, *Cases*, I., 48–94; Austin Scott, "Holmes *vs.* Walton: the New Jersey Precedent" (*American Historical Review*, IV., 456–469). For Pinckney's plan, see *ibid.*, IX., 735–747; also American Historical Association, *Annual Report*, 1902, I., 111–132. On the compromises, see Max Farrand, "Compromises of the Constitution" (*American Historical Review*, IX., 479–489).

THE ADOPTION OF THE CONSTITUTION

For bibliography, see Paul L. Ford, *Bibliography and Reference List*, mentioned above; and J. Franklin Jameson, in American Historical Association, *Annual Report*, 1902, I. The most essential material is included in Jonathan Elliot, *Debates*, II., III., IV. Ample treatment in George Bancroft, *History of the Constitution*, II., and G. T. Curtis, *History of the Constitution*, II. A few works treating the subject monographically or containing special collections of sources are indispensable, notably J. B. McMaster and F. D. Stone, *Pennsylvania and the Federal Constitution, 1787–1788* (1888); Samuel B. Harding, *The Contest Over the Ratification of the Federal Constitution in the State of Massachusetts* (*Harvard Historical Studies*, 1896), a thoroughly satisfactory monograph with a good bibliography;

Orin G. Libby, *The Geographical Distribution of the Vote of the Thirteen States on the Federal Constitution, 1787–1788* (University of Wisconsin, *Bulletin, Economics, Political Science, and History Series*, I., No. 1, 1894), containing a good bibliography. Use can be made of *Debates and Proceedings in the Convention of the Commonwealth of Massachusetts . . . 1788* (1856); Joseph B. Walker, *A History of the New Hampshire Convention . . . 1788* (1888); Belknap Papers (Massachusetts Historical Society, *Collections*, 5th series, vols. II. and III.; 6th series, vol. IV.); *Debates and other Proceedings of the Convention of Virginia* (2d ed., 1805); "Letters on . . . the Federal Constitution in Virginia" (Massachusetts Historical Society, *Proceedings*, 2d series, 1903).

The most important material showing the differences of opinion concerning the Constitution is to be found in Paul L. Ford, *Essays on the Constitution of the United States, Published during its Discussion by the People, 1787–1788* (1892); Paul L. Ford, *Pamphlets on the Constitution of the United States, Published during its Discussion by the People, 1787–1788* (1888). Twenty-two of these essays and pamphlets appear in E. H. Scott, *The Federalist and Other Constitutional Papers* (2 vols., 1894). For a discussion of the movement for a second convention, see the essay by E. P. Smith, in *Essays in the Constitutional History of the United States in the Formative Period, 1775–1789*, edited by J. F. Jameson (1889), which contains a number of other essays helpful on this period.

There are several editions of *The Federalist* besides those contained in the collections of Hamilton's writings; the best edited by P. L. Ford (1898); a good one edited by H. B. Dawson (1863); another edited by E. G. Bourne (1901); another edited by E. H. Scott (1894). The authorship of the disputed numbers of *The Federalist* is discussed by E. G. Bourne and P. L. Ford in the *American Historical Review*, II., 443–460, 675–687. Important for studying the origin of the Constitution are James H. Robinson, "The Original and Derived Features of the Constitution" (American

Academy of Political and Social Science, *Annals*, I., 203–243); Alexander Johnston, "The First Century of the Constitution" (*New Princeton Review*, IV., 175–190); W. C. Morey, "The Genesis of a Written Constitution" (American Academy of Political and Social Science, *Annals*, I., 529–557); Charles E. Stevens, *Sources of the Constitution of the United States Considered in Relation to Colonial and English History* (1894).

THE CHARACTER OF THE CONSTITUTION

The books and articles on this subject are legion. Attention may be called especially to the able treatment in J. I. C. Hare, *American Constitutional Law* (2 vols., 1889), the earlier chapters; Roger Foster, *Commentaries on the Constitution of the United States* (1 vol. published, 1895–). Joseph Story, *Commentaries on the Constitution* (Cooley's or Bigelow's ed., 1873 or 1891, 2 vols.). For the state-sovereignty interpretation, the best treatments are Alexander H. Stephens, *A Constitutional View of the Late War between the States* (2 vols., 1868–1870); John R. Tucker, *The Constitution of the United States* (2 vols., 1899). The contemporary notion of the Constitution as a compact analogous to the social compact is given in A. C. McLaughlin, "Social Compact and Constitutional Construction" (*American Historical Review*, V., 467–490).

INDEX

ABDRAHAMAN, Tripolitan ambassador, 106, 107.
Adams, John, peace commissioner, 6; in Holland, 7; negotiations, 24–29; on Jay, 31; minister to England, 102–105; and Tripolitan ambassador, 106.
Adams, Samuel, and Constitution, 279, 293.
Amendment, of Confederation, attempts at, 53–55, 79, 82–86, 171–173, 175; of Constitution recommended, 295, 304, 311.
Ames, Fisher, Federalist, 291.
Annapolis convention, genesis, 179–181; call, 181; meeting, 182.
Anti-Federalists, location, 281, 289, 299, 305; in Virginia, 298.
Armed Neutrality, 9.
Armstrong, John, Newburg address, 65.
Army, American, discontent in, 59; half-pay, 59; address to Congress, 60; agitation, 60–68; and Union, 62; Newburg address and Washington, 63–67; pay for officers, 67; Cincinnati, 67; mutiny, 68; land bounties, 113; bibliography, 326.

BALDWIN, ABRAHAM, vote on representation, 233; on grand committee, 235.

Barbary States, depredations, 90; demands, 106.
Barrell, Nathaniel, Federalist, 294.
Bedford, Gunning, of small-state party, 209, 230, 238; on grand committee, 234.
Belknap, Jeremiah, on financial crisis, 82.
Bibliographies of period 1781–1788, 318; of adoption of Constitution, 318, 334.
Bill of rights, in Ordinance of 1787, 121; demand for, in Constitution, 283, 288, 305.
Biographies of period 1781–1788, 320–322.
Boone, Daniel, in Kentucky, 131, 132.
Boonesborough, settled, 132.
Boundaries, peace negotiations, 11, 24, 27–29; French attitude, 14; West Florida, 27, 29, 91, 92.
Bowdoin, James, and Shays's rebellion, 161–164; defeated for re-election, 164; Federalist, 291.
Brearley, David, of small-state party, 216.
Butler, Pierce, in Federal convention, 190, 255.

CANADA, Franklin desires, 11.
Chase, Samuel, Anti-Federalist, 295.

337

END OF VOL. X.